SELECTED PAPERS AND LECTURES ON GHANAIAN LAW

SAMUEL KOFI DATE-BAH

LL.B (GHANA), LL.M (YALE), Ph.D (LONDON)
Former Professor of Law
Retired Justice of the Supreme Court of Ghana and Fellow of the Ghana
Academy of Arts and Sciences.

ISBN: 978-9988-3-1078-3

Published by Digibooks Ghana Ltd.
P. O. Box BT1, Tema, Ghana
Tel: +233-303-414-720 / +233-246-493-842
Email: admin@digibookspublishing.com
Website: http://www.digibookspublishing.com

To

Eugenia Date-Bah for her love, support and constant prodding.

TABLE OF CONTENTS

FOREWORD

It is with much pleasure that I introduce *Selected Papers and Lectures on Ghanaian Law*, authored by the distinguished academician and retired jurist of the Supreme Court of Ghana, His Lordship Justice Samuel Kofi Date-Bah. I was privileged to be one of his students in 1976 at the Faculty of Law, University of Ghana and also worked with the learned jurist and academician during his illustrious years on the Supreme Court. After his book: titled *Reflections on the Supreme Court of Ghana* which was a seminal piece, I am not surprised that the respected jurist has produced another book which is a collection of brilliant and carefully analysed papers and lectures presented and delivered by our esteemed jurist. Through the chapters of this book, the author has once again demonstrated his commitment to the development of scholarship and Ghana's jurisprudence in particular.

As the table of contents reflects, the book is structured into four parts with chapters addressing a range of topical legal issues some of which relate to the administration of justice in Ghana by the Judiciary. Through the chapters, the distinguished author also discusses issues of governance and business aided by the law. Part I deals with the Legal System and Legal Education in Ghana. It has three chapters discussing issues like Law and Development: the Ghana legal system as an instrument of development reflective of the Ghanaian spirit; Legal education in Ghana; The Legon Law Faculty's Contribution to Legal Education, Governance and socio-economic development of Ghana. Part II deals with the Judiciary and discusses issues such as the role and function of the Judiciary under the 1992 Constitution; the Supreme Court's role in the protection of liberty; the influence of the landmark case of *Re Akoto* on the Supreme Court's protection of liberty in Ghana; Judges' remuneration and promotion; the impact of the Commercial Court; and the contribution of Justice William Atuguba to constitutionalism in Ghana.

Part III, which is on Human Rights and Good Governance, addresses issues such as Emergency powers in emerging democracies - the case of Ghana; Religion, Human Rights and democracy in the Ghanaian context and the Constitutional mandate of the Council of State. The last Part deals with Business Law and discusses topics like: evolution of business law in Ghana; African States' ratification of the United Nations Convention on Contracts for the International Sale of Goods; and, lastly, Observations on Arbitration.

The author's treatment of different topics from the legal system, the Judiciary, Human Rights, Business law and the contribution of the University of Ghana's Law Faculty, will become a source of reference on which members of the legal community may rely in order to make informed decisions in the development of law in Ghana. The author's discussion of the impact of Justice William Atuguba on constitutionalism in Ghana gives the reader an understanding of how the law has been used as a tool to fuel the development of our country. The author also proceeds to list and discuss some distinguished personalities who have been in national leadership positions in the governance of Ghana, all being products of the Legon Faculty of Law.

It is regrettable, however, that during the ten years of his invaluable contribution to the judiciary, the distinguished author had few cases in his specialised area of the law, that is, the Law of Contract, to write his usual erudite judgments.

The number of cases discussed in this book and his review of judgments of the Supreme Court clearly demonstrate the author's commitment to the rule of law and constitutionalism in Ghana. Like the *Reflections on the Supreme Court of Ghana* , I am more than certain that this book, *Selected Papers and Lectures on Ghanaian Law*, will find its way to library shelves of not only members of the legal community but also of members of other professions and the public in general.

It is my prayer that jurists who have distinguished themselves in public life will in future draw inspiration from this invaluable work produced by Professor Justice Samuel Kofi Date-Bah for the advancement and enrichment of the law in our jurisdiction.

JUSTICE ANIN YEBOAH
Chief Justice of the Republic of Ghana
Chief Justice's Chambers
Accra

PREFACE

This book shines a light on various aspects of Ghanaian law, ranging from the Ghanaian legal system, legal education in Ghana, human rights and good governance to business law. It is presented in short easy to read Chapters. I did not set out to write such a book. Rather, it is an aggregation of various papers and lectures I have written as a result of invitations received to speak to various audiences. I am glad to share more widely, through this book, the ideas that I discussed with particular groups.

The book is thus a bonus. It is the result of the initiative of my wife, Eugenia (Dr. Eugenia Date-Bah FGA), who urged me to put together various lectures, papers and presentations that she knew I had prepared over the years but had not published. They were spread over several files on different computers. It is through her drive and prodding that some of these scattered papers were retrieved. She was also invaluable in the initial editing of my manuscript for the book. She eliminated infelicities of language and made suggestions on structure. I am obviously very grateful to her for her industry and editorial skills. Augustus Agyemang, an astute lawyer, did me the favour of reading through the whole manuscript and giving me very constructive comments on it. His assistance was valuable and is much appreciated.

The papers and lectures upon which this book is based were written after my appointment to the Supreme Court of Ghana in 2003. Accordingly, being a judge played a role in receiving many of the invitations for the lectures and presentations that have resulted in the Chapters in the book. I remain proud and grateful for my decade on the Supreme Court. Some of the invitations also relate to the fact that I used to be an academic.

Finally, I am grateful to the Chief Justice of Ghana, Mr. Justice Anin Yeboah, for readily agreeing to write the Foreword to this book. My aspiration is that this book will contribute to the dissemination of knowledge on Ghanaian law, by being read both outside and inside Ghana.

Samuel Kofi Date-Bah
31st October 2020

TABLE OF CASES

TABLE OF DOMESTIC LEGISLATION

TABLE OF FOREIGN LEGISLATION

TABLE OF TREATIES AND OTHER INTERNATIONAL INSTRUMENTS

TABLE OF CONSTITUTIONS

TABLE OF ABBREVIATIONS

A C	Law Reports, Appeal Cases (England)
ADR	Alternative Dispute Resolution
All ER:	All England Reports
AMJG:	Association of Magistrates and Judges of Ghana
AU:	African Union
CCWL:	City and Country Waste Limited
CHOGM:	Commonwealth Heads of Government Meeting
CHRAJ:	Commission for Human Rights and Administrative Justice
CISG:	United Nations Convention on Contracts for the International Sale of Goods (Vienna, 1980)
CLEA:	Commonwealth Legal Education Association
CRC:	Constitutional Review Commission
CUTS:	Consumer Unity and Trust Society of India
D.Ct:	Divisional Court Reports
ECOWAS:	Economic Community of West African States
FC:	Full Court Report
FGA:	Fellow of the Ghana Academy of Arts and Sciences
GARIA:	Ghana Association of Restructuring and Insolvency Advisers
GDP:	Gross Domestic Product
GIMPA:	Ghana institute of Management and Public Administration
GLR:	Ghana Law Reports
GNP:	Gross National Product
ICC:	International Chamber of Commerce
ICSID:	International Centre for the Settlement of Investment Disputes
JAC:	Judicial Appointments Commission
KB:	Law Reports, King's Bench (England)
K-F	King-Farlow's Gold Coast Judgments

KNUST:	Kwame Nkrumah University of Science and Technology
MOU:	Memorandum of Understanding
NCCE:	National Centre for Civic Education
NGOs:	Non-Governmental Organisations
NPART:	Non-Performing Assets Recovery Trust
OECD:	Organisation for Economic Cooperation and Development
PNDCL:	Provisional National Defence Council Law
PPA:	Power Purchase Agreement
QB:	Law Reports, Queen's Bench (England)
Ren:	Renner's Gold Coast Reports
RGL:	Review of Ghana Law
SME:	Small and Medium Enterprises
SCGLR:	Supreme Court of Ghana Law Reports SM
UGLJ:	University of Ghana Law Journal
UKPC:	Judicial Committee of the Privy Council of the United Kingdom
ULF:	Uniform Law on the Formation of Contracts for the International of Sale of Goods
ULIS:	Uniform Law on International Sale of Goods
UNCITRAL:	United Nations Commission on International Trade Law
UNIDROIT:	International Institute for the Unification of Private Law
WAEMU:	West African Economic and Monetary Union
WTO:	World Trade Organisation

CHAPTER 1

INTRODUCTION

This book is a compendium of selected lectures and papers, principally on Ghanaian law, prepared by the author for diverse fora in Ghana and abroad during the past decade and a half. Its contents deal with a wide range of topics expected to be of interest, not only to Ghanaian lawyers, but also to lawyers in general and other persons interested in the legal process in developing countries. The variety of topics treated means that the book can be regarded almost as a mini Reader on Ghanaian law. On the whole, the chapters are relatively short and easy to read, as the lectures/ papers upon which they are based, were delivered within limited time frames to their audiences. They have been consolidated into one book to reach a wider readership than the audiences to which they were initially addressed.

While the chapters are principally on Ghanaian law, they nevertheless contain comparative perspectives. Additionally, two of the chapters deal with topics that stretch beyond Ghanaian law. For example, Chapter 18 deals with competition law in the West African subregion. Furthermore, Chapter 19 makes a case for all African jurisdictions to sign and ratify the United Nations Convention on Contracts for the International Sale of Goods ("CISG"). With the coming into force of the Agreement Establishing the African Continental Free Trade Area on 30th May 2019, this is very apposite advice. The application of uniform rules on international sale of goods contracts should facilitate inter-African trade.

The chapters vary in their levels of technicality, depending on the audience to which they were originally addressed. They have been edited to remove the initial and other expressions of pleasantries and, in some cases, also updated. There is some overlap in a couple of the papers since they are on topics that require convergent discussion.

The Chapters have been grouped into four Parts comprising: the Legal System and Legal Education; the Judiciary; Human Rights and Good Governance; and, finally, Business Law. Part I, on the Ghana Legal System and legal education in Ghana, canvasses a range of issues, including the relevance of Ghanaian *volkgeist* and culture to the efficacy of law in Ghana and the extent of the "digestion" of the law received in Ghana from foreign sources. It also contains a discussion of the role of the judiciary in assisting with the digestive process referred to above and with the development process in general. Furthermore, the role of Parliament in deploying law as an instrument in the development process is highlighted. It also assesses the role of law in general in the development process. Additionally, Part I discusses issues relating to legal education in Ghana, ranging from the right balance to be struck between municipal and international legal subjects to the role that the first Law Faculty, established in Ghana, has played in national life and development. One of the Chapters sets out deliberately to provoke a debate on what the right balance between local and transnational/ international legal studies should be. The review of the historical origins of legal education in Ghana, carried out in the context of assessing the contribution of the University of Ghana's Law Faculty to education and progress in the country, is particularly pertinent to the contemporary debate in Ghana on professional legal education and access to it. It demonstrates that "the founders" of Ghanaian legal education established a paradigm customised to Ghanaian needs, which should be abandoned only after careful thought. There are interesting jurisprudential underpinnings to much of the discussion in Part I.

Part II brings together papers on the Ghanaian judiciary and courts. It examines the function of judges under the 1992 Constitution and the ramifications of this function. It commends the judiciary's role in the protection of the political freedom and human rights available under this Constitution. The purposive approach to the interpretation of the Constitution and statutes is advocated in the interest of justice. Also, the limits to judicial law making are explored and clarified. Judicial independence and accountability are discussed, in the context of the Latimer House Principles of the

2

Commonwealth, in addition to other issues pertaining to judges. The impact of the notorious and much discussed *Re Akoto*[1] case on liberty in Ghana is again assessed, from this writer's perspective. The impact of Justice Atuguba on the course of law and justice during his long tenure on the Supreme Court bench is considered in a testimonial lecture. Apart from a consideration of the role of the courts in enforcing human rights and protecting political freedom, one of the Chapters also considers the courts' role in the determination of commercial disputes and the importance of this role in the development process.

Part III contains three chapters on human rights and two on good governance. It begins with the modalities for fighting corruption and building a robust ethics infrastructure to promote integrity in Ghana. It stresses that the campaign to combat corruption has to be multifaceted and it dilates on many of its aspects. Another Chapter examines the constitutional provisions in Ghanaian law governing the use of emergency powers. Human rights may need to be abridged in times of emergency and Article 31 of the 1992 Constitution sets out the framework for the abridgment of such rights. Emergency powers under Article 31 of the 1992 Constitution have never been invoked in the history of the Fourth Republic. However, during the Covid-19 health emergency, the Government, rather than declaring a state of emergency under Article 31 of the Constitution, opted instead to enact the Imposition of Restrictions Act,2020[2] which gave the President authority to impose restrictions on the human rights specified in Article 21 of the 1992 Constitution. These rights relate to freedom of speech and expression; freedom of thought, conscience and belief; freedom to practise any religion and to manifest such practice; freedom of assembly; freedom of association; right to information; and freedom of movement. These freedoms and rights are made expressly subject, in Article 21, to the imposition of restrictions, on the right to movement within Ghana of any persons that are required in the interest of defence, public safety, public health or the running of essential services. The imposition of restrictions on the freedom of entry into Ghana or

---

1   [1961] 2 GLR 523

2   Act 1012

3

movement in Ghana of a person who is not a citizen of Ghana is also permitted. The Constitution further allows the enactment of a law that is reasonably required for the purpose of safeguarding the people of Ghana against the teaching or propagation of a doctrine which exhibits or encourages disrespect for the nationhood of Ghana, the national symbols and emblems, or incites hatred against other members of the community[3]. The Imposition of Restrictions Act, 2020, gave the President power to impose these permitted restrictions, subject to the specific provisions of the Act. Such restrictions are, however, required to be reasonably justifiable in terms of the spirit of the 1992 Constitution[4].

Other Chapters in Part III discuss freedom of religion, as a human right under the 1992 Constitution, and the role of the Council of State as an adviser to the President of the Republic. There is a consideration of the interpretation to be given to the phrases "on the advice of" and "in consultation with," when used in relation to views expressed by the Council of State to the President, in accordance with various provisions in the 1992 Constitution. A Chapter also considers the Supreme Court decisions interpreting Article 181(5) of the 1992 Constitution which prescribes Parliamentary approval for international business transactions entered into by the Government.

Finally, Part IV deals with business law. It discusses the evolution of business law in Ghana since independence, focussing on contract law and company law. It outlines the competition law scenario in West Africa. It presents a case for the ratification of the CISG by Ghana and other African States and ends with some observations on international commercial arbitration as it relates to Ghana.

Conclusion

This author's aspiration is that the papers and lectures in this book will inform readers on developments in Ghanaian law and generate discussion of that law. In developing countries, getting the law on governance and business right is an important strategic

---

3   See Article 21(4)(c), (d) and (e) of the 1992 Constitution.

4   Article 21(4),

step in the development process. The contents of this book are thus germane to development strategy and should be of interest to all who work and think about the development process. They should also be of relevance to comparative lawyers seeking an insight into Ghanaian law. Finally, it is the author's hope that Ghanaian lawyers, particularly, will find material useful for their craft in the book.

PART I:

THE LEGAL SYSTEM AND LEGAL EDUCATION IN GHANA

CHAPTER 2

LAW AND DEVELOPMENT: THE GHANA LEGAL SYSTEM AS AN INSTRUMENT OF DEVELOPMENT REFLECTIVE OF THE GHANAIAN SPIRIT[5]

Introduction

Politicians in Africa often say that without peace there can be no development. This is a truism which also underscores an aspect of the role of law in development. Development processes can only advance under conditions of law and order. The expression, "law and order," referred to here, points to public law provisions in addition to the facilitating provisions of private law. Public law means: first, the criminal law, which restrains unacceptable conduct that needs to be prohibited in the interest of society. Such restraint by the State enables access by individuals and other legal entities to the necessary space to be able to innovate and to produce the goods and services needed by society. Secondly, the term also includes the constitutional and administrative law that provides a framework for structuring the State's power to secure the peace, mentioned earlier, and to provide a mechanism for giving legitimacy to the political and administrative classes to wield the State's power of coercion. Finally, comprised in the notion of public law is tax law which enables the mobilisation of revenue to meet the needs of society. Therefore, a discussion of the role of public law inevitably will loom large in any dialogue on the role of law in development.

Public law issues tend to be subsumed under the contemporary theme of the rule of law and good governance. Perceptions of the relevance of the rule of law and good governance to the development process are based on the assumption that law has a capacity to

---

5   This Chapter is based on two papers: one was presented at a symposium of the 38th Law Week Celebration of the Law Students' Union, University of Ghana, Legon, on 23rd March, 2011 and the other paper was presented at the Harvard African Law Association's Harvard African Law and Development Conference 16th – 18th April 2010, in Cambridge, Massachusetts, USA.

affect social behaviour. This proposition is now almost axiomatic. What merits further discussion is the extent of the law's capacity to affect social behaviour. One of my Professors at the University of Ghana in the 1960s, Professor Bob Seidman, formerly an Emeritus Professor at the Boston University School of Law, recognized this issue when he wrote:

> "Pound called it the question of the limits of law. The central question for law and development becomes the analysis of the limits of law in conditions of development."[6]

In other words, what, in relation to the development process, is capable of being done through law and what must be achieved through other means? I would say that much can be achieved through the instrumentality of law. I believe that law is an instrument of social control which can be deployed to achieve the goal of development, alongside other instruments. In utilising this instrument, one should be well-informed about its use, potential and limits.

It is pertinent, at this point, to advert to Professor Seidman's view of the role of law in development. According to him:[7]

> "In sum, law and development concerns a study of how to use the legal order to ensure (a) higher productivity and more equitable distribution, (b) effective (i.e. non-symbolic)law,(c) legality and (d) greater democracy. Only if the legal order meets these objectives will development take place. One can achieve these objectives only if one can analyse the causes of the difficulties that give rise to them."

I am quite persuaded that the crafting of an appropriate legal and constitutional framework for promoting greater democracy is an important contribution that law can make to the development process. I am also attracted to Prof. Amartya Sen's idea of development as freedom. His argument is as follows:[8]

---

6   Robert B. Seidman, "On teaching Law and Development", in 1986 *Third World Legal Studies (TWLS)* 53 at 54.

7   *Ibid.*

8   Prof. Amartya Sen, *Development as Freedom*(Alfred A. Knopt, New York, 2001) at 3

"Development can be seen, it is argued here, as a process of expanding the real freedoms that people enjoy. Focussing on human freedoms contrasts with narrower views of development, such as identifying development with the growth of gross national product, or with the rise in personal incomes, or with industrialization, or with technological advance, or with social modernization. Growth of GNP or of individual incomes can, of course, be very important as *means* to expanding the freedoms enjoyed by the members of the society. But freedoms depend also on other determinants, such as social and economic arrangements (for example, facilities for education and healthcare) as well as political and civil rights (for example, the liberty to participate in public discussion and scrutiny)....If freedom is what development advances, then there is a major argument for concentrating on that overarching objective, rather than on some particular means, or some specially chosen list of instruments."

When development is viewed in these terms, the role of law in it can easily be appreciated.

Brief Snapshot of the Ghana Legal System

The Ghana legal system comprises the totality of the laws in force in the country and the ground rules governing how they work. A good place to start in any journey of discovery of the nature of the Ghana legal system is Article 11 of the 1992 Constitution. This Article sets out a list of the different elements comprised in the laws of Ghana. These are: the Constitution; enactments made by or under the authority of the Parliament established by the 1992 Constitution; Orders, Rules and Regulations made under a power conferred by the Constitution; the law in existence prior to the coming into force of the 1992 Constitution, to the extent that it is in conformity with the Constitution; and the common law. The common law, as used in Article 11, refers not only to the transplanted English common law, but also to the rules of customary law. Customary law is defined in the Article to mean: "the rules of law which by custom are applicable to particular communities in Ghana."

11

Volksgeist and the Ghana Legal System

It is clear from the constitutional listing above of the sources of law in the Ghanaian legal system that it is a somewhat eclectic system. Thus, the Ghanaian legal system is pluralistic. This implies, in my view, that it is difficult to say it embodies the *"volksgeist"*, or the national spirit, of the Ghanaian people. Savigny's concept of the *"volksgeist"* has some helpful explicatory aspects that assist us to understand the role of law in society. Savigny was, of course, the German legal philosopher (1779-1861) who propounded the jurisprudential theory of the *"volksgeist"*[9]. He stresses that a legal system is part of the culture of a people.

This observation is likely to draw the comment from critical people that where the legal system of a country contains many legal transplants, it is doubtful whether it can realistically be asserted of that law that it is part of the culture of a people. In such countries, including, of course, Ghana, making the law part of the culture of a people remains work in progress. Nevertheless, the efficacy of law as an instrument of social change and development depends to a large degree on law becoming a part of the culture of the people.

Indeed, there is a degree of tension between the instrumentalist conception of law and the notion of the *volksgeist*. The instrumentalists are in a hurry for change and development and want to use the law as a major tool in this endeavour. Transplantation of law is often seen by them as one of the techniques available to strengthen the efficacy of law as an instrument of change. On the other hand, if law must reflect the national spirit to be truly effective, then the transplanted laws will need a gestation period to become a part of the culture of the people.

I must confess that I am by instinct an instrumentalist. I am optimistic that the law can be used as an instrument of change in a country such as Ghana which needs to be transformed to reach its welfare/development goals. However, I admit that the empirical evidence is rather thin on the ground as to whether law does really make a difference in real life when it is used in an instrumental

---

9   See, e.g., J.W. Harris, *Legal Philosophies*(Oxford Universities Press, Oxford, 2004 (2nd Ed)) 235

way. What is clear is that instrumentalists, like me, have to be more humble and take much more serious account of the sociology and anthropology of change. Furthermore, they should be prepared to accept that, among the spectrum of various instruments of change, law may not be the primary one.

Law and Development in Ghana

It is in this context that I want to examine the Ghana legal system as an instrument of development that is also reflective of the Ghanaian spirit. When one refers to the Ghanaian spirit, one runs straight into the broadside attack of the critics of Savigny's *volksgeist*, who assert that to speak of the spirit of a people or a nation is to postulate a degree of unity of thought and action in that nation or people of which there is little evidence. If we are to be honest, we would also accept that in Ghana the Ghanaian identity is not a finished product and is still in the process of consolidation. Accordingly, the "Ghanaian spirit" which the law is supposed to reflect is a problematic concept which is not easy to delineate.

In spite of these conceptual and theoretical difficulties, it remains a viable aspiration for Ghanaians to expect their law and legal profession to make a contribution to the process of development and that that contribution should reflect Ghanaian mores. By consensus, development is the most dominant imperative on the Ghanaian landscape. The law and lawyers will be regarded by the general Ghanaian public as irrelevant if they do not engage with the national desire for development.

The common law of Ghana is defined in article 11(2) of the 1992 Constitution as comprising: "the rules of law generally known as the common law, the rules generally known as the doctrines of equity and the rules of customary law including those determined by the Superior Court of Judicature." Of these rules, the common law and the doctrines of equity are foreign transplants, received in Ghana as a result of colonisation. It is customary to identify the Supreme Court Ordinance, 1876 as the reception statute by which these English transplants made their entry into the Ghanaian legal system. To what extent have the courts and successive legislatures of Ghana adjusted these foreign transplants and imbued them with a Ghanaian spirit? It is clearly the responsibility of both the Ghanaian legislature and judiciary to develop Ghanaian law in such a way as to make it more and more effective. That implies enabling the general Ghanaian public to accept Ghanaian law, including its foreign transplants, as part of their culture.

The judiciary, inevitably, has a crucial role in imbuing these foreign transplants with a Ghanaian spirit. It has the responsibility of developing the rules of the common law, equity and customary law and interpreting the Constitution and statutes in the light of Ghanaian circumstances to reach outcomes that are right for Ghana. In my view, a judiciary that is most useful to the development process and to the task of adaptation of these foreign implants, which are such an important element of our legal system, is one that is mindful of its law-making role. This role is, of course,within the conventional restraints on the exercise of judicial power under the common law system. It must also take account of the needs of the development process as one of the overarching purposes of the law. Within the known constraints on the exercise of judicial power, the judiciary has to craft ingenious solutions, reflective of local Ghanaian conditions, to the public and private law issues that arise from the process of development.

Justice Cardozo has pronounced an eloquent enunciation of what constitutes these conventional restraints on judicial power. He has written:[10]

> "The judge, even when he is free, is still not wholly free. He is not to innovate at pleasure. He is not a knight-errant, roaming at will in pursuit of his own ideal of beauty or of goodness. He is to draw his inspiration from consecrated principles. He is not to yield to spasmodic sentiment, to vague and unregulated benevolence. He is to exercise a discretion informed by tradition, methodized by analogy, disciplined by system,and subordinate to "the primordial necessity of order in the social life."

---

10   See Justice BN Cardozo, *The Nature of the Judicial Process* (1921). 141

Within these restraints, however, there is no question that judges have a law-making role. As Lord Bingham, probably the finest judicial mind in England for a century, has said:

> "It used to be said that judges did not make law but merely declared what the law had always been. This is a view which has few, if any adherents today. Some judges, such as the late Lord Denning, are proud of their role in developing the law; most are more reticent. But cases are brought raising novel questions, and the judges have to answer them. Their answers will often make law, whatever answer they give, one way or the other. So the judges do have a role in developing the law, and the common law has grown up as a result of their doing just this. But, and this is the all-important condition, there are limits."[11]

My point is that in a legal system such as the Ghanaian with many foreign legal transplants still waiting to be embedded in the local culture, judges need to grasp their limited law-making role with enthusiasm in order to attune the foreign imports to local circumstances and adjust them to the imperatives of development. To do this is not to supplant the legislature, but rather to supplement its efforts. If the legislature does not like the results of particular exercises of judicial creativity, it can always undo them.

The judiciary is, however, a junior partner in the task of making Ghanaian law an instrument of development reflective of the Ghanaian spirit. Our elected representatives gathered in Parliament are supposed to reflect the national spirit, ethos and aspirations. Parliament therefore bears the frontline responsibility for making our law an effective instrument of change. This role, however, implies that Parliament and the Ministers who introduce Bills to it should take account of the sociology and anthropology of change when doing so. In other words, Members of Parliament owe an obligation to Ghana not merely to scrutinise the technical provisions of particular Bills laid before them, but also to exercise judgment over whether the measures they introduce are in tune with Ghanaian mores and the Ghanaian spirit and likely, after an

---

11   Bingham, *The Rule of Law* (Allen Lane, London, 2010) at 45

appropriate gestation period, to be accepted as part of Ghanaian culture. This is a factor that they will have to consider in their assessment of the efficacy of the proposed legislative measure.

The re-introduction and sustenance of multi-party democracy in Ghana is beginning to have a transformative impact on our society. Perceptions of the relevance of the rule of law and good governance to the development process are based on the assumption that law has a capacity to affect social behaviour. In making available an appropriate legal and constitutional framework for promoting greater democracy, the legal system makes an important contribution to the development process. The idea, espoused by the Nobel Laureate Prof. Amartya Sen, of development as freedom, which has already been referred to above, is again invoked in support of this proposition.[12]

When development is viewed in terms of freedom, the role of law in it can easily be appreciated. The instrumental role of the law to which I have already made reference can sometimes bring the law into conflict with the culture of a people. The role of law in social change can sometimes be to modify certain aspects of the culture of a people. Thus some degree of balancing may need to be undertaken by lawmakers when the law is being used as an instrument to aid development and social transformation. It is not enough for the law to be reflective of the current national spirit, if change is needed in that spirit to enable progress to be made.

I have thus far discussed the rules of the common law and equity and also of statutes. Let me finally touch briefly on customary law which is the third principal category of the sources of law for the Ghanaian legal system. The customary law, being law that has developed from the practice and usage of particular communities in Ghana, is steeped in Ghanaian culture. There can hardly be a complaint that it does not reflect the Ghanaian spirit. However, the task of adaptation of the customary law is of a different order. It is that of the modernisation of aspects of it to adjust it to contemporary Ghanaian mores. The National House of Chiefs is given a role in this task by the 1992 Constitution. Article 272(b)provides that the House

---

12   See Prof. Amartya Sen, *Development as Freedom* (Alfred A. Knopt, New York, 2001) at 3

has a duty to "undertake the progressive study, interpretation and codification of customary law with a view to evolving, in appropriate cases, a unified system of rules of customary law, and compiling the customary laws and lines of succession applicable to each stool or skin." Further, it is given the responsibility to "undertake an evaluation of traditional customs and usage with a view to eliminating those customs and usages that are outmoded and socially harmful."

I will next discuss aspects of the role of law in development, using Ghanaian illustrations. Since 1992, Ghana has embarked on yet another endeavour to make a constitutional regime work. (It is now into its Fourth Republic after its Independence in 1957. Ghana therefore has quite a track record in constitutional experimentation.) It is my hypothesis that there is a relationship between this constitutional regime and the development process.

I believe that since 1992, a firm foundation is being laid for constitutionalism in Ghana. This is a major gain, when viewed from the law and development perspective. The Supreme Court of Ghana commands respect and its decisions are not only universally accepted, but also regularly sought by those seeking to enforce the Constitution. The 1992 Constitution of Ghana confers exclusive original jurisdiction on the Supreme Court in all matters relating to the enforcement or interpretation of the Constitution and also in all matters arising as to whether an enactment was made in excess of the powers conferred on Parliament or any other entity under the Constitution.

The role of constitutionalism

Constitutionalism is about having limits to the powers of constitutional bodies and enforcing those limits. The judiciary, through its exercise of the power of judicial review, is accordingly a vital actor in this process. The Ghana Supreme Court has been quite effective in protecting the legal framework of the liberal multi-party democracy whose *grundnorm* is the 1992 Constitution. An example here would be appropriate. To my mind, this case illustrates the contribution of law to development in Ghana.

17

At first sight, the case (*Ahumah Ocansey v The Electoral Commission; Centre for Human Rights & Civil Liberties v The Attorney-General and The Electoral Commission* [2010] SCGLR 575), which was decided by the Ghana Supreme Court, would appear to have little to do with law and development. The main issue raised in the case, which in fact consisted of two consolidated cases, was whether prisoners were entitled to vote.[13] In spite of article 42 of the 1992 Constitution which provides that every citizen of Ghana of eighteen years of age or above and of sound mind has the right to vote and is entitled to be registered for the purposes of public elections and referenda, the Attorney-General had argued in this case that it was in the public interest that convicted offenders are punished, kept under lock and key and not allowed to vote. The Supreme Court rejected this contention and held that there was no justification for denying prisoners the unqualified right to vote. This right was conferred on all adult Ghanaians who are sane by article 42 of the Constitution. As I said in that case:

> "Nothing in the core values and spirit of the 1992 Constitution justifies the restriction on prisoners' right to vote that is advocated by the learned Attorney-General. There is thus no basis for implying the restriction argued for by the Attorney-General to qualify the clear and unambiguous language of article 42."

This case is important because it buttresses the inviolability of universal adult suffrage in the Ghanaian constitutional and legal system. The case's reaffirmation of the primacy of the right to vote strengthens the system of democratic representative government which underpins the concept of development as freedom. Again, if I may quote a passage from my judgment in that case:

> "Article 42, although it is not contained in Chapter 5 of the Constitution, which is on "Fundamental Human Rights and Freedoms",is for me the first of the fundamental human rights of our Constitution. For without the general right to vote, the system of representative democratic government set out in

---

13 *Ahumah Ocansey v The Electoral Commission; Centre for Human Rights & Civil Liberties v The Attorney-General and The Electoral Commission* [2010] SCGLR 575

the Constitution would fall away and be emptied of content. Without a democratic representative system of government, constructed on the bedrock of universal adult suffrage, the likelihood would be that the rights enshrined in Chapter 5 would be ineffective. It was thus very wise that the framers of our Constitution deemed it appropriate to embody the principle of universal adult suffrage as a specific entrenched provision in our Constitution".

The Supreme Court in this case held that statutory provisions, which laid down that prisoners in lawful custody were not to be regarded as resident in the prison for electoral purposes,were void, because they were in conflict with an express provision of the Constitution. These statutory provisions had the effect of disenfranchising prisoners. The Supreme Court, by thus limiting the power of the executive and the legislature and preventing them from disenfranchising prisoners, bolstered the progress towards constitutionalism in Ghana.

Constitutionalism and a framework of respect for human rights are vital to securing an appropriate enabling environment for development.[14] The liberty to discuss alternative economic strategies and ideas and to mobilize mass political support for such strategies and ideas is essential to development. This liberty creates an opportunity for enterprise, innovation and ingenuity which is of great value in the development process. It is government's prerogative to determine the extent and shape of its intervention in the process. Its political complexion will, of course, affect the nature of its intervention. The judiciary's role is in enforcing and promoting constitutionalism. This is an important contribution to development and is a manifestation of the role of law in development.

The effect of judicial philosophy

The judiciary's efficacy in performing this role is bound to be affected by the judicial philosophy that it espouses, whether wittingly or unwittingly. Judges' perception of what their role is in relation to

---

14   Cf. S.K.B. Asante, *Reflections on the Constitution, Law and Development*, The J.B. Danquah Memorial Lectures, Series 35, March 2002. (Ghana Academy of Arts and Sciences, Accra, 2002) 39.

law-making is part of any such judicial philosophy. Let me thus begin a discussion of this issue with a quotation from Lord Reid of the English House of Lords, speaking extra judicially:[15]

> "There was a time when it was thought almost indecent to suggest that judges make law – they only declare it. Those with a taste for fairy tales seem to have thought that in some Aladdin's cave there is hidden the Common Law in all its splendour and that on a judge's appointment there descends on him [or her] knowledge of the magic words Open Sesame. Bad decisions are given when the judge has muddled the pass word and the wrong door opens. But we do not believe in fairy tales anymore."

Lord Reid is here, of course, making fun of the declaratory theory of the judicial function. According to this, judges do not make law; they merely discover pre-existing law, through their trained eye. This view of the judicial function is now clearly *passé*. There is no doubt that judges do make law. The debate has now shifted to the extent to which they make law or should make law.

My own view, of course, is that judges do make law sometimes, but not all the time. Indeed, they make law far less often than they merely apply existing law. But their perception of whether or not they have the right to make law, albeit in constrained circumstances, can be important to the role they are able to play as agents of change in the development process. Why do judges make law? An answer to this question is provided by the Australian judge, Justice Brennan in the Australian case of *Gala v Preston* (1991) 172 CLR 243 at162:

> "The purpose of judicial development of legal principle is to keep the law in good repair as an instrument of resolving disputes according to justice as it is understood in contemporary society, subject to statute … In a society where values change and where the relationships affected by law become increasingly complex, judicial development of the law is a duty of the courts – more especially when legislative law reform languishes."

---

15 See "The Judge as Law maker" (1972) 12 *Journal of the Society Public Teachers of Law 22* at 22.

This justification for judicial law-making has a special resonance in relation to the Ghanaian legal system, where the law reform function of the legislature has lagged behind. In those areas where the courts can interstitially fill the gaps left unattended by the legislature, there is particular need for activism by the judges.

Even the great positivist, John Austin, recognized the need for judicial law-making. I would like to quote, in this connection, a passage from his *Lectures on Jurisprudence:*[16]

> "...I must here observe that I am not objecting to Lord Mansfield for assuming the office of a legislator. I by no means disapprove of what Mr. Bentham has chosen to call by the disrespectful, and therefore, as I conceive, injudicious, name of judge-made law. For I consider it injudicious to call by any name indicative of disrespect what appears to me highly beneficial and even absolutely necessary. I cannot understand how any person who has considered the subject can suppose that society could possibly have gone on if judges had not legislated, or that there is any danger whatever in allowing them that power which they have in fact exercised, to make up for the negligence or the incapacity of the avowed legislator. That part of the law of every country which was made by judges has been far better made than that part which consists of statutes enacted by the legislature. Notwithstanding my great admiration for Mr. Bentham, I cannot but think that, instead of blaming judges for having legislated, he should blame them for the timid, narrow, and piecemeal manner in which they have legislated, and for legislating under cover of vague and indeterminate phrases, such as Lord Mansfield employed in the above example, and which would be censurable in any legislator."

Indeed, Austin expresses himself in favour of greater judicial activism than he witnessed in his day.[17]

---

16   Ed. Campbell at 218-9:

17   Thus Austin also said in his *Lectures on Jurisprudence*, op.cit. p. 644: "The truth is, that too great a respect for established rules,and too great a regard for consequence and analogy,has generally been shewn by the authors of judiciary law."

Austin's insights confirm the nature of orthodox judicial law making and its limitations. Judges are generally not inclined to make new law unless they need to. In any case, in making new law they tend to develop the law by analogy from the existing law. Accordingly, judges do not establish revolutionary change. That is for the legislature. It is this restraint that Austin complains about.

This judicial law making role can be illustrated with a case from the Ghanaian jurisdiction. This is the Supreme Court case of *CCWL* v *Accra Metropolitan Area.*[18] The facts of the case were that a waste disposal contract was awarded to a private company by a city council in breach of statutory provisions regarding the award process. The contract on which the company sued was thus adjudged to be illegal. However, in the meantime, the company had rendered services to the city which were worth a considerable amount of money on any reckoning. On these facts, the issue which the Supreme Court had to resolve was whether restitution should be made to the company for the value of its services, even though the contract on which it had sued was illegal. Applying the received case law from the English jurisdiction would have meant denying the company any relief. However,this area of law has long been regarded as not satisfactory and so the decision made by the Supreme Court was deliberately intended to develop the Ghanaian law in this area, departing from the strict English law. The Supreme Court identified the issue to be resolved as follows:

> "The common law doctrine of illegality of contract is complex and its effect often unjust. Consequently, some common law jurisdictions (such as New Zealand, through its Illegal Contracts Act 1970) have undertaken legislative reform of the effects of the doctrine. The facts of this case pose the issue whether this Court should, in this jurisdiction, wait for such legislative reform or whether it would be appropriate for this final Court to take a decision which constitutes a step in a stepwise judicial reform of the law to achieve a just result on the facts of this case. .... On the facts of this case, what is difficult is not the determination of whether the contract sued on was illegal or not. Rather, the difficulty is with determining

18   [2007-2008] SCGLR 409.

the legal consequences of such determination. It is with regard to the effect of a determination of illegality that this Court will need to be creative in order to serve the needs of justice."

It was in furtherance of this need to be creative that the Court reached the following conclusion:

"The critical issue is whether this Court is entitled to grant the Plaintiff restitutionary relief in respect of the services actually rendered the Defendant or whether the illegality of the contract is also a defence to the restitutionary claim. It is open to this Court to base an alternative restitutionary claim on the Plaintiff's claim for the recovery of the value of its services, indorsed on its Writ, although the Plaintiff's intent was to found that claim on the contract that we have held to be illegal. The Plaintiff can legitimately argue that a restitutionary claim by it is not equivalent to enforcing the illegal contract. The Plaintiff is bound by the unenforceability of the illegal contract. Nevertheless, in the interest of justice, it is reasonable for the Plaintiff to seek to reverse the unjust enrichment of the Defendant through its retention of the benefit of the Plaintiff's services without any payment for them at a reasonable rate, not necessarily coincident with the contract rate negotiated under the illegal contract. In the English case law, the illegality of a contract has been held to be an effective defence to even a restitutionary claim, unless the parties are not *in pari delicto* (or equally at fault).

...We do not think that we ought int his Court to be constrained excessively by the weight of the English case law in finding a just outcome in this case. Rather, we are encouraged to develop Ghanaian law in this area by some of the ideas contained in the English Law Commission's Consultation Paper No. 154 on *Illegal Transactions: The Effect of Illegality on Contracts and Trusts*. This Consultative Paper, after an extensive and erudite review of the complex English law in the area, concludes as follows (at p.91):

... The adoption of some type of discretionary approach has the support of the vast majority of academic commentatorsin this area; and it is the approach which has been followed in those jurisdictions where legislation has been implemented. Moreover,we have not been able to devise a new enlightened regime of "rules" that would provide satisfactory answers to all disputes involving illegal contracts. In our view, a balancing of various factors is required so that, put quite simply, the law on illegal contracts does not lend itself to a regime of rules."

We have decided to adopt this structured discretionary approach to the resolution of issues arising from illegality of contracts. The approach is to be fleshed out on a case by case basis. On the facts of the present case, balancing the need to deny enforceability to the contract sued on by the Plaintiff against the need to prevent the unjust enrichment of the Defendant, and, considering that in relation to the Defendant's non-compliance with the statutory provisions binding on it, the Plaintiff was not *in pari delicto* in a broad sense, we have come to the conclusion that the Plaintiff must be paid reasonable compensation for the services it rendered to the Defendant."

A recognition by the judiciary of its role in the development process has to be accompanied by an interpretative stance that advances the needs of development. In my experience, I have found that a purposive approach to interpretation is the one that best meets the needs of a progressive judiciary. Judges have the crucial responsibility of serving as a bridge between the cold words of a Constitution or a statute and their application to real life situations. In this task, judges inevitably have to interpret the words of the Constitution or statute. The type of interpretative stance that judges adopt has come to be given labels like "purposive", "golden rule" etc. In the Ghanaian case of *Asare v Attorney-General*, referring to the so-called "rules of interpretation", I said[19]:

---

19   [2003-2004] SCGLR 823 at 833

""Rules" of interpretation are not to be understood as binding courts in the same way as the *ratio decidendi* of a case is binding on subsequent courts. The so-called "rules" of interpretation are merely guides or aids to judges in deciphering the meaning of words they are required to interpret. As Lord Reid said in *Maunsell v Olins*[20] :

> "They are not rules in the ordinary sense of having some binding force. They are our servants, not our masters. They are aids to construction: presumptions or pointers. Not infrequently one "rule" points in one direction, another in a different direction. In each case we must look at all relevant circumstances and decide as a matter of judgment what weight is to be attached to any particular"rule"."

This is a helpful *dictum* reminding us that the task of interpretation is always complex, usually involving the balancing of competing interests, and the "rules" of interpretation, whether the "Literal Rule", "the Golden Rule", "the Mischief Rule" or the "Purposive Approach", are to be applied in the context of particular enactments in order to achieve justice. What I have stated above has been merely to emphasise that I consider the purposive approach to be more likely to achieve the ends of justice in most cases."

The role of legislation

The judiciary alone, however, cannot devise and maintain a framework of law conducive to development. Indeed, in the fast-moving contemporary economic and political circumstances, the role of the legislature is key to what the law can achieve as an instrument of change and development. Legislation needs to address the dual role of law as both a facilitator and regulator of economic activities and enterprise.

An example of the kind of intervention which needs to be made by legislation in support of development and where judicial law-

---

20   [1975]1 All ER 16 at 18

making does not have a comparative advantage is the Electronic Transactions Act, 2008 of Ghana (Act772). The object of the Act is:[21]

"to provide for and facilitate electronic communications and related transactions in the public interest, and to

a. Remove and prevent barriers to electronic communications and transactions;

b. Promote legal certainty and confidence in electronic communications and transactions;

c. Promote e-governance services and electronic communications and transactions with public and private bodies, institutions and citizens;

d. Develop a safe, secure and effective environment for the consumer, business and the Government to conduct and use electronic transactions;

e. Promote the development of electronic transaction services responsive to the needs of consumers;

f. Ensure that, in relation to the provision of electronic transaction services, the special needs of vulnerable groups and communities and persons with disabilities are duly taken into account;

g. Ensure compliance with accepted international technical standards in the provision and development of electronic communications and transactions;

h. Ensure efficient use and management of the country domain name space; and

i. Ensure that the interest and image of the Republic are not compromised through the use of electronic communications."

Clearly in a digital age, this framework legislation is needed to expedite the more widespread application of information and communication technology to the transactions and processes which feed economic growth and development. It is a particular manifestation of the facilitating and regulatory role of law that needs to be carried out through legislation in modern economies. This

---

21   See section 1 of the Act.

role of legislation in the development process was recognized in the following recommendation by African leaders and industrialists who met in Gaberone, Botswana in June 1995 to deliberate on the private sector:

> "Governments should promulgate clear, coherent and stable laws and regulations, especially relating to the private sector, which should be widely disseminated. In addition, governments should establish the appropriate institutional framework to administer, implement and to ensure transparent and orderly enforcement of these laws and regulations."[22]

There is no doubt that legislation has a crucial role to play in the development process. The instrumental role of law in the process will often need to be carried out through legislation that enables judges and administrators to implement the needed change, facilitation or regulation. The efficacy of particular legislation will depend on the issues relating to the limits of law identified at the beginning of this Chapter and on the efficiency and integrity of the judiciary and public servants, among other factors. Legislation is a useful tool in providing for a legal infrastructure that enables the carrying out of economic activities that fuel economic growth. For instance, the Petroleum (Exploration and Production) Law 1984 [23] provided the framework within which petroleum agreements were concluded which have led to the discovery of oil and gas in Ghana. Prior to the production of oil and gas in the country for the first time, there was a demand across the political spectrum for more legislation to govern the distribution of the revenue that would be generated by this new source of wealth and also to provide for local content in the goods and services consumed by the industry.

Implementation of legislation and other laws by the judiciary

Regarding the implementation of legislation by the judiciary, the Ghanaian Constitution makes provision for a judiciary whose independence is guaranteed. This independence has a significant impact on the efficacy of the courts. The courts enjoy greater

---

22   Quoted in Asante, *op.cit.*67

23   PNDCL 84

credibility among those seeking access to justice, if they are believed to be free from government control. The Superior Courts, consisting of the Supreme Court, the Court of Appeal and the High Court, are established directly by the Constitution and Parliament has no authority to vary their jurisdiction or add to their number. Parliament may only create inferior courts. The formal source of the legitimacy of the Judiciary in Ghana is Article 125(1) of the 1992 Constitution which provides that:

> "Justice emanates from the people and shall be administered in the name of the Republic by the Judiciary which shall be independent and subject only to this Constitution."

Article 125(3) also states that:

> "The judicial power of Ghana shall be vested in the Judiciary, accordingly, neither the President nor Parliament nor any organ or agency of the President or Parliament shall have or be given final judicial power."

The Ghana judiciary thus has a high degree of autonomy in determining how to implement legislation. The Chief Justice has the discretion to determine what Divisions of the High Court may do what. In the exercise of this discretion, the Chief Justice has established the Fast Track Division of the High Court and also the Commercial Division of the High Court.[24] These have made a major impact on the delivery of justice and the implementation of laws.

The judicial process also serves as a backdrop to the facilitation provided by private law generally to the development process. The enforcement and enforceability of property rights and contracts are essential to the functioning and development of the economy in Ghana and virtually all developing States. Indeed, those parts of the legal system needed by private enterprises for the making and implementation of private investment decisions have legitimately been described as constituting the legal infrastructure of private

---

24   See Date-Bah, "Developing a New Commercial Court in Ghana" (2007) 42 *Texas International Law Journal 619*

investment.[25] It is this legal infrastructure that enables the deal-making in the market-place which drives contemporary market economies. The courts' role in the maintenance of this legal infrastructure is yet another of their contributions to the role of law in development.

Conclusion

How much of the development process is achievable through law and how much through other means remains a subject for investigation which no doubt will receive the scholarly attention that it deserves in institutions of higher learning. This short Chapter has sought to show through Ghanaian examples that law does have apart to play in the process of development, but that there are other factors also in play which need to be given due attention.

The legal system which Ghana has inherited has a rich tapestry of different sources of law. Not all the rules of law emanating from these various sources can be said to be reflective of the "Ghanaian spirit", whatever that means. It is, therefore, the continuing responsibility of the Ghanaian Parliament and Judiciary to customise foreign legal transplants to Ghanaian needs and culture and also to update our customary law to bring it into tune with contemporary Ghanaian culture. In adjusting the law to the needs of Ghanaian culture, our lawmakers should be mindful always of the overarching goal of Ghanaian society, which is development. What I am urging is a continuous process of law reform to make the Ghanaian legal system responsive to the needs of national development. I have advocated the view that developing and sustaining a system of good governance and the rule of law will serve this national need.

---

25 Cf. S.K. Date-Bah, "Private Investment and Law in a Developing Economy: Reflections" in *Ghana Academy of Arts and Sciences, Law & Religion: Inaugural Lectures* (Accra, 2006)19 at 35.

LEGAL EDUCATION IN GHANA:
INTERNATIONAL AND LOCAL DIMENSIONS[26]

Introduction

While all countries need to find a balance between local and international elements in legal education, it is my general impression that in many countries the international and transnational dimensions of law are not given sufficient weight in legal education programmes. Accordingly, the theme for this chapter is that legal education should pay more attention to international and transnational dimensions than is now customary in many of the legal systems of the Commonwealth. Legal educators everywhere, to my mind, need to work seriously to redress any imbalance. In this Chapter, Ghana is used to illustrate this general theme and focus attention on the more general discussion which should take place in legal education circles regarding the right balance to be struck between local and international considerations. It is intended to provoke a debate on what that right balance should be.

The Chapter briefly considers some of the local and international aspects of legal education in Ghana. It then goes on to examine the issue of what more is required to give Ghanaian legal education a transnational element that is fit for purpose in the twenty-first century.

Studying the common law has an international dimension, except perhaps in the largest jurisdictions. For a small to medium jurisdiction such as the Ghanaian, many of the issues for which the common law has fashioned answers may not have arisen in local litigation. Accordingly, the case law of other common law jurisdictions has to be studied to fill the gaps in the local case law. On the other hand, right from the date of introduction of English

---

26   This Chapter is based on a paper that was the author's key note address to the Commonwealth Legal Education Association in Glasgow in April 2015.

law into Ghana, the colonial authorities preserved the application of the indigenous customary law. That body of law is local to Ghana and plays its role alongside the common law in the Ghanaian legal system. Additionally, there is, of course, Ghanaian legislation. The country's resultant pluralistic legal system implies that there are both international and local elements that any system of legal education for Ghana will have to incorporate. This is quite apart from the need to study public international law, private international law and the various elements of transnational law. It is clear that merely teaching the common law from other jurisdictions, the local common and customary laws and local statutory and constitutional law in Ghana would not amount to delivering a transnational legal education in the country. More transnationalism in educational perspectives is needed because of the increased interdependence in the modern world on international trade and investment, increased social interaction across national boundaries and political cross-penetration.

The Origins of Legal Education in Ghana

The modern legal profession in Ghana, trained in the common law, dates back to the late nineteenth century. The formal reception of English law into the then Gold Coast was in 1876 by the Supreme Court Ordinance, 1876. Initially some Ghanaians were allowed to practise before the local colonial courts without any formal legal training. Soon however, young Ghanaians went to the Inns of Court in London for legal training as barristers and returned to practise before the local courts. Professional legal training remained an overseas activity for Ghanaian lawyers until late 1958, when the Ghana Law School was established.

The origins of legal education in Ghana today, therefore, are traceable to the establishment of the Ghana Law School. That School, although local, had an international dimension right from the start as the moving spirit behind its establishment was Geoffrey Bing, QC, an English barrister and former Member of the UK Parliament, who was then Attorney-General of Ghana. Thus, although the Ghana Law School constituted the first attempt to localise the training of lawyers in Ghana, it was introduced through a foreign protagonist. Among the reasons advanced by Bing for championing the establishment of the Ghana Law School was the need to increase the supply of lawyers in the country and to provide an opportunity for able Ghanaians to study for legal qualification part-time in the evenings. The Ghana Law School provided non-University part-time legal education for those who could not make it to the United Kingdom for legal training. Bing was also a political adviser of Dr. Kwame Nkrumah, Ghana's leader at Independence, and the political advantage to Nkrumah of diluting the ranks of the British trained lawyers, who tended to be conservative and opposed to Nkrumah, with a supply of locally trained ones would not have been lost on him.

The origins of university-based legal education in Ghana are traceable to a decision by the Council of the University College of the Gold Coast in 1956 to establish a Department of Law. The appointment by the Ghana Government of an International Advisory Committee, comprising Professors L.C.B. Gower of the London School of Economics, Zelman Cowen, a Vice-Chancellor of an Australian University and Arthur Sutherland of the Harvard Law School, facilitated the implementation of this decision. The Committee produced a Report on Legal Education in Ghana which recommended two routes to the practice of law in the country. One route was through a four-year LL.B degree programme at the University, followed by a year's practical training at the Ghana School of Law. The other route was through a diploma programme offered by the Ghana School of Law, followed by a year's practical training at the same institution.

The Department of Law at the University College of Ghana was established in 1958 and admitted its first students in October 1959. It later became the Faculty of Law in 1962, after the University College of Ghana became the independent University of Ghana[27]. The two institutions: namely, the Faculty of Law at the University of Ghana and the Ghana School of Law, have played critical roles in establishing legal education in Ghana, combining local and international dimensions.

---

27   Recently, the Law Faculty has been renamed the School of Law of the University of Ghana.

Interplay between English and American Influences on Ghanaian Legal Education

International influence on Ghanaian legal education has come principally from England and the United States of America. The first Head of the Department of Law at the University College of Ghana was an English solicitor, Professor Lang. He was also the first Director of Legal Education appointed by the General Legal Council,the regulator of the legal profession in Ghana, to take charge of the Ghana School of Law. He served for about two years. His approach to legal education was naturally derived from his country of origin. He established a system of lectures and tutorials at the University. He was succeeded in both his roles at the University and the Ghana Law School by Professor William Burnett Harvey,an American from Michigan University.

Professor Harvey was quite critical of the system of instruction in place on his assumption of office. He thought that it relied excessively on the learning of rules and doctrines. While he accepted that a certain level of information about rules and doctrines was inevitable in legal education, he did not consider the learning of such information to be the principal objective of legal education. Rather, his view was that what was critical were the skills of case analysis, statutory interpretation and the ability to develop useful doctrinal generalisations from prior experience. These skills he did not consider could be communicated through lectures to which students were mere listeners. Students needed to be more active participants in class and needed to prepare before lessons. In short, he was in favour of the Socratic method widely in practice in the US. His view was that students developed by performing or attempting to perform lawyer's tasks under the guidance of the law teacher. The law teacher's task was to organise the cases and other materials to stimulate the student to sharpen his analytical skills.

The contrasting pedagogical approaches to legal education by Professors Lang and Harvey have continued to compete even in contemporary Ghana. The didactic lecture remains in competition with the Socratic method. It is for individual law lecturers to determine what particular pedagogical methods to adopt. When

I taught contract law to first year students at the Faculty of Law at the University of Ghana in the 1970s, I deployed the Socratic method, because of my experience as a student at the Yale Law School. Some colleague lecturers used the straight lecture method, but still allowed, and even encouraged, students to ask questions during lectures. This eclecticism took place within the context of a legal education programme which was itself eclectic. The lecture method,however, appears to have won against the Socratic method, as the main method of instruction in Ghanaian legal education institutions today.

The Ghanaian legal education programme, championed by Dean Harvey and put in place after the amendment of Professor Lang's initial programme, was justified by a position paper from the Law Faculty dated October 1962. It stated that:

"4.   The circumstances of certain of the new countries may justify "crash programs" for the training of minimally qualified legal technicians. We see no persuasive evidence that these circumstances obtain in Ghana today. Therefore, in projecting its program, Ghana is entitled to concentrate on the production of lawyers who are soundly and liberally educated, entitled to full acceptance and respect in the international legal community.

5.   No existing system of legal education provides a model fully responsive to Ghana's conditions and needs. British University education in law, which achieves magnificently in the development of analytical skills and historical perspective, can perhaps afford to be extremely non-professional in view of the ancient instructional programs of the Inns as well as the pre- professional apprenticeships and courses of study required of solicitors. In America the University law schools long tended toward excessive, narrowing professionalism. A high degree of professionalism can be defended there, however, in view of the fact that law is post-graduate education, the student having pursued his general studies beyond the secondary school level and very commonly having earned a B.A. or equivalent degree

before entering law school. The German system involves an interesting combination of legal and non- legal instruction. The Universities are able, however, to shape their programs in reliance on the student's having three years of referendar study and practical observation after leaving the University and before entering his profession. Thus the underlying assumptions of the various foreign models are not valid in Ghana. This country must devise its own model, borrowing from abroad whatsoever is useful but feeling no initial commitment to any pattern merely on the basis of familiarity."

This justification for the system of legal education, proposed by the Law Faculty and adopted by the University and the General Legal Council, also explains the current legal education system in Ghana, although it has been tweaked and has evolved since those early heady days of 1962. From its early days, the Ghanaian legal education system was, and has remained, customised to Ghanaian needs. A relevant fact is that there was an early "Ghanaianisation" of the Law Faculty because a dispute broke out between the Ghana Government and Dean Harvey and some of the American law teachers who had been recruited by him. This led to a mass departure of most of them in 1963. The subsequent predominance of Ghanaians on the Law Faculty meant that there was consolidation of the customisation of the legal education programme to Ghanaian needs.

Current State of Legal Education in Ghana[28]

Ghana's legal education provision has now evolved beyond the two original institutions described above. Legal education providers now include four public universities as well as several privately-owned university colleges. The four public universities are: University of Ghana, at Legon, Accra; Kwame Nkrumah University of Science and Technology ("KNUST") in Kumasi; University of Cape Coast in Cape Coast; and the Ghana Institute of Management and Public Administration (or GIMPA) in Accra. The privately-

---

28   It should be stressed that what follows is true only as of 2015. Subsequently, additional Faculties of Law have been established.

owned Colleges, which are all affiliated to the KNUST Law Faculty are: Mount Crest University College, Central University College, Wisconsin University College and Kaaf University College. Other privately-owned institutions, such as Zenith University College and the Empire African Institute, prepare students to sit for external LL.B degrees of the University of London, under its International Programmes. Lancaster University Ghana also runs a programme for a Lancaster degree and another privately-owned college prepares students for a London Metropolitan University LL.B degree. The original Ghana School of Law has also now grown and has three campuses for the professional/vocational training of lawyers.

The curriculum of the University of Ghana's School of Law (formerly the Law Faculty) may be used as a microcosm of that of the other institutions of legal education in Ghana. (The Faculty of Law of the University of Ghana was renamed "the School of Law" in 2015 after an internal restructuring of the University.) Both the curriculum put in place under the leadership of Professor Harvey in 1962 and that which preceded it under the leadership of Professor Lang,included subjects of transnational import: namely, comparative law, conflict of laws and public international law. These subjects are of even greater relevance in the contemporary more globalised legal world. Although, ideally, Law Faculties and Law Schools currently need to pay more attention to legal systems beyond their own domestic law, unfortunately in contemporary Ghana, imparting knowledge of the domestic legal system has predominated over expanding education on transnational law.

Thus, comparative law, for instance, has virtually disappeared from the LL.B curriculum of the University of Ghana's School of Law. Although it is nominally in the syllabus, it is not taught. This is a pity since comparative law, as we all know, is the systematic study and comparison of different legal systems. The methods evolved in this discipline provide a useful tool for expanding the transnational dimensions of legal education. There is, however, some countervailing progress in the School of Law's introduction of some more detailed courses of transnational interest such as: international trade and investment law, natural resources law, environmental law and international human rights law. Public international law and conflict of laws also remain on the curriculum.

The full curriculum for the LL.B degree at the University of Ghana comprises: Ghana Legal System, Legal Method, Law of Contract, Constitutional Law, Torts, Immovable Property, Criminal Law, Public International Law, Administrative Law, Jurisprudence, Equity, Law of Succession, International Trade and Investment Law, Natural Resources Law, Intellectual Property Law, Conflict of Laws, Commercial Law, International Human Rights Law, Gender and the Law, Environmental Law, Criminology, ADR, Taxation, International Human Rights Law, English for Law Students and Logic for Law Students. There is thus little doubt that subjects dealing with domestic Ghanaian law predominate.

The Law Faculties of sister Ghanaian Universities and University Colleges follow a similar trend. In addition, KNUST and Cape Coast Universities incorporate elements of professional skills training in their curricula. The KNUST curriculum, by way of further illustration, offers the following subjects: Ghana Legal System and Method, Constitutional Law, Law of Contract, Law of Torts, Criminal Law, Land Law, Equity and Trusts, Administrative Law,Introduction to Trial Advocacy, Conflict of Laws,Commercial Law, Public International Law, Jurisprudence, Legal English and Study Skills, Legal Drafting, Analytical and Research Skills, Law Clinic and Environmental Law. There are also electives including: Intellectual Property Law, Labour Law, Law of Evidence, Revenue and Taxation Law, International Human Rights Law, International Trade and Investment Law, Medical Law and Ethics, Petroleum and Natural Resources Law,Criminology,Family Law, Sports Law, Computers and the Law and Gender and the Law.

Transnationalism

The issue which arises is whether the need of many Ghanaian lawyers for transnational legal skills is adequately addressed by the existing local legal education system. This is an issue that probably confronts the legal systems of many other countries.

To equip lawyers trained in Ghana with the skills needed to succeed in the modern international market place and in the socially and politically interwoven world that we inhabit, the Ghanaian institutions of higher learning which teach law should systematically consider the international and transnational dimensions of law and embody imaginative elements in their curricula. This is an issue which is probably a live one for many jurisdictions. There is thus currently a great opportunity for imaginative curriculum development to meet the needs of the contemporary world. This opportunity needs to be seized by legal educators such as those at this meeting. How you do it is best left to you. My task is merely to highlight the need for it. We need to take to heart the credible argument that has been made by comparatists for years, namely that comparative law teaches respect for legal cultures of other peoples, through which students eventually come to understand their own domestic law better. Quite apart from such respect, I consider that an expanded teaching of comparative law should help in a better functioning of the legal transactions and activities of our globalised world.

Since the late 1950s and the early 1960s when the rudiments of the legal education system in Ghana were laid down, the world has become much more interconnected technologically, economically and politically. Legal education in Ghana and elsewhere has to respond to this more globalised context. It is no longer adequate to teach conflict of laws and public international law in the traditional fashion. Students need to be made aware of new developments, such as the creation of parallel law by international arbitrators which does not necessarily coincide with the law that issues from state institutions such as municipal courts and international courts. Law students need to be equipped with the skills to deal with this arbitral law and similar phenomena.

In view of the above, restoring the teaching of comparative law in Ghanaian legal education institutions is an important part of the required strategy for giving greater emphasis to the transnational dimensions of law. Comparative legal studies are, in my view, an essential part of the international dimensions of Ghanaian legal education which need to be given a boost. Unfortunately, the training of Ghanaian comparative law teachers has been problematic, since not enough people have been attracted into this specialisation. More needs to be done to encourage young graduates to specialise in comparative law. Comparative law introduces students to legal concepts and methods different from what they are used to in their domestic legal system. It thus enables them to understand better the view point of lawyers from other jurisdictions with whom they have to interact in the contemporary globalised milieu. A trend seems to be evolving by which comparative law courses are taught at the postgraduate level in some Ghanaian institutions. For instance, the Faculty of Law at Kwame Nkrumah University of Science and Technology has proposed, to the National Accreditation Board, an LL.M programme which includes a course in Comparative Constitutional Law, besides courses in international law and municipal law.

Another way of infusing comparative law dimensions into the curriculum is to integrate comparative law aspects into the teaching of the main bread and butter LL.B subjects, such as contract and torts. For this to happen, however, the teachers of these subjects must themselves have some level of comparative legal education.

It is worth mentioning that the curriculum for the Lancaster University Law School, Ghana, includes a course on Introduction to Comparative Law and also Courts, Law and Politics in Comparative Perspectives. The University of London International Programmes LL.B curriculum also includes a course on "Introduction to Islamic Law," but none on general comparative law. Thus, apart from the Lancaster University Law School in Ghana, my critique of the curricula of legal education providers in Ghana applies also to the non-Ghanaian providers.

Beyond comparative law, there should be an endeavour to view law more transnationally and to reflect this transnational view in legal education. States cannot afford to be legally islands unto themselves, so to speak. This is probably true of all States these days. I understand transnational law to be the aggregation of international law and domestic law (both of host states and foreign states)applicable to cross-border cases, problems and issues. Increasingly, in these contemporary times, such law may be "soft law", in the sense that the norms applicable to particular problems or issues may not be made by State institutions, such as Parliaments or courts, but by private entities such as commercial arbitral tribunals, industry-wide rule making bodies, or by particular companies through the corporate best practices they have accepted. Greater effort is required to make students aware of the hard and soft law which make up transnational law. Students need to be introduced to the output of bodies such as UNIDROIT (the International Institute for the Unification of Private Law) and UNCITRAL (the United Nations Commission on International Trade Law), the decisions of regional bodies such as the African Court of Human and People's Rights, the European Court of Justice, the Inter-American Court of Human Rights, the Directives and Regulations of the European Union and the decisions of arbitral tribunals set up by the ICC (International Chamber of Commerce) and ICSID (the International Centre for the Settlement of Investment Disputes).

It has become trendy to speak, in some circles, of "global governance". By this is meant that a combination of hard and soft law across borders increasingly governs important aspects of the modern world. To understand how this governance works, prospective lawyers have got to be educated to be able to decipher the various standards and rules laid down by both formal and informal networks of both domestic and international governmental and non-governmental institutions.

Conclusion

In short, the local elements of legal education in Ghana are well taken care of in the curricula of the local institutions of legal education, with the exception of those that teach for external degrees whose awarding institutions cannot be expected to customise their degrees to the needs of Ghana. However, there is a need for Ghanaian legal education providers to raise their game in relation to the international dimensions of legal education. There needs to be a revival of comparative law and greater emphasis on transnational law in an endeavour to equip students with the knowledge and skills needed to solve contemporary legal problems of a globalised world. What the right balance is between domestic and transnational/international law is the subject for a debate that will continue. I hope that this Chapter has drawn attention to the need for that debate.

CHAPTER 4

THE LAW FACULTY OF THE UNIVERSITY OF GHANA'S CONTRIBUTION TO LEGAL EDUCATION, EDUCATION IN GENERAL, GOVERNANCE AND SOCIO-ECONOMIC DEVELOPMENT IN GHANA[29]

Introduction

This Chapter is an abbreviated and aggregated version of the two Golden Jubilee Lectures of the University of Ghana's Faculty of Law, which I delivered in 2009. The University of Ghana is located at Legon, in Accra, and so sometimes the place name Legon is used to refer to it.

The contribution of the University of Ghana's Law Faculty to legal education and education in general in Ghana has to be considered within the context of the history of legal education in the common law world and the dual purpose of law teaching in universities. Universities in the common law world seek to impart vocational/professional skills to law students, whilst also endeavouring to give them a sound university education. There is thus a balance to be struck between the vocational and the academic and that balance is judged differently in different universities.

Legal Education at the University of Ghana, Legon

As indicated in the preceding chapter, it was not until a decade after the establishment of the University College of the Gold Coast that a Department of Law was founded at Legon. This was in 1959. The founding Head of Department was Professor JHA Lang, an English solicitor. At that time, there were basically two paradigms of legal education in the common law world, in terms of pedagogy. In the United States of America, there was the Socratic method using

---

29 This Chapter is based on an abridged and aggregated version of two lectures I delivered on 5th and 6th March 2009, in commemoration of the Golden Jubilee of the Law Faculty of the University of Ghana. The presentations were made at the British Council Hall, Accra.

case books, which pedagogic method had been established by the famous Professor Langdell (1806-1906) at the Harvard Law School. The focus of this method was to impart technique, rather than any quantified amount of knowledge of black letter law. As is well-known, the method consists of students reading, ahead of classes, certain assigned cases and then being asked probing questions about the cases by the law lecturer. The ensuing interaction between law teacher and student helps the student to develop the capacity to analyse cases and distil from them the principles that are needed for effective statements of the common law. The method continues to dominate law teaching in the US.

In England and the Commonwealth, on the other hand, law tended to be taught in fairly didactic lectures, with students getting their chance to ask questions and discuss ideas in more detail in tutorials. The Legon Law Faculty was founded on the English pedagogical paradigm. When I was admitted as a student to the Law Faculty in 1962, there was a well-established tradition of lectures and tutorials. Lecturers prepared their lecture notes on the black letter law and delivered them. Whilst a few questions by students in the course of these lectures were permitted, it was always understood that not too many such interruptions were desirable. In tutorials, however, the participation of students was actively encouraged. This paradigm of law teaching meant that legal education at Legon was very black letter law oriented. The legal education was thus very normative. Students learnt many rules and there was not much focus on the impact of these rules on the ground. In effect, one could say that law was taught as one of the humanities and not as a social science.

For non-lawyers, and even for lawyers, it is helpful to state that legal reasoning tends to take the form of what the students of logic call a syllogism. A typical syllogism may be expressed as follows:

If $X = Y$

And $Y = Z$

Then $X = Z$.

The first line, i.e. X = Y, is referred to as the major premise. The second line, i.e. Y = Z is called the minor premise, while the third line is referred to as the conclusion.

An example of a syllogism would be:

It is an offence to steal.
The accused has stolen.
Therefore, the accused has committed an offence.

Much of the legal education that I received at Legon was intended to equip me to formulate the major premiss in this syllogism. The major premiss in legal reasoning is usually the proposition of law which is sought to be applied to a set of facts. Formulating the right legal proposition requires skill and generations of lawyers who have passed through Legon have been taught the skill. The minor premiss in the syllogism will be established in court situations through the law of evidence and the advocacy skills of the lawyer. It is thus not a principal focus of legal education. However, the capacity to construct a valid argument from the major premiss and the minor premiss in order to reach a valid conclusion is an important part of legal education. It is this core of legal education, as it has been imparted at Legon, which makes me assert that law has been taught as one of the humanities, rather than a social science at Legon. Up to the time when I left the Law Faculty in 1981 and, I suspect, up to today, the empirical method has not been a significant feature of law teaching there.

If you are studying sociology at Legon, you are taught research methods, including quantitative techniques, which enable you to administer questionnaires and other empirical investigative methods and to evaluate the results of such investigations. Law teaching and research at Legon have, to the best of my knowledge, not moved in this direction. As a young law Lecturer at the Faculty in the 1970s, I had some pretensions towards the empirical method. I was influenced by the work of Professor Stewart Macaulay of the University of Wisconsin, who had done empirical work to verify the underlying values of contract law in Wisconsin. I thus embarked on empirical work in Accra to ascertain what values underlay the contract formation of various actors on the Ghanaian scene. I sent students into Makola market in Accra and various other relevant places with questionnaires seeking to elicit the values that underlay the contracting behaviour of the people who were interviewed. Those were the days when such surveys would be analysed by being recorded on punch cards. That was as far as I got. I never got to analyse the results for one reason or another. This story is told in order to motivate the new generation of legal academics to embark on work at the empirical level. Law in action is worthy of investigation. We cannot continue to live in our normative cocoon.

A caveat needs to be sounded here though. The fact that a legal argument is expressed in syllogistic form does not mean that it is only logic that is leading to the conclusion of the argument. There is always the matter of the inarticulate major premiss. The values of the judge may have influenced him in the construction of the major premiss of the syllogism, thus influencing the conclusion of the argument. Justice Oliver Wendell Holmes (1841 – 1935) makes this point in the following passage from his article on *The Path of the Law* [30]:

> "The training of lawyers is a training in logic…The language of judicial decision is mainly the language of logic. And the logical method and form flatter that longing for certainty and for repose which is in every human mind. But certainty generally is an illusion, and repose is not the destiny of man. Behind the logical form lies a judgment as to the relative worth and importance of competing legislative grounds, often an inarticulate and unconscious judgment it is true, and yet the very root and nerve of the whole proceeding. You can give any conclusion a logical form."

In effect, then, beneath a legal argument which may have been expressed in perfect syllogistic or logical form, the more percipient legal analyst may discover underlying values or philosophical underpinnings which throw light on the conclusion reached by the judge. That is why one legal commentator (McLeod) has said:

---

30   (1897) 10 Harv. L.R. 461

"Many people find that one of the most enduring pleasures of studying law is playing the game of 'hunt the inarticulate major premise', and you may often find that your reading of even the dullest of cases can be enlivened by trying to get behind the words and the doctrine in order to penetrate the mind of the judge as an individual human being."[31]

The capacity of a lawyer to lay bare such underpinnings will often depend on his broader humanities education. That is why right from the inception of the Legon Law Faculty, it was considered essential for all law students to study also some non-legal subjects to broaden their discernment.

The law degree programme at Legon has evolved over the years. At the outset in 1959, the Department of Law at the University College of Ghana was established as part of the Faculty of Arts and Social Sciences.[32] The LL.B programme that was introduced by the Department was a four-year semi-professional qualification. The regulations governing admission to the Ghana Bar at the time required that the holders of this LL.B should undertake a further year of practical training at the Ghana Law School in Accra, ran by the General Legal Council, before such holders could be admitted to the Ghana Bar.

During the 1962-63 academic year, the University of Ghana entered into negotiations with the General Legal Council which resulted in an extensive revision of the law degree programme offered by the University. As a result of those negotiations, the General Legal Council delegated all teaching of law to the Faculty of Law, established in place of the Law Department in 1962.[33] The University thus took over the teaching responsibilities of the Ghana Law School, with the Law School closing down in July 1964. At the same time, the University restructured its degree programme into one for two degrees: a three-year non-professional law degree, which was to be called the Bachelor of Arts (Honours)in Law (or BA(Hons)Law).

---

31   McLeod, *Legal Method* (Palgrave, 1999) 3rd Ed. 5

32   See *Annual Report 1962-63 by the Vice-Chancellor* (University of Ghana, 1963) 26

33   *Ibid.*

This was to be followed by a two-year professional Bachelor of Laws (LL. B) degree. The LL. B was to be a professional qualification that was to enable admission to the Ghana Bar, without more.

The *Annual Report* of the Vice-Chancellor of the University of Ghana for 1962-63, points out the benefits of these changes in legal education as follows:[34]

> "The curricular revisions approved and made applicable to all present students in the Faculty provide a number of significant advantages:
>
> 1. The amount of instruction in non-legal subjects has been increased, thus assuring a more broadly and liberally educated Bar.
>
> 2. The disciplinary and cultural aspects of legal education have been made available within a three-year degree to students who will not seek full professional qualification.
>
> 3. All instruction in Law has been consolidated within a full-time Faculty, able to support their teaching with necessary research.
>
> 4. The total cost of programmes of legal education will be reduced through the elimination of duplicate facilities."

The *Annual Report* further states that:

> "In connection with the revision of degree structures, all existing course syllabuses were reviewed and revised, and syllabuses prepared for new courses. The Faculty are therefore prepared for the coming year with a carefully considered curriculum responsive to the development needs of Ghana."

These developments at the Law Faculty attracted the Vice-Chancellor's attention. In his address at the first Congregation of the University of Ghana on 23rd February 1963, the then Vice-Chancellor, the late Dr Connor Cruise O'Brien said:

---

34   At 27

"The Dean of the Faculty of Law, Professor Harvey, has reached agreement with the General Legal Council of Ghana on a curriculum leading to a degree at this University which will at the same time mean admission to the legal profession in Ghana. The curriculum designed by the Faculty of Law is a wide and liberal one, including subjects like English or French literature, of which the layman normally does not think as part of the lawyer's training. I have no doubt that this humane conception of preparation for the law – which does not, of course, exclude exacting professional courses – is the correct one, which will benefit in the future, not only the Bar and Bench of Ghana, but through them the life of the country generally."

It was in the midst of these curricular changes that I entered the University of Ghana in 1962 as a student. Therefore, I can attest to the well-rounded education that I received in consequence of it. I had the good fortune that the period of training of my class, and of a few subsequent classes, was abridged from five to four years. I have a hazy recollection of courses in Logic, English, Economics and African Studies which I had to take, in addition to the law subjects.

The two-degree structure was abolished in 1965. From that year onwards and for many years after, the structure of the legal programme taught by the Law Faculty was a three-year LL.B, followed initially by one year of practical training, which was later (in 1970) extended to two years. The first year of the practical training was to continue to be offered at Legon, while the second year was to take place at the Law School's premises at Makola in Accra. The justification for this re-organisation was stated as follows in a Memorandum prepared by the Law Faculty:

"At the moment the Faculty of Law prepares students for two degrees – B.A. (Honours) in Law and the LL.B. The duration of these courses are three years for the B.A.(Honours) in Law, and two years for the LL.B. Normally a student can only proceed to the latter after having obtained the former degree. This in effect means that the student spends five academical sessions to obtain both degrees. To be enrolled as a Legal

Practitioner in Ghana – the objective of most students who enter the Faculty – a student must normally have obtained both degrees.

The LL.B. Degree, which appears to be a post-graduate degree, is such only in name. The students working for that degree are, to all intents and purposes, undergraduates. They do not engage in any research projects, nor, indeed, do they study any subjects beyond the undergraduate level. In fact, in all cases, they are studying the subjects for the very first time. This LL. B course was originally intended as a "practical course" for students who wished to be enrolled as Legal Practitioners in Ghana. As it is now, it is not practical in any way, and it is at best only an extension of the B.A. course which precedes it.

After watching this arrangement in operation for over two years, the members of the Board of the Faculty of Law are convinced that it is very unsatisfactory. The scheme we suggest now would change this situation fundamentally. We, in effect, suggest that the Faculty should prepare students for only ONE undergraduate degree. That the "practical course" for future Legal Practitioners should be re-organised to reflect its essentially practical character, and that responsibility for this course should, in the long run, at least, be with the General Legal Council of Ghana rather than with the Faculty of Law. The General Legal Council has asked the Faculty to organize and run, for the time being, this course on its behalf. We are at the moment negotiating with the Council on the arrangements for the practical course.

The Board of the Faculty of Law suggests that the present three-year first-degree course should be retained. It is however suggested that the degree awarded should be an LL. B and not the BA Honours in Law degree as hitherto. This designation is more in line with the practice all over the world and is, of course, more descriptive of the degree."

The quest for teaching law in a broad humanities framework at Legon has continued till today. I remember that, in the 1970s, the

Faculty initiated the so-called 3:2:1 programme as the structure of the LL.B. The 3:2:1 programme for the LL. B meant that, in the first year, the law was only one of three subjects that the student pursued. In the second year, the student dropped one of the subjects to concentrate on studying law alongside another subject. It was only in the Final Year that the student devoted himself or herself exclusively to the study of the law.

It is my understanding in 2009 that the Faculty recruits only graduates into its two-year LL.B programme. Thus, students import into their legal training the broader university education that they have already acquired before enrolling to study law. Subsequent to the delivery of the lectures on which this Chapter is based, the School of Law has introduced an additional stream of admissions that allows entry by holders of the West African School Certificate.

The point, however, is not only that legal training at Legon has always been conducted within a broad humanities context, but that the way law has been taught at Legon has meant that the study of the law has itself been an education. In my view, there is a distinction between University legal education in Ghana and the vocational legal education that the Ghana Law School is currently required to provide. Although the law is a professional subject, it has to stretch the mental horizon of its students at a theoretical level as well,when taught at the University. In other words, it has to be taught in such a way as to be comparable in intellectual challenge to the other great disciplines of the humanities, such as history,philosophy,literature and so on. It is not part of my task here to dilate on how this is to be done. Nevertheless, in whatever way that it is done, the result of legal education should not be mere knowledge of a finite amount of black letter law. It should also result in the capacity of the law graduate to lay bare the philosophical and value underpinnings of the black letter law. The law graduate should possess insights into the structure, values and dynamics of the society in which he or she is to practise his or her profession.

At this juncture, I want to draw a contrast between academic education in the law and the vocational legal education with which the Law School is charged. The Law School has to impart to its students practical skills to grapple with the problems of the legal services marketplace, including the needs of both private and public clients and stakeholders. Although the vocational dimension is not the principal objective of law teaching in the University, nevertheless it cannot be ignored and the Faculty of Law over the years has laid a solid foundation on which the Ghana Law School, whether institutionally separate or integrated into the Law Faculty at Legon, has built its practical and professional training.

Earlier I referred to the study of law in the University of Ghana as being an education. I would now like to illustrate what I mean by that. As we all know, the study and analysis of decided cases from the courts is at the very core of legal training in the common law tradition. A sensitive analysis of cases can be very revealing about the society from which the cases emanate and the cases can therefore serve as raw material for a level of reflection about societal issues which, to my mind, qualifies as an educative process. Let me begin my illustration by quoting the words of one of Ghana's most distinguished judges, Apaloo J., as he then was. He later became one of the longest serving and erudite Chief Justices of Ghana. In *Wankyiwaa v Wereduwaa*[35], he said:

> "That brings me to the question whether customary law provides a remedy for mere vituperation which falls short of slander as defined by Sarbah. I cannot think of any reason why on principle there should be none. The fact that the law of England provides no remedy is quite beside the point. The society of England is different from the society of Ghana. In this country, where words of abuse are taken seriously, it would, in my opinion, be socially intolerable if customary law provided no sanctions against a man who finds pleasure in injuring the feelings of his neighbour by vituperation. The Juaso/ Bompata Local Court, which tried this case as of first instance, did not feel itself inhibited by any rule of customary law from awarding damages to the plaintiff for insult. Although the Kumasi East District Court B reversed this judgment on appeal, nothing turned on the fact that abuse by itself could not give rise to an action for

---

35   [1963] 1 GLR 332, at 335.

damages according to customary law. Indeed, the judgment of that court itself proceeded on the basis that such action was cognizable in accordance with custom. Judges who sat in this Court and in the Supreme Court have said time and again that native custom is peculiarly within the bosom of the native courts. Unless there is authority to the contrary, and none was produced by either counsel, I am prepared to hold that abuse by itself is a wrong redressible by damages according to customary law. The fact that the words of abuse were spoken in the heat of a quarrel is no doubt a matter that the good sense of a tribunal would take into consideration as a mitigating factor, but it does not by itself negative liability."

From this passage, it is evident that Justice Apaloo clearly identified a need to acknowledge a local value requiring protection from insult. He saw this value as an interest worthy of recognition by the law. This is a value, however, that is in conflict with what underlies the English law of defamation. Influenced by the English value, another of our great Ghanaian judges, Taylor J. as he then was, disagreed with Justice Apaloo in *Nkrumah v Manu*[36] saying:

"I must say though that it is about time the customary law of slander took on a more enlightened garb and moved so to speak with the demands of modern times. When village communities were small and the written word was unknown to customary law the only means of social and commercial intercourse was the spoken word. It was therefore essential for the preservation of the peace of those small communities that idle insults which ridicule and may therefore ruin a person be discouraged by the body politic. With the very drastic changes which modern civilization has imposed on community and rural life throughout the country it seems to me that the law has more serious problems than silly vituperation..."

The issue opened up by these contrasting judicial views is one that may be said to be intellectually challenging and whose debate can contribute to the education of students who study both sides of the

---

36   [1971] 1 GLR 176 at 181-82

argument. It is as challenging as some of the issues one would expect to encounter in sociology and the sociology of change. It shows that some legal issues cannot be resolved by reference to internal legal consistency criteria only and that reference has to be made to the external social framework. In an article that I wrote in my youth on this and other issues[37], I pointed out that protecting a claim against insult is not necessarily a sign of lack of enlightenment, as Justice Taylor implies. I undertook comparative legal research that showed that Roman law and modern systems of law that derive from it have given protection to the interest against insult. I concluded as follows[38] :

> "This brief excursus into comparative law has been meant to show that the customary law is not alone in providing a remedy against insult and affronts to personal dignity and that it is no sign of backwardness for it to provide such a remedy. The issue is thus not one relating to enlightenment or lack of it. Rather, it is one as to the desirable purpose of the tort of defamation."

Apart from the study of such rules with a social intersection, even the study of some of the core rules of the law, typically viewed as part of the material for internal exegesis of legal doctrine, can in themselves be an education. An illustration of such core rules would be: the rule against perpetuities in the law of immovable property or the doctrine of consideration in the law of contract or the liability to pay damages for nervous shock or psychiatric injury caused by another's negligent conduct. All these can generate such difficulty that the mastery of the doctrine or rule and the analytical tools needed to apply the doctrine or rule eminently constitute part of an educational process. The mental agility needed to be in command of these areas of the law is an indication of the educative processes involved. One could multiply examples of such rules of social significance or of particular difficulty. It is however not my intention to do so. All that I am asserting is that the acquisition of the skill to deal with such rules in order to deploy them for the solution of problems is a process that educates the mind.

---

37   See Date-Bah, "*Reflections on the Law of Defamation in Ghana*"(1973)10 U.G.L.J. 129

38   *Ibid* at 135.

The Law Faculty's Contribution to Education in General

I now advert briefly to the Legon Law Faculty's contribution to education in general. I believe that I have given readers, particularly those who did not pass through the Faculty, a flavour of the Faculty's activities sufficient to verify my working hypothesis. My contention is that the instructional course that the Law Faculty delivers contributes significantly to general education in this country. In my view, the non-legal subjects studied with core legal subjects, the difficulty of some of the core legal subjects and the way in which law has been taught at Legon over the years and the intellectual experience required to master the subject-matter thrown at students lead to such cultivation of the students' minds that I have no hesitation in asserting that what the Legon Faculty of Law does contributes to general education in Ghana. Furthermore, the considerable corpus of published works and research (both books and articles) which have emanated from the Legon Law Faculty have contributed to the advancement of knowledge and learning in Ghana and represents a major contribution to general education in Ghana. This is particularly so as the majority of such publications are devoted to the study and elucidation of issues relating to Ghanaian society.

New Directions

What of the future? While I have no doubt that the legal training imparted at the University of Ghana's law Faculty has led to sound general education of most of the lawyers who have passed through the portals of our redoubtable *alma mater*, an issue which arises for me is whether, looking to the future, the paradigm of legal education, administered at Legon, would benefit from some modification. It is almost axiomatic to state that legal education must not be static but must change with changes in society. There is also need to learn from experience gained in sister common law jurisdictions.

In this light, I think that an infusion of a clinical element in the curriculum at Legon would be beneficial. Given that both Legon and the Law School at Makola are located in Accra, the management of the two institutions should consider the joint establishment of a legal clinic that would enrich the vocational dimensions of the legal education that they both deliver. Considering the different objectives of University legal education and the Law School's vocational education, the relevant authorities should give this clinical education more weight in the Law School than at Legon. Nevertheless, there would be value in even the Legon students beginning to have familiarity with clinical legal education.

I find useful the following definition of "clinical" proposed by the English academic Richard Grimes that[39]

> "'clinical' is used to describe a learning environment where students identify, research and apply knowledge in a setting which replicates, at least in part, the world where it is practised. This might be in a court room or before a tribunal. It may be in correspondence between opposing sides in litigation, or it may occur during the course of a transaction. It almost inevitably means that the student takes on some aspect of a case and conducts this as it would (or ought to!) be conducted in the real world."

From this definition, it is clear that clinical legal education can have various manifestations. I think that the teaching of Alternative Dispute Resolution (or ADR) is an inculcation of a "lawyering skill" which fits into this definition of clinical legal education. I understand that ADR teaching has in fact started at Legon. This is a forward-looking move that is to be commended.

During the development of the idea of clinical education in US law schools, one of its early prevalent forms was that of the Legal Aid Clinic. This served as a means of delivering legal services to the poor, with funding from private foundations and offices of public defenders. Students in such Clinics have the opportunity to participate in a wide range of legal services, such as drafting legal documents and representing clients, under the supervision of qualified legal practitioners. Is this a form of clinical education

---

39   Richard Grimes, "The theory and practice of clinical legal education" in Webb and Maughan (Eds.) *Teaching Lawyers' Skills* (Butterworths, London, 1996) 137 at138

capable of adoption and adaptation by the Law School and the Legon Law Faculty jointly? Shall we, as one of my Professors at the Yale Law School, Professor Kessler, used to say, leave this question as a cliff-hanger?

I believe that the Faculty is achieving its mission. This mission was expressed thus in a Position Paper on "An Integrated Program of Legal Education for Ghana", prepared by the Faculty in 1962:

> "No existing system of legal education provides a model fully responsive to Ghana's conditions and needs. British University education in law, which achieves magnificently in the development of analytical skills and historical perspective, can perhaps afford to be extremely non-professional in view of the ancient instructional programs of the Inns as well as the pre-professional apprenticeships and courses of study required of solicitors. In America the University law schools long tended towards excessive, narrowing professionalism. A high degree of professionalism can be defended there, however, in view of the fact that law is post-graduate education, the student having pursued his general studies beyond the secondary school level and very commonly having earned a B.A. or equivalent degree before entering law school. The German system involves an interesting combination of legal and non-legal instruction. The Universities student's having three years of referendar study and practical observation after leaving the University and before entering his profession. Thus, the underlying assumptions of the various foreign models are not valid in Ghana. This country must devise its own model, borrowing from abroad whatever is useful but feeling no initial commitment to any pattern merely on the basis of familiarity."

What has happened at Legon over the last fifty years has been an endeavour to devise a Ghanaian model of legal education.

The Faculty's Contribution to Governance

Next, I will consider the Legon Law Faculty's contribution to good governance in Ghana. "Good governance" is, of course, the buzz phrase these days. Everybody is for good governance. Good governance is not possible without lawyers. Good governance implies accountable government limited by law. Lawyers are indispensable in the task of ensuring that the agencies of the State stay within the law and do not abuse the rights of citizens and residents. I propose at this juncture to examine the Legon Law Faculty's contribution to governance by outlining some of the activities of its alumni and also the achievements of some of its current and former members in governance. The research output of members of the Faculty on governance, published in the University of Ghana Law Journal, will also be reviewed. Regarding socio-economic development, the discussion will locate the Faculty's contribution within the general context of the role of law and lawyers in social and economic development.

With regard to governance, among the motivations of the Department of Law's founders was to contribute to the good governance of Ghana. Subsequently the Legon Faculty of Law had a similar motivation. One can say that the contribution of the Faculty of Law to governance in Ghana has been through the careers and activities of its alumni and Faculty members and the ideas whose ventilation it has facilitated through its courses of instruction and through the medium provided by the University of Ghana Law Journal.

I need only list a few of the alumni and alumnae of the Faculty in our contemporary political and governmental life to demonstrate how much the Faculty's legal education has contributed to the governance of our nation. First, one has to mention the late President John Evans Atta Mills, President of the Republic of Ghana and the Right Honourable Ebenezer Bagyina Sekyi Hughes and Right Honourable Doe Adjaho, past Speakers of Parliament. With regard to the judiciary, we can refer to the first female Chief Justice of the land, Her Ladyship Justice Georgina Theodora Wood, and,before her, her predecessor in office,the late Justice George

Kingsley Acquah. Other Chief Justices who should be mentioned are His Lordship Justice Anin-Yeboah (who assumed office in 2020) and before him Her Ladyship Justice Sophia Akuffo. When we come to the leadership of Parliament, the Majority Leader in 2009, the Honourable Alban S.K. Bagbin (and his predecessor the Honourable Abraham Ossei Aidoo) are both alumni of the Faculty of Law. The Attorney-General in 2009, the Honourable Mrs Betty Mould-Iddrisu, her predecessor the Honourable Mr. Joseph Ghartey and several of their predecessors in office are products of the Legon Law Faculty. Subsequent Attorneys-General have all also been alumni of the Legon Law Faculty: the Honourable Ben Kumbuor; the Honourable Martin Amidu; the Honourable Marietta Brew Appiah-Oppong; and the current Attorney-General, the Honourable Gloria Akuffo. Finally, one should mention Ms Anna Bossman, who is currently Ghana's Ambassador to France and in 2009 was the Acting Commissioner of the Commission for Human Rights and Administrative Justice (or CHRAJ) ,an important governance institution,. Her successors in office have also been alumni of the Legon Law Faculty: Ms Lauretta Lamptey and Mr. Joseph Whittal.

Worth noting is also the fact that all the members of the Supreme Court in 2009 were alumni of the Legon Faculty of Law. They were: Justices William Atuguba, Sophia Akuffo, Allan Brobbey, Julius Ansah, Sophia Adinyira, Rose Owusu, Jones Dotse, Anin-Yeboah, Paul Baffoe-Bonnie and me. Members of the current Supreme Court (as of 31st October 2020) are also all alumni of the Legon Law Faculty. They are: Justices Julius Ansah, Jones Dotse, Paul Baffoe Bonnie, Nasiru S. Gbadegbe, Yaw Appau, Gabriel Pwamang, Samuel K. Marful-Sau, Agnes M.A. Dordzie, Nene Abayaateye Ofoe Amegatcher, Prof. Nii Ashie Kotey, Mariama Owusu, Avril Lovelace Johnson, Gertrude Torkornoo, Clemence J. Honyenuga, Issifu Omoro Tanko Amadu, Prof. Henrietta Joy Abena Nyarko Mensa-Bonsu, and Emmanuel Yonny Kulendi. Indeed, the other superior court Justices are also predominantly Legon law graduates.

Apart from the current contribution of alumni to governance, one could mention the governance activities of several ex-members of the Legon Faculty of Law. Professor Ekow Daniels served in the government of the First Republic as Deputy Attorney-General. He was also Minister of the Interior, and then of Education, in the Third Republic. Nana Dr. SKB Asante, an Acting Head of the Department of Law in the early 1960s, was Solicitor-General and later Deputy Attorney-General in the government of the Second Republic. Professor G K A Ofosu-Amaah, then a lecturer, was appointed Director of Special Branch during the same Republic. During the Fourth Republic, Professor Ofosu-Amaah served as Chairman of the Securities and Exchange Commission. The late Professor Kwamena Bentsi-Enchill, one of the pioneers of the Department of Law, who became a Professor on his return from America during the Second Republic, was appointed a Justice of the Supreme Court during the Second Republic. The late Professor A N E Amissah, who was a Dean of the Faculty in the 1970s, was the Attorney-General under the Supreme Military Council and was also a member of the Court of Appeal, which used to be the highest court of the land during his membership of it. At one time in the 1970s, he was also chairman of the Law Reform Commission.

The late Justice Nii Amaa Ollennu, who was an Honorary Professor at the Faculty, served as the Speaker of the Parliament of the Second Republic. During the Third Republic, Professor S O Gyandoh was appointed the Ombudsman. Furthermore, during the PNDC era, Dr. Kwesi Botchway and Mr. Kwamena Ahwoi served as Ministers in the regime. Finally, in the Fourth Republic, Professor E V O Dankwa has served on the Law Reform Commission, as also has the late Professor A K P Kludze, its Chairman in 2009. The late Professor Kludze, the late Mr. Justice Kwame Afreh and I have, in the course of the Fourth Republic, been appointed to the Supreme Court. Mr. Tsatsu Tsikata served as the Chief Executive of the Ghana National Petroleum Corporation both during the PNDC period and during the earlier years of the Fourth Republic. Finally, Professor Henrietta Mensa-Bonsu was a member of the Truth and Reconciliation Commission appointed by President Kufour in the Fourth Republic and Professor Nii Ashie Kotey served as the chief executive of the Forestry Commission, on leave of absence from the Faculty. Both Professors Mensa-Bonsu and Kotey have, subsequent to the delivery of the Golden Jubilee Lectures in 2009, been appointed Supreme Court Justices.

This is not an exhaustive account of the governance activities of members and ex-members of the Law Faculty, but it serves to illustrate the fact that the Law Faculty is not a cloistered institution. Its members have always had an "applied knowledge" orientation and have shown a willingness to engage with the society whose law they have taught to students.

The University of Ghana Law Journal has also served as an important medium for the canvassing and exchange of ideas on governance and other issues. Starting out as the Legon Law Journal in 1962, a cyclostyled student journal, the first printed volume was produced in 1964 by the Faculty and it has continued in publication since then.

Right from the very first issue, the University of Ghana Law Journal contained material pertinent to the issues of governance. The first Dean of the Faculty, Professor William Burnett Harvey, had published, in the maiden issue, an article on "A Value Analysis of Ghanaian Legal Development since Independence," which was his inaugural lecture at the University. The article can be said to have started a tradition of vigorous participation by Faculty members in discussions on legal issues relating to governance. In a wide-ranging review of legal developments affecting the evolution of the independent Ghanaian State, Dean Harvey had some percipient remarks on the role of the doctrine of *stare decisis,* or of binding judicial precedent, in the Ghanaian legal order. He said[40]:

> "Article 42 of the Republican Constitution speaks to this question with superficial clarity:
>
>> "The Supreme Court shall in principle be bound to follow its own previous decisions on questions of law, and the High Court shall be bound to follow previous decisions of the Supreme Court on such questions, but neither court shall be otherwise bound to follow the previous decisions of any court on questions of law."
>
> This article appears to be an unequivocal declaration of independence for the superior courts in so far as the decisions

---

40   WB Harvey, "A Value Analysis of Ghanaian Legal Development Since Independence,"[1964] 1 UGLJ 4

of non-Ghanaian courts are concerned. The stability of legal institutions and the relative conservatism of judicial attitudes, however, make it inevitable that English decisions will enjoy for a long time a high degree of persuasiveness in Ghana. One may hope never the less that the Supreme Court and High Court will not be reluctant to re-examine long-established English precedents to determine their responsiveness to the developing needs of this country."

This issue of governance that the Dean thus identified is still with us, although much progress has been achieved since the1960s in loosening the link between the Ghanaian legal system and the English legal system. These days the first port of call in research on the Ghanaian common law is Ghanaian decided cases. It is only if these do not disclose an authoritative Ghanaian judicial determination on the issue concerned that the inquirer would look to foreign decided cases. Cases from jurisdictions other than the English are also increasingly resorted to, though it is true that English cases continue to be referred to the most.

Dean Harvey concludes his discussion on *stare decisis* under the 1960 Constitution of Ghana as follows:

"These questions do not represent a mere academic exercise. They go to the heart of the role of the judiciary in keeping the tension between stable legal institutions and social needs and values within tolerable limits. It seems to me at least doubtful that legislative bodies in most countries today have either the time or the interest for making those periodic adjustments in established doctrine that social change may demand. Within rather broad limits I think the courts are the agencies best equipped to perform this function. I would therefore hope that the Supreme Court of Ghana in interpreting the Constitution and defining its own role in the processes of legal change will shun English judicial passivity and claim for itself a more affirmative, creative function."

These were very thought-provoking remarks, particularly in those early years. They certainly left an indelible mark on some of us who were privileged to listen to that inaugural lecture. I must confess that I was converted to the concept of the judicial role that he advocated. Up to today I remain convinced that, in a developing country context, judges should adopt an activist role in adapting the law to the requirements of social change, always subject, of course, to the constraints imposed on the judicial process by the Constitution.

The next illustration of a Faculty member's contribution to discourse on a governance issue is Professor S. O. Gyandoh's article on "Principles of Judicial Interpretation of the Republican Constitution of Ghana"[41] in the 1966 volume of the University of Ghana Law Journal. This article is a critique of an approach to the judicial interpretation of the 1960 Republican Constitution which had been set out by Mr Bennion in his book on that Constitution (*The Constitutional Law of Ghana*)[42]. Professor Gyandoh observes that some of the principles embodied in the approach advocated by Mr. Bennion are too mechanistic and stifling of judicial creativity.

He subjects the principles of interpretation, articulated by Bennion, to scholarly analysis and concludes his article in the following words:

> In this survey and critical examination of the general principles underlying constitutional interpretation, with special reference to the now suspended Republican Constitution of Ghana, attempts have been made to point out expressly and by implication the inadequacy—one may say without exaggeration, the total lack—of principled criteria for the determination of the meaning of the Constitution in Ghana. This nation, it is submitted, can ill-afford to shirk the task of consciously developing such principles. The greater part of this burden will surely fall on our higher courts of Law, which must regard themselves as the custodians of the high ideals for which the nation stands. But the burden will not be theirs alone. All of us—teachers, legal practitioners, litigants or potential litigants who claim that rights granted them under the Constitution have been infringed, indeed all citizens—

---

41   [1966] 3 UGLJ 37.

42   (Butterworths, London, 1962)

must play our part in preserving the law of the Constitution, so long as this law is of our own making. If this article helps to sharpen our awareness of some of the problems involved in this noble task, the nit will have achieve done of its humblest, though crucial, objectives."

The issue of governance that Professor Gyandoh raises is a very legitimate one, which is as relevant today as in 1966 when he wrote his article. Since then, the courts have, of course, had much more opportunity to evolve principled criteria for constitutional interpretation. What is important is that a member of the Faculty of Law was tabling for debate an issue of governance that was crucial for the development of democracy in our nation. The current predominant view which has evolved from the case law of the Supreme Court would appear to be that, while there is no one size fits all approach to constitutional interpretation, a purposive approach is preferred.

Justice N. A. Ollennu, an Honorary Professor of Law at Legon, in his article on "Judicial Precedent in Ghana"[43], in the 1966 volume of the University of Ghana Law Journal, returns to the *stare decisis* theme raised in an earlier volume by Professor Harvey. He expresses a view on the doctrine of judicial precedent as it applies to the Supreme Court which continues to be valid till today. This is what he wrote:

"Now what is the proper interpretation to be given to the words "shall in principle be bound to follow its own previous decisions on questions of law"? Are they to be interpreted in the same way as the principle of stare decisis as operates in England in the House of Lords or the Court of Appeal, namely, that the Supreme Court has no option but to follow its previous decision even though it is manifestly wrong unless it can show that that previous decision was given per incuriam? Our view is that the words "in principle" are intended to create an elastic rule, to save the Supreme Court in embarrassing situations and to enable it tore-examine its own previous decision to correct or differ from it when it finds such decision to be either manifestly wrong, not only because

---

43   [1966] 3 UGLJ 139

it was given per incuriam, but because of inconsistency with some principle of law or custom, and is therefore a decision which for some good reason or the other should not be followed. In our view the Article lays down a flexible rule intended to enable the court to mould and develop the law, the common law no less than the customary law, to meet the needs of economic and social changes which are taking place in our new and developing nation, without the necessity to resort to Parliament each time to rectify an error in the law brought about by a wrong decision".

This article on judicial precedent was an important contribution to that particular governance issue and must have had an influence on settling the issue. Other Faculty contributions to the national conversation on governance worthy of mention in this context include another article by Professor SO Gyandoh in the 1968 volume of the University of Ghana Law Journal on "The role of the judiciary under the constitutional proposals for Ghana"[44], and articles by: Professor W. C. Ekow Daniels in the 1974 volume of the Journal on "The meaning and scope of Executive Power in Ghana Today"[45]; Dr. Richard Turkson in that same volume on "Ministerial control of public corporations in Ghana;"[46] Professor C.E.K. Kumado on" The National Redemption Council (Establishment) Proclamation (Amendment) Decree, 1975: An exercise in revolutionary constitutionalism?"[47] in the 1975 volume; Professor E V O Dankwa and Professor C. Flinterman on "Judicial Review in Ghana" in the 1977 volume[48]; Mr. F. S. Tsikata on "Limits of Constitutional Law" in the 1978 volume;[49] Professor C E K Kumado on "Chieftaincy and the Law in Modern Ghana"[50] and on "Forgive us our trespasses: an examination of the indemnity clause in the 1992 Constitution of Ghana"[51]; and Professor EK Quashigah on "The constitutional right

---

44   [1968] 5 UGLJ 133.

45   [1975] 11 UGLJ 109

46   [1975] 11 UGLJ 83

47   [1975] 12 UGLJ 124

48   [1975] 14 UGLJ 1

49   [1978] 15 UGLJ 17

50   [1991-92] 18 UGLJ 194

51   [1993-95] 19 UGLJ 83.

to freedom of assembly and procession in Ghana in the light of the decision in the public order case and the Public Order Act."[52] This is only a selection in tended to give a flavour of the output of members of the Legon Faculty of Law on governance issues. It should be stressed also that I have confined myself to only publications in the University of Ghana Law Journal. Faculty members, of course, published through other journals as well inside and outside Ghana.

In addition to publishing on governance issues, members and ex-members of the Faculty of Law have contributed directly to the shaping of various Constitutions of the Ghanaian Republic. For instance, in 1978-79, Dr. Thomas A Mensah, a former Acting Dean of the Faculty, and Professor Gyandoh, a former Dean of the Faculty,were influential in fashioning the Constitution for the Third Republic. Furthermore, the Committee of Experts set up in 1991 to prepare proposals for a draft Constitution for Ghana had as its Chairman a former member of the Faculty and a serving member of the Faculty. These were Nana Dr. S.K.B. Asante, who was Chairman of the Committee and Professor E V O Dankwa, then a member of the Faculty, who was a member of the Committee. It should also be pointed out that subsequent to the delivery of the Lectures on which this Chapter is based, Professor Emeritus Albert Fiadjoe (an alumnus of, and a former law don at, the Legon Law Faculty) was appointed to chair the Constitutional Review Commission which presented its Final Report to the late President Mills in December 2011, recommending various amendments to the 1992 Constitution.

Beyond named individuals, the Faculty has made a contribution through making available trained personnel to fill many of the posts needed for the effective governance of Ghana. I refer to posts such as solicitor/secretaries of the statutory corporations; professional legal positions in the Attorney-General's Office, the Ministry of Foreign Affairs and other relevant Ministries; and judicial positions at all levels of the hierarchy of the judiciary.

---

52   [1996-99] 20 UGLJ 1.

Apart from national governance, the Faculty's influence on traditional governance is also discernible. A couple of examples are Nana Susubiribi Krobea Asante, Asokorehene (Paramount Chief of Asokore), and Nana Akuoko Sarpong, Agogohene (Paramount Chief of Agogo), both from the Ashanti Region. There are also other examples in the other regions of the country.

Looking to the future, I think that the Faculty collectively, distinct from its individual members, could do more in the area of extra-mural extension of knowledge on governance to both lawyers and non-lawyers. It should consider forming strategic alliances with government agencies, NGOs and international donors with a view to disseminating knowledge in this area. Ghana would be the better for it. What I have said is not meant to derogate from the valuable work being done already by individual members of the Faculty in this area, sometimes in association with NGOs. I applaud the work that has been done.

The Faculty's contribution to Socio-Economic Development

I consider, next, the Faculty's contribution to Ghana's socio-economic development.

Conventional wisdom is that law has a role in, and an impact on, the development process. By producing the predominant proportion of lawyers in practice in the public and private sectors in Ghana, the Faculty of Law at Legon has inevitably contributed to Ghana's socio-economic development. Let me provide an example. The present economic system in this country could not survive without the enforceability of business bargains and the protection of property rights. This important element in sustaining our economic development has been maintained thanks to the numbers of well-trained lawyers who have been produced by Legon, alongside other institutions. More particularly, the institution of credit illustrates the role of law in the economy and in economic development. Because of the global credit crunch, the role of credit in the economy was of topical interest in 2009. The lending of money and the enforcement of the obligation to repay the loan are quintessentially legal matters and lawyers are needed by banks and enterprises for the conclusion and enforcement of loan agreements and other transactions. Graduates from the Legon Law Faculty are visible in the banks and various enterprises in facilitating such transactions. By their role, they are oiling the wheels of the development process and are an exemplification of the role of the Law Faculty in the socio-economic development of Ghana.

Additionally, the considerable research output of ex-Faculty members in the area of land law has contributed to the crystallisation and consolidation of legal principles relating to land that have assisted the development process of Ghana. In this connection, one should mention Faculty stalwarts such as Justice N A Ollennu[53], Professors K Bentsi-Enchill[54], G R. Woodman[55], A K P Kludze[56] and Nana Dr. S K B Asante [57]. Faculty and ex-Faculty members have also written on the enforcement of contract and other rights, which are relevant for the development process.[58]

Similarly, our constitutional legal order could not survive without the numbers of lawyers trained by Legon, in addition to those trained by other institutions. The Legon-trained lawyers not only supply legal services to the private sector, but also to the public sector and the judiciary, whose role is crucial in the maintenance of a legal framework which is protective of contract and property rights as well as the general constitutional legal regime.

It must be said, though, that this beneficial impact of the increase in the population of lawyers in Ghana has not been universally appreciated. I remember that in one of my forays from Legon in the 1970s in to the courts, a very senior member of the Bar confronted

---

53   See Ollennu, *Principles of Customary Land Law in Ghana*(Sweet & Maxwell, London, 1962)

54   See K. Bentsi-Enchill, *Ghana Land Law: An Exposition, Analysis and Critique* (Sweet & Maxwell, 1964)

55   See, for example, G R Woodman, *Customary Land Law in the Ghanaian Courts* (Ghana Universities Press, Accra, 1996)

56   Kludze, *Ghana Law of Landlord and Tenant*

57   SKB Asante, *Property Law and Social Goals in Ghana 1844-1966* (Ghana Universities Press, 1975)

58   See, for example, Date-Bah, "*The Enforcement of Third Party Contractual Rights*" (1971) 8UGLJ 76 and "*Doctrine of Consideration and the Modification of Contracts*"(1973) 5RGL 10.

me in the Bar Dressing Room at the High Court and protested to me that the Faculty was "killing the profession". His protest was in effect against the increasing numbers of lawyers we were producing and their impact on the profession. The profession was being transformed from a small exclusive club into a much larger profession with a diffuse membership.

I have also heard, in some quarters, criticisms of some of the current products of the Law Faculty as not measuring up to the standards demanded by the market place. This is a troubling issue that needs to be confronted by the current Faculty members. I am not necessarily saying that this criticism is justified. Nevertheless, the Faculty needs to monitor the concern and address it. Additionally, I have learnt of some purported explanations for the perceived fall in the standards of achievement of recent graduates of the Law Faculty. It has been alleged that because tuition for the law degree is now no longer free, it has resulted in many students being in effect part-time. They hold down a full-time job at the same time as they study for their law degree. These are all matters which I suggest need to be considered at the Law Teachers' Conference that the Dean planned (in 2009) to convene, as part of the Golden Jubilee activities, and should then be sustained.

Another of the issues that the Law Teachers' Conference should consider is the clinical element in legal education that I touched upon earlier. I was heartened by the positive reaction of the Legon Vice-Chancellor to this suggestion. I also found his invocation of the analogy of the clinical training of doctors helpful. I think that a dialogue is called for between the staff of the Law School at Makola in Accra and the Law Faculty at Legon on the future direction of legal education in Ghana and their respective places in the grand scheme of things. I myself think that too much black letter law is taught at the Law School and not enough of the "lawyering" skills needed to enable their graduates to hit the ground running when they leave the School. In the dialogue between the Law School and the Law Faculty, they would do well to listen to the voices from industry and the profession. We have already heard of the willingness of lawyers from industry and the profession to engage constructively with the

Faculty in improving standards. I would strongly urge such offers to be taken advantage of. In addition, it would be advisable to revive the Faculty, Bench and Bar Conferences which used to be regular events some time back, in order to maintain a structured interaction between some of the principal stakeholders in the legal system.

Next, I would like to point out one other consequence of the production of fresh law graduates from Legon year on year for over forty years. It has, in my view, led to the permeation of Ghanaian society with a rights-based approach in many spheres of our national life. Such a rights-based attitude of the public and of society is conducive to the rule of law and the evolution of a democratic polity. A rights-based mentality is an important building block for constitutionalism in any nation state. Constitutionalism implies government limited by law. The State, if it is a constitutional one, is not a leviathan unconstrained by the fetters of law. If the State is thus limited by law in what it may do, it takes citizens and residents with the will to keep the State within the bounds of law to help the notion of constitutionalism to spread and grow. I thus consider this diffusion of the consciousness of rights in our society and the general legal assertiveness of the public as contributions of the Legon Law Faculty to the socio-economic development of Ghana.

Conclusion

To end, let me say that over the past 50 years, the Legon Law Faculty has evolved a rich and varied heritage in legal education. I am confident that the current members of staff and students are conscious of this heritage and will do what it takes to maintain the high standards set by their forbears. My prayer to them is to strive to innovate in response to social, economic and political change. Legal education is about enthusing a fresh generation of lawyers each time about the rule of law and the potential of law as an instrument of social ordering and development. Legal education has to inculcate these broader objectives in addition to teaching the techniques for serving the needs of the legal services market.

I am also glad to be able to confirm that the Faculty of Law of the University of Ghana has contributed significantly to the governance and socio-economic development of Ghana since its inception, as a Department of Law, in1959. There is, however, room for improving, expanding and deepening the relevance of its role. Indeed, the nature and scope of its contribution should, in my view, be one of the subjects treated in the jurisprudence course at Legon. Self-assessment and self-examination are always useful exercises. What I am saying is that the role of legal education in our society and in our economy is a worthy subject for jurisprudential study and discourse. Long may the Faculty continue to serve as a medium for the transmission of legal learning in the service of the development needs of our people!

PART II:

THE JUDICIARY

CHAPTER 5

THE JUDICIARY: A CLOSER LOOK AT ITS ROLE AND FUNCTION UNDER THE 1992 CONSTITUTION[59]

Introduction

In this short Chapter, I begin with general introductory remarks about the role of the judiciary in justice delivery, based on the 1992 Constitution of Ghana. I then proceed to discuss three particular aspects of the function of judges under the Constitution.

The formal source of the legitimacy of the Judiciary in Ghana is Article 125(1) of the 1992 Constitution which provides that:

> "Justice emanates from the people and shall be administered in the name of the Republic by the Judiciary which shall be independent and subject only to this Constitution."

In the same way as the President and Members of Parliament have their electoral mandate and the legitimacy that it accords them, judges also have this "anointment", metaphorically speaking, from the people, through the Constitution, to do justice in their name.

The delivery of justice is a very important constitutional and political objective of the Ghanaian State. Indeed the very first of the political objectives set out in the Directive Principles of State Policy, contained in Chapter 6 of the 1992 Constitution, provides (in article 35(1)) that:

> "Ghana shall be a democratic state dedicated to the realization of *freedom and justice*; and accordingly, sovereignty resides in the people of Ghana from whom government derives all its powers and authority through this Constitution." (The emphasis is mine).

59   This Chapter is based on a paper that I presented at a capacity building workshop of the Select Committee of the Parliament of Ghana on the Judicial Service, on 5th December 2009.

However, the justice that judges are able to deliver is not necessarily coterminous with the notion of justice contained in article 35(1). Justice is a very broad concept which includes more than judges alone can deliver. For instance, social justice is more within the domain of politics and politicians than of judges, although judges also have to be sensitive to the issue. I have written else where that[60]:

> "Social justice refers to fairness in the distribution of the benefits of government among members of society. Another way of expressing this is to say that social justice means the fairness of a society in its distribution of rewards and burdens among its members."

The business of judges is narrower than this and may be expressed as "doing justice according to law." The justice referred to in article 125(1), it is submitted, is justice according to law. An idea of what this justice consists of is given in Article 125(5), which states that:

> "The judiciary shall have jurisdiction in all matters civil and criminal, including matters relating to this Constitution, and such other jurisdiction as Parliament may, by law, confer on it."

It is evident from this provision that the justice the judiciary is expected to deliver is through the resolution of disputes. Human experience has shown that this dispute-resolution function is usually exercised through the following means:

a. The interpretation of the Constitution, statutes and constitutional and statutory instruments;

b. The ascertainment and application of the law, including, in the case of Ghana, the common law of Ghana and the customary law, to disputes before the courts;and

c. Performance of a junior partnership role in law-making through interstitial rule formulation.

The judiciary also has the opportunity and the capacity to contribute to the promotion of good governance, respect for the law and

---

60   See Date-Bah, On *Law and Liberty in Contemporary Ghana* (Ghana Academy of Arts and Sciences, 2008) 70-71.

constitutionalism through the efficient exercise of the three aspects of its dispute-resolution function, identified above. By means of their judgments and even extra-judicially, it is my personal belief that judges have a moral obligation to promote the values of democratic governance, through among other methods, pedagogic utterances, where appropriate. In other words, judges, in my view, have an informal educational role, in addition to their dispute-resolution function. These are the ideas to be dilated on here.

To end these introductory remarks, I should emphasise that final judicial power in Ghana may only be exercised by the Judiciary under the 1992 Constitution. Article 125(3) states that:

> "The judicial power of Ghana shall be vested in the Judiciary, accordingly, neither the President nor Parliament nor any organ or agency of the President or Parliament shall have or be given final judicial power."

Any attempt by the Executive or the Legislature to give finality to its own decision in relation to an issue that lends itself to justiciability will not be binding on the judiciary which will have the power of judicial review over that issue. The judicial remarks that I made in the case of *Adofo v Attorney-General and Cocobod*[61] illustrate the extent of judicial authority in such matters:

> "The power of judicial review of the constitutionality of legislation, which is explicitly conferred on this Court by Articles 2(1) and 130(1) of the Constitution, is one that should be vigilantly deployed by this Court in discharge of the obligation of this Court to uphold the Constitution of this land. It is a power over whose legitimacy constitutional scholars in constitutional democracies have often agonised. Because of the clarity of the provisions which vest this Court with that jurisdiction, we do not think this Court need agonise about the legitimacy of its power. The framers of the Constitution wanted this Court to exercise this jurisdiction and that is, for us, a sufficient basis for the legitimacy of the power. However, the reason why some constitutional scholars agonise over

---

61   [2005-2006] SCGLR 411

the legitimacy of the power is that judges are unelected and therefore are not electorally accountable. On the other hand, this very lack of electoral accountability is probably one of the justifications or rationales for judicial review. The Constitution expects judges to protect individuals and minorities from the power of the majority. The fundamental human rights and freedoms enshrined in Chapter 5 of the Constitution are intended to facilitate the fulfilment by judges of this expectation. The fact that judges are unelected in democracies such as ours strengthens their capacity to protect individuals and minorities because their tenure is not dependent on the short-term wishes of the majority of the electorate. Marjoritarian institutions such as Parliament and the Executive are less well-suited to the protection of the interests of individuals and minorities because of the pressure applied on them by the will of the majority which they represent."

A consideration of particular aspects of the judicial role

a. **Interpretation of the Constitution, statutes and constitutional and statutory instruments.**

Judges have the crucial responsibility of serving as a bridge between the cold words of a Constitution or a statute and their application to real life situations. In this task, judges inevitably have to interpret the words of the Constitution or statute. When judges interpret legal instruments, they tend to develop an interpretative stance or approach, whether wittingly or unwittingly. The type of interpretative stance that judges adopt have come to be given labels like "purposive", "golden rule" etc. In *Asare v Attorney-General*[62] , referring to the so-called "rules of interpretation", I said:

> ""Rules"of interpretation are not to be understood as binding courts in the same way as the *ratio decidendi* of a case is binding on subsequent courts. The so-called "rules" of interpretation are merely guides or aids to judges in deciphering the meaning

---

62   [2003-2004] SCGLR 823 at 833

of words they are required to interpret. As Lord Reid said in *Maunsell v Olins* [1975]1 All ER 16 at p 18:

> "They are not rules in the ordinary sense of having some binding force. They are our servants, not our masters. They are aids to construction: presumptions or pointers. Not infrequently one "rule" points in one direction, another in a different direction. In each case we must look at all relevant circumstances and decide as a matter of judgment what weight is to be attached to any particular"rule"."

> This is a helpful *dictum* reminding us that the task of interpretation is always complex, usually involving the balancing of competing interests, and the "rules" of interpretation, whether the "Literal Rule", "the Golden Rule", "the Mischief Rule" or the "Purposive Approach", are to be applied in the context of particular enactments in order to achieve justice. What I have stated above has been merely to emphasise that I consider the purposive approach to be more likely to achieve the ends of justice in most cases."

The message being conveyed is that the Parliamentarians, the audience of my initial address which forms the basis of this Chapter, should not take a stridently literal approach to the interpretation of the Constitution. I have sometimes noticed that literalism characterises the approach of many social commentators on the airwaves. The Supreme Court on the whole is inclined towards according the Constitution a liberal, broad and purposive interpretation.

The interpretative role of judges in relation to the Constitution gives them a crucial role in the protection of political freedom in this country. Chapter 5 of the 1992 Constitution contains an extensive Bill of Rights. The judiciary's role in enabling the enforceability of the rights contained in that Chapter and of the supplementary political, social, cultural and economic rights contained in Chapter 6 of the 1992 Constitution is central to the quality of the democratic governance that is achievable in this country.

On the whole, the record of the Ghana judiciary in the protection of political freedom under the 1992 Constitution is better than the public perception, although, in this short piece, I do not attempt to provide chapter and verse to justify this proposition. I would rather refer the audience to the book by the late Dr. Bimpong-Buta on *The Role of the Supreme Court in the Development of Constitutional Law in Ghana* [63] and the Lectures I delivered under the auspices of the Ghana Academy of Arts and Sciences in 2008 entitled *On Law and Liberty in Contemporary Ghana* [64]. For instance, the late Dr. Bimpong-Buta, at p. 616 of his book, says:

> "With regard to the development of Constitutional Law in Ghana, the picture which emerges, as demonstrated in the preceding chapters of this book, is that the Supreme Court has made distinctive contributions, for example, on the question of the underlying concepts or principles of the 1992 Constitution as examined in chapter 3, namely: the doctrines of the supremacy of the Constitution, of separation of powers, of non-justiciable political questions and of mootness. This book demonstrates that the Supreme Court's pronouncements and decisions on the application or otherwise of these concepts have thrown much light on and enriched our understanding of these concepts under Ghanaian Constitutional Law."

b. **The ascertainment and application of the law, including, in the case of Ghana, the common law of Ghana and the customary law to disputes before the courts.**

The ascertainment and application of the law take place within the context of the procedure and jurisdictional limits laid down by law. Accordingly, the Constitution and the relevant applicable statutes, such as the Courts Act 1993[65], have an important impact on the role and function of judges under the regime established by the 1992 Constitution. Furthermore, the Courts Act 1993 lays a duty on judges to promote reconciliation and the resolution of disputes by settlement, wherever practicable. Accordingly, judges are obliged

---

63   (Advanced Legal Publications, Accra, 2007)

64   (Ghana Academy of Arts and Sciences, 2008)

65   Act 459

to promote ADR (or Alternative Dispute Resolution) whenever practicable.

Regarding the hierarchy of courts established under the Constitution, Article 126(1) of the 1992 Constitution provides as follows:

> "The Judiciary shall consist of --
> a. the Superior Courts of Judicature comprising–
>   i. the Supreme Court;
>   ii. the Court of Appeal;and
>   iii. the High Court and Regional Tribunals.
> b. such lower courts or tribunals as Parliament may by-law establish."

The Supreme Court consists of the Chief Justice and not less than nine other Justices of the Supreme Court. The Court of Appeal consists of the Chief Justice and not less than ten Justices of the Court of Appeal. In addition, other Justices of the Superior Courts of Judicature may be requested by the Chief Justice to sit in the Court of Appeal for any specified period to determine a particular cause or matter. The High Court consists of the Chief Justice and not less than twenty Justices. In this court also, the Chief Justice may request any of the other Justices of the Superior Courts of Judicature to sit as High Court Justices for any period. The lower courts which have been established by Parliament are the Circuit Courts and the Magistrates Courts which are spread all over Ghana and are the principal courts of first instance.

The Supreme Court is the highest court in the land and normally decides cases in panels of five. When exercising its review jurisdiction, however, it is constituted by a panel of not less than seven judges. In addition to exercising jurisdiction as the final court of appeal, the Supreme Court also has the following other jurisdictions: original,supervisory; review; an exclusive jurisdiction to determine whether an official document shall not be produced in court because its production or the disclosure of its contents will be prejudicial to the security of the State or injurious to the public interest; and a jurisdiction to hear petitions challenging the validity of the election of a President.

The appellate jurisdiction is exercised to hear appeals from the Court of Appeal. The original jurisdiction is exercised to interpret exclusively (in the language of Article 130(1) of the 1992 Constitution):

> "a. all matters relating to the enforcement or interpretation of this Constitution; and
>
> b. all matters arising as to whether an enactment was made in excess of the powers conferred on Parliament or any other authority or person by law or under this Constitution."

This provision in the Constitution makes the Supreme Court virtually a Constitutional Court. However, in relation to the enforcement of the fundamental human rights and freedoms, it shares its enforcement jurisdiction with the High Court. The supervisory jurisdiction of the Supreme Court is exercisable over all courts and adjudicating authorities and may be exercised through the issue of writs or orders in the nature of *habeas corpus, certiorari, mandamus, quo warranto,* and prohibition. It is my view that the supervisory jurisdiction extends beyond adjudicating authorities to all persons and entities subject to judicial review at common law.

c. Performance of a junior partnership role in law-making through interstitial rule formulation.

This section starts with a quotation from Lord Reid, who was for a very long time a member of the English final court, the House of Lords, speaking extra judicially:

> "There was a time when it was thought almost indecent to suggest that judges make law – they only declare it. Those with a taste for fairy tales seem to have thought that in some Aladdin's cave there is hidden the Common Law in all its splendour and that on a judge's appointment there descends on him[or her]knowledge of the magic words Open Sesame. Bad decisions are given when the judge has muddled the password and the wrong door opens. But we do not believe in fairy tales anymore."[66]

---

66   See"The Judge as Lawmaker"(1972)12 *Journal of the Society of Public Teachers of Law 22 at 22.*

Lord Reid is here, of course, making fun of the declaratory theory of the judicial function. According to this, judges do not make law; they merely discover pre-existing law, through their trained eye. This view of the judicial function is now clearly *passé*. There is no doubt that judges do make law. The debate has shifted to the extent to which they make law or should make law.

My own view is that judges do make law sometimes. They need to make law in order to fill in the gaps of the existing law, inappropriate circumstances. However, they make law far less often than they merely apply existing law. The English judge, Lord Devlin, once expressed the view that 90% of the time of English judges is spent in the "disinterested application of known law".[67] Justice McHugh of the Australian High Court has also confirmed that this percentage is right in relation to Australian judges as well.[68] I am not in a position to assert, in relation to Ghana, what percentage of cases involve judicial law-making. However, it would be safe to assert that in the majority of cases before our courts, the judges and magistrates have no discretion but to apply existing law. This is particularly so for the lower courts, who are bound by precedent and rarely have the opportunity for creativity. But even for the lower courts, if a case of first impression comes up, they can, and indeed are obliged to, make law. In other words, if a case presents an issue on which no binding precedent exists, the lower court can, and has to, make a new rule and apply it. I have in mind here, of course, common law situations and not, for instance, disputes relating to statutory penal law. This is because the common law does not have a doctrine of *non liquet*. In other words, a court cannot refuse to decide a case on the ground that there is no rule governing the issue in controversy. The scope for judicial law-making increases as one goes up the hierarchy of the courts. The most room for judicial law-making is usually in the highest court, which in Ghana is the Supreme Court. This court is bound by no other decisions, except its own decisions and it may even depart from its own decisions, if it sees the need to do so.

---

67   See, "The Judge as Lawmaker" in *The Judge*(1979) Ch. 1 at 3.

68   See his speech at the Australian Bar Association Conference in 1998 in London, on "The Judicial Method".

Some have argued that judges in common law jurisdictions, which are less mature in the sense of not having very many issues in the common law already settled by case law, should be more activist in order to fill in the gaps of the law. I will not venture an opinion on this argument here. There is need to stress, however, that there are acknowledged limits to judicial law-making. The very nature of the judicial process imposes a limit on the extent of judicial law-making. This limit is well-expressed by Justice McHugh, the Australian judge that I earlier referred to. He has said[69]:

> "The law-making function of the judiciary is not unfettered. There is a real difference between judge-made law and the creation of law by a popularly elected legislature. Any encroachment into the legislative sphere is constitutionally impermissible and democratically unpalatable. Although this ideal is easy to state, the dividing line is not easy to draw. As Justice Stephen Breyer of the Supreme Court of the United States has been reported as saying, a "bright line" between permissible and impermissible judicial creativity does not exist. That said, there is no doubt that "judicial law-making is of a different nature and order from legislative enactment. It occurs in different circumstances, in response to different stimuli, and is subject to restrictions that do not constrain the legislature's freedom of action". Rather than a usurpation of the legislative role, the judiciary's law-making function may be seen as a complementary dimension to governmental law-making as a whole.

First, courts only make law in the context of determining a legal dispute which is initiated by the parties to the dispute. The courts resolve issues which litigants define. In the words of Chief Justice Doyle, "the law making [of courts] is opportunistic."

Second, the natural inclination of most judges is to place a premium on certainty and predictability which are important characteristics of a stable legal system. Stability instils confidence in the institution of the judiciary and in the law.

---

69   *Ibid.*

Because judicial law-making operates retrospectively, the rule of law would be seriously threatened if law-making was a routine function of courts.

Third, in most cases, judges make law only when changes in society require the law to be developed to meet the consequences of those changes. Changing social conditions are central to the development of the law by the judiciary. Unlike political parties, judges have no agenda to be implemented. Moreover, judges know that it is no easy task to identify and measure social change or to assess the effect of an alteration of the law which responds to that change. The courts are largely dependent on litigants, interveners and *amici curiae* to provide relevant information for the determination of the issues in dispute. Additionally, it is the appellate courts that are the principal judicial law-makers and their procedures are not geared towards the elaboration of relevant non-legal material. Awareness of these difficulties naturally makes the judiciary develop the law cautiously and only when it is clear that the needs of society demand it or the state of the law requires that the existing rules or principles be rationalized."

Conclusion

In this short Chapter, one can only give a broad and impressionistic overview of the role and function of the judiciary under the 1992 Constitution. There is no doubt that the role accorded the judiciary is important and one that cannot be effectively discharged without the active support of the other two branches of government, namely, the Executive and the Legislature. I think that I would be speaking for all judges and magistrates if I were to declare that the judiciary counts on Parliament's support for the achievement of the important constitutional function that the people of Ghana have assigned to the judiciary. This support is needed particularly in relation to adequate budgetary allocation and recognition of the need for judicial independence.

CHAPTER 6

JUDICIAL INDEPENDENCE AND THE RULE OF LAW IN GHANA, A MICROCOSM OF WEST AFRICAN COMMONWEALTH JURISDICTIONS[70][71]

Introduction

After briefly pointing out the relevance of the notion of independence of the judiciary to the rule of law, this Chapter will focus on the extent of the judiciary's independence in Ghana. Ghana will be regarded here as a microcosm of the West African Commonwealth Region. I had originally intended to discuss briefly material from Nigeria and Sierra Leone as well, but had to exclude that option because of the constraints of time. Nevertheless, it remains true that Ghana is a microcosm of the judicial systems in place in Nigeria, Sierra Leone and the Gambia.

Judicial independence and the rule of law are two of the pillars identified in the Latimer House Principles as essential for the functioning of a democratic state. The formal name of the Principles is the Commonwealth Principles on the Accountability of and the Relationship between the Three Branches of Government. These Principles are based on Guidelines which were initially fashioned at Latimer House, Buckinghamshire, in England by a conference in June 1998 under the auspices of the Commonwealth Parliamentary Association, the Commonwealth Legal Education Association, the Commonwealth Magistrates' and Judges' Association and the Commonwealth Lawyers' Association. The Conference brought together distinguished judges, Parliamentarians, practising lawyers and legal academics. The product of the Conference was

---

70 This Chapter is based on a paper that the author gave as a public lecture to the Commonwealth Legal Education Association, West African Regional Chapter, at the British Council Hall, Accra, in March 2015.

71 Some of the material used in this lecture was adapted from my book entitled *Reflections on the Supreme Court of Ghana* published by Wildy, Simmonds & Hill Publishing, London (2015).

the Latimer House Guidelines on Parliamentary Supremacy and Judicial Independence. The Guidelines were then subjected to a process of revision and fine-tuning, after they had been considered first by Commonwealth Law Ministers in Port of Spain, Trinidad and Tobago, in 1999. They were finally distilled into the Principles by a Committee of Law Ministers, including the Ghanaian Minister, agreed by Commonwealth Law Ministers, and eventually endorsed in 2003 by Commonwealth Heads of Government at the CHOGM in Abuja, Nigeria.

The fundamental values of the Commonwealth, identified by the Heads of Government and declared in the Final Communique of the Abuja Meeting, included the following:

> **"Fundamental Political Values**
>
> 7. Heads of Government reaffirmed their commitment to the fundamental political values of the Commonwealth as set out in the Singapore and Harare Declarations and subsequent CHOGM Communiqués, and reinforced by the Millbrook Action Programme. They reiterated their commitment to non-racism, international peace and security, democracy, good governance, human rights, rule of law, the independence of the judiciary, freedom of expression, and a political culture that promotes transparency, accountability and economic development".

These values show how important the independence of the judiciary and the rule of law are to the systems of government chosen by Commonwealth States.

I. The rule of law

The rule of law is a much discussed notion. However, as my principal focus here is on the independence of the judiciary, I will only give a brief indication of what I understand by the rule of law. At its barest minimum, it means that all the organs of the State are subject to law and are accountable in accordance with the law. The *Magna Carta*, whose 800th Anniversary was celebrated in June 2015, embodied this basic notion. Some claim that it is the origin of the idea of the Rule of Law. However, others trace it back to the classical Greeks. By the *Magna Carta*, the English barons were able to extract from King John, in June 1215, the concession that the King or the Sovereign was subject to the law. In effect, this was an acknowledgement that the institutions of the State were subject to the law. The rule of law in a modern context probably connotes more than that; and should. It probably offers also a measuring rod for the contents of the law. For me, there was no rule of law in Nazi Germany nor in Apartheid South Africa, even if the governments there enacted law and purported to follow that law.

Although I am not of a natural law persuasion, the rule of law for me connotes a qualitative assessment of the content of a nation's law. That is why I am glad that the national law in the three West African Commonwealth States (that is, Ghana, Nigeria and Sierra Leone) has a measuring rod within it, namely their Constitutions. These West African jurisdictions are emerging democracies with democratic aspirations. To abbreviate the discussion, the fair and impartial application of law in States with democratic constitutions would approximate to the rule of law. It is obvious that fair and impartial application of the law requires an independent judiciary.

Lord Bingham in his book, entitled *The Rule of Law*, captures the essence of the concept of the Rule of Law as follows[72]:

> "The core of the existing principle is, I suggest, that all persons and authorities within the state, whether public or private,should be bound by and entitled to the benefit of laws publicly made, taking effect (generally)in future and publicly administered in the courts."

To this definition, I would add an element identified by Lord Steyn of the United Kingdom House of Lords in *R(Alconbury Developments Ltd and Others) v Secretary of State for the Environment, Transport and the Regions*,[73] where he said: "...the rule of law enforces minimum standards of fairness, both substantive and procedural."

---

72 Tom Bingham, *The Rule of Law* (Allen Lane, London, 2010) 8

73 [2001] UKHL 23, [2003] 2 AC 295.

II. Judicial Independence

An independent judiciary is indispensable to the rule of law because, in modern governments with written constitutions, the executive and legislative branches of governments are answerable before the courts, if they exceed their powers. Under the Westminster model of democracy, Parliament is supreme and therefore not answerable to the courts on the contents of its legislation. However, in all the West African Commonwealth jurisdictions, the Constitution, and not Parliament, is supreme. Accordingly, even Parliament in these countries is answerable to the Judiciary, if it exceeds its powers. The citizen thus has the right to challenge before the courts any acts or omissions of the executive or the legislature considered to be in breach of the Constitution or the law. This system can only work if independent judges are in place to adjudicate on these legal suits.

Independence of the judiciary has two dimensions: the institutional and the personal. Personal independence relates to the commitment of individual judges to the judicial values that ensure their impartiality and fairness. I am here referring to values such as eschewing corruption and not allowing ethnic and other particularistic considerations to affect judicial determinations. Institutional independence of the judiciary, on the other hand, relates to the constitutional, statutory and other arrangements put in place to assure the independence of the judiciary. Issues that are customarily dealt with under institutional independence include: separation of powers; security of tenure for judges, including appropriate provisions on the appointment process of judges, the conditions of service of judges and the process for the removal of superior court judges; financial and administrative autonomy of the judiciary; and measures to ensure judicial accountability. Accountability measures are what make judicial independence justifiable. It would be unacceptable to have independent but unaccountable judges. Below, I dilate first on issues relating to institutional independence before discussing the personal independence of judges.

(i)   Institutional Independence of the Judiciary

The Latimer House Principles, earlier referred to, provide useful benchmarks for assessing the standards embodied in the Ghanaian constitutional and statutory provisions on the independence of the Judiciary. The Latimer House Principle on the independence of the Judiciary states the following:

"(IV) Independence of the Judiciary

An independent, impartial, honest and competent judiciary is integral to upholding the rule of law, engendering public confidence and dispensing justice. The function of the judiciary is to interpret and apply national constitutions and legislation, consistent with international human rights conventions and international law, to the extent permitted by the domestic law of each Commonwealth country.

To secure these aims:

a.   Judicial appointments should be made on the basis of clearly defined criteria and by a publicly declared process. The process should ensure: equality of opportunity for all who are eligible for judicial office; appointment on merit; and that appropriate consideration is given to the need for the progressive attainment of gender equity and the removal of other historic factors of discrimination;

b.   Arrangements for appropriate security of tenure and protection of levels of remuneration must be in place;

c.   Adequate resources should be provided for the judicial system to operate effectively without any undue constraints which may hamper the independence sought;

d.   Interaction,if any, between the executive and the judiciary should not compromise judicial independence.

e.   Judges should be subject to suspension or removal only for reasons of incapacity or misbehaviour that clearly renders them unfit to discharge their duties.

f. Court proceedings should, unless the law or overriding public interest otherwise dictates, be open to the public. Superior Court decisions should be published and accessible to the public and be given in a timely manner.

g. An independent, effective and competent legal profession is fundamental to the upholding of the rule of law and the independence of the judiciary."

I now consider the Ghanaian constitutional provisions relating to the independence of the judiciary and assess them against the above benchmarks set out in the Latimer House Principles.

The 1992 Constitution contains elaborate provisions intended to ensure the independence of the Ghana Judiciary. The Judiciary is defined in the Constitution as follows:

"**126.**

(1) The Judiciary shall consist of -
    (a) the Superior Courts of Judicature comprising-
        (i) the Supreme Court;
        (ii) the Court of Appeal; and
        (iii) the High Court and Regional Tribunals.

    (b) such lower courts or tribunals as Parliament may by law establish."

Although the Constitution defines the Judiciary in terms of the courts,it is reasonable to interpret the reference to the courts as one to the judges and magistrates who man the courts. In effect, all the courts in the land (meaning the judges and magistrates) are defined as constituting the Judiciary.

In this connection, the first constitutional provision I would like to consider is Article 125(3) of the 1992 Constitution which provides as follows:

"The judicial power of Ghana shall be vested in the Judiciary, accordingly, neither the President nor Parliament nor any organ or agency of the President or Parliament shall have or be given final judicial power."

This exclusive vesting of final judicial power in the Judiciary implies that Parliament cannot itself apply criminal sanctions for contempt of Parliament, as some other Parliaments in the Commonwealth can. For instance, in Australia, The Parliamentary Privileges Act 1987 allows Parliament to enforce criminal sanctions for contempt of Parliament. The Act sets out penalties for committing contempts before the Australian Parliament and its committees. Fines and imprisonment are possible by order of a resolution of Parliament. However, in contrast to the Ghanaian system, Australia operates the Westminster constitutional model, which does not have the same degree of separation of powers as the Ghana Constitution requires.

One way of viewing article 125(3) of the 1992 Constitution of Ghana is to see it as the source of legitimacy of judicial power in the country. The people vest judicial power in the Judiciary directly and independent of the executive and legislature. In the same way as the President and Members of Parliament ground their legitimacy on their electoral mandate, the judiciary's mandate to exercise judicial power derives from this constitutional delegation of power from the people. Judges are anointed, so to speak, by the people to do justice on their behalf.

Besides separating judicial power from the other powers of government, Ghana's 1992 Constitution goes on, in Article 127, to provide expressly for the independence of the judiciary in broad terms as follows:

"**127.**

1. In the exercise of the judicial power of Ghana, the Judiciary, in both its judicial and administrative functions, including financial administration, is subject only to this Constitution and shall not be subject to the control or direction of any person or authority.

2. Neither the President nor Parliament nor any person acting under the authority of the President or Parliament nor any other person whatsoever shall interfere with Judges or judicial officers or other persons exercising judicial power, in the exercise of their judicial functions; and all organs

and agencies of the State shall accord to the courts such assistance as the courts may reasonably require to protect the independence, dignity and effectiveness of the courts, subject to this Constitution.

3. A Justice of a Superior Court, or any person exercising judicial power, shall not be liable to any action or suit for any act or omission by him in the exercise of the judicial power.

4. The administrative expenses of the judiciary, including all salaries, allowances, gratuities and pensions payable to or in respect of, persons serving in the judiciary, shall be charged on the Consolidated Fund.

5. The salary, allowances, privileges and rights in respect of leave of absence, gratuity, pension and other conditions of service of a Justice of the superior court or any judicial officer or other person exercising judicial power, shall not be varied to his disadvantage.

6. Funds voted by parliament, or charged on the Consolidated Fund by this Constitution for the Judiciary, shall be released to the Judiciary, in quarterly instalments.

7. For the purposes of clause (1) of this article, "financial administration" includes the operation of banking facilities by the Judiciary without the interference of any person or authority, other than for the purposes of audit by the Auditor-General, of the funds voted by Parliament or charged on the Consolidated Fund by this Constitution or any other law, for the purposes of defraying the expenses of the Judiciary in respect of which the funds were voted or charged."

These constitutional provisions are now analysed below.

a. Administrative and Financial Autonomy

Clauses 4, 6 and 7 of Article 127 of the 1992 Constitution of Ghana provide a constitutional basis for administrative and financial autonomy of the Judiciary. In Ghana, the Chief Justice heads an administration for the Judiciary that is distinct, separate from, and relatively independent of the Executive and the Legislature. Judges and magistrates and their supporting staff are employees of the Judiciary, as an institution, and the Judicial Service, respectively, and not of the Executive. This may be contrasted with the system in the United Kingdom, for instance, where the courts are run by Her Majesty's Courts and Tribunals Service, which is a unit within the Executive. It is an Executive agency sponsored by the Ministry of Justice. It used to be part of the Lord Chancellor's Department until the constitutional reforms of 2005 in the United Kingdom, after which it became a part of the Ministry of Justice. In this context, the courts do not include the independent judges who manage themselves. Thus, the service which administers the courts in the UK is under the authority of the Ministry of Justice, while in Ghana it is headed by the Chief Justice and separated from the executive branch of government.

The administrative and financial independence of the Ghanaian judiciary is, however, not unqualified because of the practical realities of government. The budget process in relation to the Judiciary and Judicial Service illustrates the limits to the independence of the Judiciary. Clauses 3 to 6 of article 179 of the 1992 Constitution state as follows:

"3.	The Chief Justice shall, in consultation with the Judicial Council, cause to be submitted to the President at least two months before the end of each financial year, and thereafter as and when the need arises -

a.	the estimates of administrative expenses of the Judiciary charged on the Consolidated Fund under article 127 of this Constitution; and

b.	estimates of development expenditure of the Judiciary.

4.	The President shall, at the time specified in clause (1) of this article, or thereafter, as and when submitted to him under clause (3) of this article, cause the estimates referred to in clause (3) of this article to be laid before Parliament.

5. The estimates shall be laid before Parliament under clause (4) by the President without revision but with any recommendations that the Government may have on them.

6. The development expenditure of the Judiciary, if approved by Parliament, shall be a charge on the Consolidated Fund."

Accordingly, the President is not to cut the budget estimates of the Judiciary by executive action. He is obliged to submit the Judiciary's budget estimates to the Legislature, without revision, although he is authorised to make recommendations on it to the Legislature. In practice, because of the President's influence on Parliament through the governing party, his recommendations on the Judiciary's budget are likely to be accepted. However, the constitutional provisions do ensure that Parliament gets to consider the Judiciary's budget estimates in their original form, without the usual revisions carried out by the Finance Ministry to the budget estimates of Ministries, Departments and Agencies.

According to Article 127(6) of the 1992 Constitution, funds voted by Parliament, or charged on the Consolidated Fund, for the Judiciary,shall be released to the Judiciary, in quarterly instalments. The Government does not, however, always comply with this provision. Unfortunately, there is no effective and practical sanction for such non-compliance. The usual remedy of suing to enforce a constitutional provision which has been breached does not necessarily work in this context. This is one of the weak links in the system of financial autonomy that the Constitution provides for the Judiciary. When the Executive fails to release the Judiciary's approved subventions on time, the only remedy that the Judiciary has been able to resort to, in practice, is to hold discussions with the Executive with a view to expediting such release. This is an inadequate remedy which implies that the Executive can in practice impair the autonomous financial functioning of the Judiciary.

A more unqualified independence would come from a funding arrangement for the judiciary that did not depend on the Executive and the Legislature. This would be unusual in the constitutional practice of States, but still deserves serious consideration. One technique would be to allocate to the judiciary through the Constitution a fixed percentage of national revenue. This could be a crude measure in that it could undershoot or overshoot. In other words, the quantum of revenue delivered by this constitutional measure could be more or less than the requirements of the Judiciary. The technique could thus be refined by a constitutional provision allowing Parliament to modify the projected allocation to the Judiciary through a super-majority, such as a two-thirds or three-quarters of the members of Parliament. Through such a constitutional arrangement, there would be a presumptive annual budgetary provision to the Judiciary which would automatically flow from the Consolidated Fund to the Judiciary, unless the legislature exercised its discretion to modify the quantum of the revenue going to the Judiciary.

All in all, however, the constitutional provisions on administrative and financial autonomy for the Ghana Judiciary measure up reasonably well against the Latimer House Principles, although there is still scope for improvement. The provisions, in theory, ensure that resources are provided for the judicial system to operate effectively without undue constraints that hamper judicial independence. However, there are issues as to the adequacy of the resources made available to the judiciary and the timeliness of the payment of subventions to this third branch of government.

b. Independent Appointment and Security of Tenure of Superior Court Justices

Clause 5 of Article 127, combined with articles 144 and 146 of the 1992 Constitution, make provision for considerable security of tenure for Superior Court Justices in Ghana.

The mode of appointment of Justices of the Supreme Court is specified by article 144 of the 1992 Constitution. It provides for their appointment by the President, acting on the advice of the Judicial Council, in consultation with the Council of State and with the approval of Parliament. Thus both the Executive and the Legislature are involved in the process. The intention of the framers of the Constitution, as confirmed by practice, appears to be that nominations should be made by the Judicial Council, although the appointment is by the President. The names of nominees, recommended by the Judicial Council, are forwarded to the President who places them before the Council of State for their views. If the views of the Council of State are positive, the President then forwards the names to the Speaker of Parliament for Parliamentary vetting.

It should be noted, however, that Presidents in the Fourth Republic have not considered themselves bound by the advice of the Judicial Council in relation to nominations for appointment to the Supreme Court. Presidents have on occasion refused to accept some nominees recommended by the Judicial Council. Though the Judicial Council has expressed regret at this, it has not challenged the legality of such refusal in court. There is thus no judicial decision clarifying the meaning of "acting on the advice of the Judicial Council" in article 144(2)[74]. Under a Constitution on the Westminster model, such as that in force in Ghana between 1957 and 1960, the Governor-General was obliged to follow the advice given him on judicial appointments. However, this convention and understanding have not survived into the Republican era. Ordinarily, Presidents tend to accept the nominees of the Judicial Council as, it has to be remembered, the Attorney-General (the President's principal legal adviser) and four nominees of the President serve on the Judicial Council. The President thus has ample opportunity to influence the nominations by the Judicial Council. Therefore though the appointment process for Supreme Court Justices enjoys a degree of independence from the Executive, it is not hermetically sealed from the influence of the executive. Furthermore, because the constitutional provision requires Parliament's prior approval, Parliament has a veto power over the appointment of any Supreme Court Justice.

---

74   It should be pointed out, however, that subsequent to the delivery of this Lecture, a judgment of the Supreme Court has interpreted this expression. See *Ghana Bar Association & Ors v Attorney-General and Judicial Council.* [2015-2016] 2 SCGLR 871. This decision is discussed in Chapter 12 below.

Although the above shows that roles are assigned to both the President and Parliament in the appointment process of Supreme Court Justices, the crucial role of the Judicial Council ensures that the Judiciary and the Bar play important roles as well in the process. The appointment of Justices of the Supreme Court thus involves an interactive process between stakeholders identified by the Constitution. In this connection, a disclosure of the composition of the Judicial Council is pertinent. The membership is as follows:[75]

"a. the Chief Justice who shall be Chairman;

b. the Attorney-General;

c. a Justice of the Supreme Court nominated by the Justices of the Supreme Court;

d. a Justice of the Court of Appeal nominated by the Justices of the Court of Appeal;

e. a Justice of the High court nominated by the Justices of the High Court;

f. two representatives of the Ghana Bar Association one of whom shall be a person of not less than twelve years' standing as a lawyer.

g. a representative of the Chairmen of Regional Tribunals nominated by the Chairmen;

h. a representative of the lower courts or tribunals;

i. the Judge Advocate-General of the Ghana Armed Forces;

j. the Head of the Legal Directorate of the Police Service;

k. the Editor of the Ghana Law Reports;

l. a representative of the Judicial Service Staff Association nominated by the Association;

m. a chief nominated by the National House of Chiefs; and

n. four other persons who are not lawyers appointed by the President."

The mode of appointment of the other Superior Court Justices, that is High Court and Appeal Court Justices and Chairmen of Regional Tribunals, is similar to that for Justices of the Supreme Court,

---

75 See article 153 of the 1992 Constitution.

except that there is no role for Parliament and the Council of State in relation to them.

The mode of appointment of superior court Justices in Ghana is in my view compliant with the standards spelt out in the Latimer House Principles. Judicial appointments are made on the basis of clearly defined criteria, which are set out in the 1992 Constitution. These stipulate that for a person to be qualified for appointment to the High Court, he or she must be of high moral character and proven integrity and be of at least 10 years standing as a lawyer; for appointment to the Court of Appeal, the period of standing as a lawyer is longer that is, 12 years, otherwise the qualification is the same as for the High Court; and finally the period of standing as a lawyer for appointment to the Supreme Court is 15 years, otherwise the qualification is the same as for the High Court. In other words, they also have to be of high moral character and proven integrity. The appointment process is publicly declared and offers equality of opportunity for all eligible for judicial office. Appointment is on merit, with provision made for the sitting of qualifying examinations and the assessment of a sample of the written legal output of the candidates.

Article 146, clauses 1 and 2 provide as follows:

"(1) A Justice of the Superior Court or a Chairman of the Regional Tribunal shall not be removed from office except for stated misbehaviour or incompetence or on ground of inability to perform the functions of his office arising from infirmity of body or mind.

(2) A Justice of the Superior Court of Judicature or a Chairman of the Regional Tribunal may only be removed in accordance with the procedure specified in this article."

Accordingly, Justices of the Superior Courts of Judicature in Ghana have security of tenure from the date of their appointment till their retirement, unless they are adjudged to be guilty of stated misbehaviour or incompetence or have been found to be unable to perform the functions of their office by reason of infirmity of body or mind.

The Constitution makes provision for an elaborate impeachment process, which is the only way by which a Superior Court Justice may be removed from office. The Supreme Court has held that the impeachment process cannot be circumvented by indirect means of removing a judge. In both *Tuffour v Attorney-General*[76] and *Ghana Bar Association v Attorney-General and Anor*[77] the Court held that an action whose effect was to remove a Chief Justice from office could not be maintained, since the special procedure prescribed by the Constitution for the removal of judges had not been followed. That procedure involves three superior court Justices and two non-lawyers determining whether a judge has been guilty of misconduct or incompetence, if the Chief Justice determines that there is a *prima facie* case established against the judge[78]. The judges who are members of the impeachment committee are nominated by the Judicial Council, while the non-lawyers are nominated by the Chief Justice, on the advice of the Council of State.

In *Ghana Bar Association v Attorney-General*, the plaintiffs sought, *inter alia,* to declare the appointment of a Chief Justice null and void, on the ground that he did not satisfy the constitutional requirement of being a person of high moral character and proven integrity. The Attorney-General raised a preliminary objection to the jurisdiction of the Supreme Court and this was unanimously upheld. Justice Edward Wiredu, in the course of his judgment, explained the law as follows[79]:

> "Though the plaintiff's indorsement has been couched in a way so as to make it appear a constitutional issue, its ultimate result will be otherwise if her claim succeeds on the allegations made. In *Yiadom I v Amaniampong* [1981] GLR 3, SC this court held the view that where the issue sought to be decided is clear and it is not resolvable by interpretation, or enforcement of the Constitution, this court ought to resist any invitation to pronounce on the meaning of the constitutional provision. In the instant case, the allegations upon which the plaintiff's

---

76   [1980] GLR 637

77   [1995-96]1GLR 598; [2003-2004] 1 SCGLR 250

78   See article 146(4) of the 1992 Constitution.

79   [1995-96] 1 GLR 598 at 611.

action is founded touch on the character and integrity of the second defendant as Chief Justice. Any person against whom such an allegation is established would not be entitled to hold the high office not only of a Chief Justice but also as a justice of any of the superior courts of which the second defendant is a member ex officio. It is my respectful view that the Supreme Court will itself be violating the Constitution, 1992 by assuming jurisdiction to embark on an inquiry into the plaintiff's allegation by treating this issue as purely constitutional. Under this same Constitution, 1992, a special procedure for embarking on such exercise for removing a judge is exclusively to be determined by a process within the contemplation of article 146."

The security of tenure of Superior Court Justices is further buttressed by the provision in article 127(5) of the 1992 Constitution which states that the salary, allowances, privileges and rights in respect of leave of absence, gratuity, pension and other conditions of service of a Justice of the superior court or any judicial officer or other person exercising judicial power, shall not be varied to his disadvantage. This provision gives the protection of the levels of remuneration referred to in the Latimer House Principles and is an important element in the financial security of Superior Court Justices. Finally, in relation to the financial security of Superior Court Justices, article 71 of the 1992 Constitution includes Superior Court Justices in the category of public servants whose remuneration is independently determined in accordance with the process embodied in that article.

c. Impeachment and other Sanctions for Interference with the Independence of the Judiciary

It will be recalled that article 127(2) lays a constitutional obligation on the President, Parliament and any persons acting on the authority of these two not to interfere with judges in the exercise of their judicial functions and to accord the courts such assistance as they may reasonably require to protect their independence, dignity and effectiveness. Theoretically, this provision raises the possibility of the President or any of his Ministers or the Speaker or Members of Parliament being sanctioned for breach of this constitutional obligation. In the case of the President, sanctioning would have to be by the process of impeachment. Where the President acts in wilful violation of a provision of the Constitution, the process for the removal of the President provided for in article 69 of the 1992 Constitution can be activated. Although the impeachment process provides for a determination of a *prima facie* case by a tribunal chaired by the Chief Justice and consisting of herself/himself and the four most senior Supreme Court Justices, ultimately whether the President is impeached is a political decision since the determination is made by a resolution of Parliament made by secret ballot.

The President would be responsible for sanctioning any of his Ministers who acts in wilful violation of the Constitution, whilst Parliament,acting under its Standing Orders, would be responsible for applying sanctions to any of its Members who acted in wilful violation of the Constitution.

In the alternative, a citizen may bring a constitutional suit in the Supreme Court against the President, Vice-President or a Minister, or the Speaker or any Member of Parliament, claiming that they have acted in breach of article 127(2). If the action succeeds, the Supreme Court may, under article 2(2) of the Constitution make such orders and give such directions as it may consider appropriate to give effect to its declaration. Under article 2(4), failure to obey or carry out the terms of an order or direction made by the Supreme Court constitutes a "high crime" under the Constitution and shall, in the case of the President or Vice-President, constitute a ground for removal from office under the Constitution.

d. Judicial accountability

The judiciary's independence under a democratic system has to be counterbalanced by measures to ensure its accountability. The rule of law requires that the independent judges who enforce it are themselves accountable. The judiciary is also subject to the law and to the need for ethical standards. It is not and should not be above the law. To fulfil its role in society, therefore, the judiciary needs to get its house in order on the issue of accountability. The usual measures available to ensure accountability of judges are codes of conduct, administrative mechanisms to monitor compliance with the standards set in the codes of conduct and effective impeachment procedures to remove errant judges. All these measures have been deployed in relation to the Ghanaian judiciary.

The Chief Justice, as the administrative head of the judiciary, and the Judicial Council, as the constitutional body charged with assisting the Chief Justice in the performance of her/his duties with a view to ensuring efficiency and effective realization of justice,[80] are the principal actors in the formulation of policies and measures to ensure the accountability of the judiciary.

The Latimer House Principles correctly indicate that[81]:

> "The principles of judicial accountability and independence underpin public confidence in the judicial system and the importance of the judiciary as one of the three pillars upon which a responsible government relies."

Judges in Ghana and elsewhere in the Commonwealth are not subject to the electoral accountability that the Executive and the Legislature are subject to in a democracy. This absence of electoral accountability for the judiciary does not, however, denote a lack of accountability. The accountability of the judiciary merely takes different forms. These forms include: peer review by members of the profession; criticism, through the media, by lay members of the public and also by members of the Executive and the Legislature; and legislative reversal of judicial precedent or lines of development of case law disapproved of by the Legislature. There is also self-regulation by the judiciary itself through its codes of conduct and other accountability measures.

Whilst the judiciary is not bound to follow the advice or prescriptions offered in criticisms by members of the profession and of the wider public, nor by strictures from the Executive or the Legislature, the exercise of the democratic right of free speech

---

80   See article 154(1) of the 1992 Constitution

81   Principle VII (Accountability Mechanisms).

to scrutinise the judgments and conduct of judges, subject always to due compliance with the contempt of court laws, serves as an avenue for securing their accountability. The fundamental human right of freedom of expression is thus also an important vehicle for securing the accountability of judges. The exercise of this freedom by the Legislature and the Executive should, however, not be untrammelled and probably needs some constraints in the broader democratic interest. The judiciary, under Ghana's written constitution, is given the role of a watchdog against abuse or excess of power by the Executive or the Legislature. As the Latimer House Principles put it: "Best democratic principles require that the actions of governments are open to scrutiny by the courts, to ensure that decisions taken comply with the Constitution, with relevant statutes and other law, including the law relating to the principles of natural justice. "The Executive and the Legislature may therefore on occasion wish to react vigorously to the restraining action of the judiciary. Because of the greater political power of the Executive and the Legislature, their unbridled attack on the judiciary can undermine the authority of the courts. Accordingly, there is the need in Ghana to develop conventions on how the Executive and Legislature may react to judicial decisions, without undermining the authority of the courts.

e. Personal Judicial Independence

All Superior Court Justices of Ghana are obliged by the Constitution to take an oath, prior to their assumption of office, by which they swear, *inter alia,* to perform the functions of their office "without fear or favour, affection or ill-will". This oath epitomises the judge's duty to be personally independent. Judges should reach their determinations without succumbing to pressure, wherever it may come from. This personal independence is facilitated by the institutional independence that I have dwelt on thus far.

The Judiciary, in concert with employees of the Judicial Service, who are not judges or magistrates, needs to continue to monitor adherence to the judicial values that underpin personal judicial independence.

Rule 1 of the *Code of Conduct for Judges and Magistrates in Ghana* states that:

> "An independent and honourable judiciary is indispensable to justice in our society. A judge should maintain and enforce high standards of conduct, and should personally "observe those standards so that the integrity and independence of the judiciary is preserved."

The Chief Justice, with active support of the Judicial Council, has put in place processes for enforcing the judicial values embodied in this Code of Conduct. For instance, she has established a committee to investigate complaints made against individual judges and another one to advise on ethical standards. This augurs well for the further strengthening of the judiciary's independence in Ghana.

Conclusion

Apart from brief remarks on the rule of law, this Chapter has focussed on the independence of the judiciary in Ghana. The constitutional provisions on independence of Ghana's judiciary provide a solid basis for the institutional independence of the judiciary. Also, the code of conduct which has been put in place by the Ghana Judiciary is an important tool for buttressing the personal independence of judges. The judiciary has adequate institutional mechanisms in place for monitoring and sanctioning non-compliance with the code. In practice, however, stakeholders need to work constantly at it to ensure that the independence of the judiciary continues and flourishes further. Financial autonomy is an area that requires further work. Public feedback and engagement are also vital in policing the personal independence of judges. Vigilance is required of all the three branches of government and of the general public in order to ensure that the Ghana judiciary is and remains independent.

CHAPTER 7

THE SUPREME COURT OF GHANA'S ROLE IN THE PROVISION OF JUDICIAL RELIEF AGAINST HUMAN RIGHTS ABUSES[82]

Introduction

This Chapter presents a brief sketch of the Ghanaian Supreme Court's role in the enforcement of human rights. It begins with an overview of the system for the enforcement of human rights in Ghana, before focussing on the Supreme Court's role. The Chapter is based on a paper prepared to contribute to a comparative basis for discussion at the First Summit of High, Regional and International Courts held in Mexico City in November 2012.

Overview of the current system for the enforcement of human rights in Ghana

Apart from the enforcement of human rights through litigation in the courts, the 1992 Constitution of Ghana provides for a parallel channel for the protection of human rights through recourse to the Commission on Human Rights and Administrative Justice. This body, popularly known locally as CHRAJ, is an independent body directly established by the Constitution for the vindication of human rights.

Chapter 18 of the 1992 Constitution of Ghana deals with this Commission on Human Rights and Administrative Justice ("CHRAJ"). Its *raison d'etre* is stated as follows[83]:

> "358. The constitutional experience of many countries, including ours, demonstrates that a catalogue of constitutional rights together with provisions for judicial enforcement is in

---

82 This Chapter is based on a paper presented at the First Summit of Presidents of High, Regional and International Courts, November 8-9 2012, Mexico City.

83 Committee of Experts, *Proposals for a Draft Constitution of Ghana*, (Accra,1992) para. 358

adequate to ensure meaningful enforcement of fundamental rights and freedoms on the ground. The Committee accordingly proposes the establishment of a Commission on Human Rights and Administrative Justice which would sensitize people to their constitutional rights, investigate violations of such rights, and assist individuals in prosecuting them."

The passage above is from a Report by a Committee of Experts set up by the Military Government which preceded the establishment of the Fourth Republic of Ghana in January 1993. The Committee's Report formed the basis for deliberation at the Consultative Assembly which produced the 1992 Constitution. The passage provides evidence that the objective of the framers of the Constitution was to provide for the establishment of an institution which would be effective in investigating violations of the fundamental human rights of individuals in Ghana.

The Ghana Supreme Court has construed the mandate of CHRAJ to be investigative and educational and not adjudicative. The determination of human rights by adjudication remains the preserve of the courts. The leading case establishing that CHRAJ's functions are investigative and educational, and not adjudicative, is *CHRAJ vAttorney-GeneralNo.2*[84]. In that case, Justice Charles Hayfron-Benjamin said:[85]

> "Act 456 was, of course, made in pursuance of authority granted to Parliament under chapter 18 of the 1992 Constitution. The functions–and this is the expression used in article 218 of the Constitution – which the plaintiff commission may exercise, are taken almost verbatim from the Constitution and restated in section 7 of Act 456. Similarly, the manner in which such functions may be exercised, is copied verbatim from article 219 and are also contained in sections 8 and 9 of the Act. Taken together, it is clear that the objects or functions of the plaintiff commission are investigative and educational. For the purposes of effective exercise of its investigative

---

84   [1998-99] SCGLR 871

85   At 882-883

functions, the plaintiff commission has certain powers akin to those of the regular courts and tribunals. But it must be said that, in exercising those powers, the commission does not thereby constitute a court or tribunal properly so-called; nor does it thereby assume any jurisdiction to do anything in its investigations. However, the plaintiff commission may institute legal action "before any Court in Ghana and may seek any remedy which may be available from that Court.""

Thus, the system for the enforcement of human rights in Ghana consists of the judicial system, which provides a forum for enforcement through litigation, and CHRAJ, which assists aggrieved persons through investigating alleged breaches of human rights as well as through helping them to enforce their rights in accordance with the available legal channels. In addition, CHRAJ has a mandate to sensitise the general population on their human rights, thus promoting the growth of a human rights culture. CHRAJ's mandate is, of course, not exclusive: the police and other law enforcement agencies also have an investigative mandate.

The Supreme Court of Ghana and the human rights provisions in the Ghanaian Constitution

The 1992 Constitution of Ghana, which is currently in force, contains what is equivalent to a Bill of Rights. This is Chapter 5 of the Constitution and is entitled: "Fundamental Human Rights and Freedoms." In addition to this primary source for the protection of human rights in the Ghanaian legal system, Chapter 6 of the same Constitution, entitled "The Directive Principles of State Policy", also contains provisions protecting human rights. The latter Chapter has been interpreted by the Supreme Court of Ghana to be presumptively justiciable, unlike in India where the directive principles of State policy have been interpreted to be non-justiciable. Accordingly, Chapter 6 of the Constitution has the potential to be a source for the enforcement of economic, social and cultural rights, although, so far there has been little litigation seeking to enforce its provisions. Apart from the provisions contained in Chapters 5 and 6 of the 1992 Constitution, there are others in that Constitution which protect human rights. Principal among them is the right of every citizen of Ghana of eighteen years or above and of sound mind to vote and to be registered as a voter for the purposes of public elections and referenda. This right is contained in Chapter 7 of the 1992 Constitution, which deals with Representation of the People. In my view, the right to vote is even more fundamental than the other rights provided for in Chapters 5 and 6 of the 1992 Constitution. It should therefore be regarded as an integral part of Ghana's Bill of Rights, even though it is not contained in Chapter 5.

The decision of the framers of the 1992 Ghana Constitution to embody in it enforceable human rights was a response to the political consequences of the absence of a Bill of Rights from the 1960 Republican Constitution of Ghana, under which the First Republic was established. The Bill of Rights provisions in the 1992 Constitution are traceable to those recommended for incorporation in the 1969 Constitution of the Second Republic. They were deliberately sought to address the human rights deficit stemming from the absence of a Bill of Rights in the 1960 Constitution. The Constitutional Commission that made proposals to the 1968 Constituent Assembly, which drew up the 1969 Constitution, declared that:[86]

> "We do not believe that any authority should be above the law. We appreciate that a Government should have authority to govern. But if that Government is not to be arbitrary and tyrannical, we conceive that restrictions there must be upon how far it can go in regulating the lives of those who are under its authority. Our people are unanimous in this that the proposed Constitution for Ghana should set out in detail the rights of the individual and of the State in what may be considered a declaration of "liberty under the law.""

The court of first instance for the enforcement of human rights in Ghana is the High Court, which is a court below the Supreme Court. Nevertheless, the Supreme Court exercises supervisory and appellate jurisdictions over this court and therefore some

---

86 (Constitutional Commission, *The Proposals of the Constitutional Commission for a Constitution for Ghana*, Accra, 1968: para. 179)

human rights cases end up before the Supreme Court. Through the adjudication of appeal cases before it, the Supreme Court is able to provide strategic guidance on human rights matters to the courts system. The Supreme Court also has an exclusive original jurisdiction to interpret the Constitution. Accordingly, where a human rights provision in the Constitution is unclear, it is the Supreme Court that interprets it.

Illustrative cases

Here are a couple of illustrative human rights cases that have come before the Supreme Court for the vindication of human rights.

Awuni v West African Examination Council[87] was an appeal from a human rights case, originally brought before the High Court, alleging the violation of the human rights of some students by an examination authority. The facts of the case were that Awuni and 12 other students sat for an examination in 2000. The Respondent was the body authorised to conduct the examination and award the relevant certificate to successful candidates. Awuni asserted that during the examination period neither he nor any of the other 12 students was questioned, reprimanded or cautioned by any person for engaging in or trying to engage in any examination malpractices. He further gave evidence that he never had any foreknowledge of any examination papers nor did he collude with the other 12 students to have foreknowledge of any examination papers.

The Respondent, however, wrote to the Headmaster of Awuni's school that its Final Awards and Examiners' Appointments Committee had cancelled the results of Awuni and the 12 other students because of their involvement in some examination irregularities and requested him to inform the candidates. The nature of the irregularity concerned was stated as follows: "It was alleged that the candidates had foreknowledge of the paper and it has been established that the listed candidates colluded among themselves." In addition to cancelling the results of the candidates, the Respondent barred them for 3 years from taking any examinations conducted by the Respondent.

---

87   [2003-2004]1 SCGLR 471

Awuni gave evidence that, before this decision by the Committee, neither he nor any of the 12 other students were privy to any enquiry, investigation or trial to establish the truth or otherwise of any allegation of examination malpractices that might have been levelled against them and that they were not given any opportunity by the Respondent to make any representations or give any testimony as to their innocence of any such allegations.

The Headmaster of Awuni's school petitioned the Respondent to review its decision. One significant paragraph of the Headmaster's petition read as follows[88]:

> "First of all, the case that the 13 students had foreknowledge of the Mathematics (Core) 2 is only an allegation, and therefore the application of rule 5b without further investigation to ascertain the veracity or otherwise of the allegation is a bit harsh on the poor students. We are dealing here with young people who have worked hard for three years in a reputable school with the hope of developing a career for themselves, and if we are not careful we may ruin their future for good."

The Respondent rejected the Headmaster's petition by a letter which contained the following very significant paragraph[89]:

> "During the conduct of the 2000 SSSCE there were allegations of foreknowledge of some of the question papers. The only means by which the Council could verify the allegations was the scrutiny of the scripts of the candidates. As a result all scripts for all subjects were scrutinized. From the scrutiny it was established that there was foreknowledge and collusion among the 13 candidates from your school in Mathematics (Core) paper 2. The Council therefore applied the prescribed sanctions."

This letter thus confirmed that Awuni and the other students were not given an opportunity to be heard before the prescribed sanctions were applied. Furthermore, evidence was given on the

---

88 [2003-2004]1 SCGLR 471 at 547
89 [2003-2004]1 SCGLR 471 at 548.

Respondent's behalf that the sole evidence of malpractice relied on by the Respondent was evidence in the examination scripts themselves.

On these facts, the Supreme Court held that the students' human rights had been infringed. Article 23 of the 1992 Constitution provides as follows:

> "Administrative bodies and administrative officials shall act fairly and reasonably and comply with the requirements imposed on them by law and persons aggrieved by the exercise of such acts and decisions shall have the right to seek redress before a court or other tribunal."

This was the provision that was held to have been infringed. In my concurring judgment in the case, I emphasized the fundamental character of the rights infringed as follows:[90]

> "First of all, it needs to be made abundantly clear, in view of the ambivalence expressed in the Court of Appeal as to whether any constitutionally guaranteed human rights of the Appellants had been breached, that Article 23 imposes binding obligations on administrative bodies and officials. In this connection, it should be noted that Article 12 provides that all the fundamental human rights and freedoms enshrined in Chapter 5 of the 1992 Constitution are to be respected and upheld by the Executive, Legislature and Judiciary and all other organs of government and its agencies and all natural and legal persons in Ghana. The Article places a duty on the courts to enforce these rights and freedoms. They are thus justiciable. Since Article 23 comes within Chapter 5, it embodies a justiciable fundamental human right. What needs analysis is the extent of the rights and duties provided for in the Article."

I went on to hold that article 23 imposes a duty on administrative agencies and officials to act fairly and reasonably. I further explained that [91]:

---

90   [2003-2004]1 SCGLR 471 at 561

91   [2003-2004]1 SCGLR 471 at 563

"My interpretation of fairness within the context of Article 23 would be that, in general, unless the circumstances make it inappropriate, for instance for reasons of practicality or of public interest or for any other cogently valid reason, it includes a principle that individuals affected by administrative decisions should be afforded an opportunity to "participate" in the decision in the sense of being given a chance to make representations on their own behalf of some kind, oral or written, to the decision-maker.

Individuals affected or to be affected by administrative decisions obviously have an interest in influencing the outcome of the decision-making process. In general, it is fair that they should be afforded an opportunity to influence the decision. Given the variety, and the width of the continuum, of contexts in which administrative decisions are taken, however, there is need for flexibility in the ways that are to be worked out to enable individuals to influence decisions about themselves.

Thus, in relation to a particular decision, the circumstances may indicate that there is no need for a formal hearing, in the sense of an adjudication. A consultation, for instance, may be adequate."

The Supreme Court held that the decision of the Respondent to cancel the results of the students should be quashed, because the denial to the students of an opportunity to be heard was in breach of the Respondent's obligations under article 23 to act fairly and reasonably in making its administrative decisions.

Another illustrative human rights case decided on appeal by the Supreme Court of Ghana is *Dexter Johnson v Republic*[92]. In this case, what was in issue was whether the death penalty for murder was unconstitutional and incompatible with the fundamental human rights of the appellant who had been convicted of a gruesome murder. Case law from other Commonwealth jurisdictions and international human rights jurisprudence provide some support for

___
92   [2011] 2 SCGLR 601

the case against the death penalty for murder as provided for in Ghanaian law. However, the Supreme Court declined to follow this line of authority in *Dexter Johnson v Republic.*

The appellant sought to invoke Article 6(1) of the International Covenant on Civil and Political Rights, asserting that Ghana has been a party to this Convention since 23 March 1976. This Article provides that:

> "Every human being has the inherent right to life. This right shall be protected by law. No one shall be arbitrarily deprived of his life."

Although the appellant accepted that the International Covenant had not been incorporated in Ghana's domestic law, he nonetheless invited the court to treat article 6(1) of it and the emphatic jurisprudence of the United Nations Human Rights Committee as a powerful persuasive guide to the interpretation of article 13(1) of the Constitution of Ghana, which provides as follows:

> "(1) No person shall be deprived of his life intentionally except in the exercise of the execution of a sentence of a court in respect of a criminal offence under the laws of Ghana of which he has been convicted."

Although I was persuaded by this argument, I was in a minority. However, I did say[93]:

> "I would accept that in the context of the international human rights jurisprudence on this issue it would be reasonable to construe article 13(1) of the 1992 Constitution purposively as prohibiting arbitrary deprivation of life, although the express language in article 6(1) of the International Covenant is absent from Article 13(1) of the 1992 Constitution. Accordingly, on this ground also, I find that the appellant's appeal against the constitutionality of his sentence must succeed."

---

93   [2011] 2 SCGLR 601 at 636

I summarized the case for the appellant as follows[94]:

> "...the common law crime of murder, which is, with some refinement relating to the primacy of intention, the basis of the statutory crime of murder embodied in section 46 of Ghana's Criminal Offences Act 1960, encapsulates a wide range and array of prohibited conduct with different degrees of culpability. As the Royal Commission on Capital Punishment 1949-1953 said in its Report (Cmd 8932, September 1953),p.6:
>
> > "Yet there is perhaps no single class of offences that varies so widely both in character and in culpability as the class comprising those which may fall within the comprehensive common law definition of murder."

This feature of murder is also stressed by the Privy Council in *Reyes v The Queen* [2002] UKPC 11, [2002] 2 AC 235, where their Lordships said (at paras 9-11 of UKPC):

9. "The penalty for murder

10. Under the common law of England there was one sentence only which could be judicially pronounced upon a defendant convicted of murder and that was sentence of death. This simple and undiscriminating rule was introduced into many states now independent but once colonies of the crown.

11. It has however been recognised for very many years that the crime of murder embraces a range of offences of widely varying degrees of criminal culpability. It covers at one extreme the sadistic murder of a child for purposes of sexual gratification, a terrorist atrocity causing multiple deaths or a contract killing, at the other the mercy-killing of a loved one suffering unbearable pain in a terminal illness or a killing which results from an excessive response to a perceived threat. All killings which satisfy the definition of murder are by no means equally heinous".

---

94   [2011] 2 SCGLR 601 at 624-5

The appellant argues that this blunderbuss nature of murder under the common law and under section 46 of the Ghanaian Criminal Offences Act, 1960 renders its mandatory penalty of death open to constitutional challenge. He contends that the penalty of death is disproportionate to some of the conduct coming within the general offence of murder and is thus a breach of the prohibition in the 1992 Constitution against inhumane and degrading punishment or treatment. For this contention, he relies heavily on the Kenyan Court of Appeal case of *Mutiso v Republic*, Crim. App. No. 17 of 2008, Judgment of 30th July 2010, which is reported in [2010] eKLR. *Mutiso* is an emphatic persuasive authority that supports the appellant's contention."

There were other Commonwealth decisions in support of this position. The majority view was, however, against this position and the death sentence for murder was upheld. In reaching its conclusion, the lead judgment for the majority delivered by Justice Dotse adopted a less internationalist approach as follows:[95]

"However, it is my humble view that in determining the issue as to whether the mandatory death sentence for murder violates the constitutional prohibition of inhuman and degrading treatment as well as the arbitrary deprivation of life etc, one will invariable embark upon an excursion as to whether mandatory death sentence for murder as we have it now in our Criminal and other Offences Act is in violation of various constitutional provisions in the Constitution 1992 vis-à-vis recent decisions of the Courts in South Africa, Zambia, Malawi, Uganda, and lately Kenya all of which have been referred to supra.

I have stated times without number that where our constitutional provisions on the subject matter are clear and there is no ambiguity, there should be no hesitation in interpreting the constitutional provisions without reference to decided cases from other jurisdictions.

---

95   [2011] 2 SCGLR 601 at 681 et seq.

In my opinion in the judgment delivered by the Supreme Court on 3rd February 2010 Suit No. CM/JI/1/2009 entitled, William Brown vrs Attorney-General and Two others, I stated as follows:-

> "I have always held the view that in interpreting a Constitution, one must resort to the Constitution itself to determine the spirit the framers of the Constitution intended to give it in its interpretation. Where the Constitution contains guidelines or principles which can be used to interpret the Constitution these must be applied. Where in the case of our Constitution 1992 there are no such express guidelines, the Supreme Court itself must fashion out its interpretative principles on a case by case basis taking into account the contextual nature of the provisions concerned. It is however my firm conviction that in fashioning out these guidelines and interpretative principles which underpin the Constitution 1992, one must first and foremost look at the Constitution itself, that failing then resort will be made to previous decisions of the Supreme Court in the 1st, 2nd and 3rd Republican Constitutions of 1960, 1969 and 1979respectively.
>
> I am also of the view that principles of constitutional interpretation and decided cases from foreign countries must be sparingly referred to and whenever these are used, the provisions of those Constitutions upon which the cases have been decided must be thoroughly digested and analysed to prevent the wholesale and corrupted adoption of foreign constitutional interpretation which have no nexus to our home grown situation".

In order to arrive at a considered, reasonable and fair minded interpretation of the constitutional provisions being relied upon by learned Counsel for the appellants to request a review and moderation in the application of the mandatory death sentence on those convicted of murder, I will adopt the same measure and yardstick stated in the unreported judgment of *William Brown vrs Attorney General*, already referred to supra."

The position of the majority of the Court and my own position are not too far apart and represent a matter of emphasis. The difference in emphasis raises the next issue for consideration, namely: what is the preferable approach for national courts to adopt when interpreting international human rights provisions embodied in national constitutions? The next section of the Chapter addresses this issue.

Interpretation of Human Rights in National Courts: National or International Perspectives

The approach that I prefer national courts to adopt generally in relation to human rights provisions in national constitutions is manifested in the following quotation. It is from a judgment that I gave in the Supreme Court of Ghana in the case of *Dexter Johnson v The Republic*, already referred to[96]:

"This court is, of course, master of what interpretation is to be put on provisions in the 1992 Constitution. In exercising that jurisdiction, however, it should be mindful of not turning this court into a philistine one, out of touch with enlightened human rights decisions made elsewhere, unless the imperatives of the Ghanaian context require it, which is not what the facts of this case indicate. It has to be remembered that human rights have a universal and international quality. These are rights which are supposed to inhere in all humans, unless there are compelling local reasons to displace them. Because of this universalist dimension of human rights, this court should be very slow to reject interpretations of human rights provisions *in pari materia* with provisions in our Constitution, when these interpretations have become widely-accepted orthodoxies in jurisdictions with a similar history to ours."

In Ghana, this approach is buttressed by the provision in Art. 33(5) of the 1992 Constitution that: "The rights, duties, declarations and guarantees relating to the fundamental human rights and freedoms specifically mentioned in this Chapter shall not be regarded as

---

96   [2011] 2 SCGLR 601 at 633

excluding others not specifically mentioned which are considered to be inherent in a democracy and intended to secure the freedom and dignity of man." This provision implies the necessity for the Supreme Court to have regard to the evolution of human rights in international and comparative law in order to fill gaps in Ghanaian law, where necessary. So while accepting Justice Dotse's emphasis that a Supreme Court should look primarily at the provisions of its national Constitution to arrive at its conclusions, there is the undoubted context of international human rights jurisprudence and the decisions of other national courts on similar issues. It would be imprudent to ignore the wisdom contained in the wealth of material available through these sources.

The Enforcement of Economic, Social and Cultural Rights under the Ghanaian Constitution: The Role of the Supreme Court

The Directive Principles of State Policy contained in Chapter 6 of the 1992 Constitution is the main source of Economic, Social and Cultural Rights under the Ghanaian Constitution. However, Chapter 5 of the Constitution, which deals with the civil and political human rights, also contains provisions which are in the nature of social or cultural rights. For instance, articles 24 and 25, in Chapter 5, provide as follows:

"**24.**

1. Every person has the right to work under satisfactory, safe and healthy conditions, and shall receive equal pay for equal work without distinction of any kind.

2. Every worker shall be assured of rest, leisure and reasonable limitation of working hours and periods of holidays with pay, as well as remuneration for public holidays.

3. Every worker has a right to form or join a trade union of his choice for the promotion and protection of his economic and social interests.

4. Restrictions shall not be placed on the exercise of the right conferred by clause (3) of this article except restrictions prescribed by law and reasonably necessary in the interest of national security or public order or for the protection of the rights and freedoms of others.

25.

1. All persons shall have the right to equal educational opportunities and facilities and with a view to achieving the full realisation of that right-

   a. basic education shall be free, compulsory and available to all;

   b. secondary education in its different forms, including technical and vocational education, shall be made generally available and accessible to all by every appropriate means, and in particular, by the progressive introduction of free education;

   c. higher education shall be made equally accessible to all, on the basis of capacity, by every appropriate means, and in particular, by progressive introduction of free education;

   d. functional literacy shall be encouraged or intensified as far as possible;

   e. the development of a system of schools with adequate facilities at all levels shall be actively pursued.

2. Every person shall have the right, at his own expense, to establish and maintain a private school or schools at all levels and of such categories and in accordance with such conditions as may be provided by law."

In addition to the right to work and to education, as prescribed above in the Ghanaian "Bill of Rights", the Directive Principles provide for other economic, social, and cultural rights, in relation to which the Supreme Court applies a presumption of justiciability. In

Ghana Lotto Operators Association & Ors. V National Lottery Authority[97], the Supreme Court, speaking through me, said[98]:

"The rights set out in chapter 6, which are predominantly the so-called ESC rights, or economic, social and cultural rights, are becoming, by international practice and the domestic practice in many jurisdictions, just as fundamental as the rights in chapter 5. The enforceability of these ESC rights is a legitimate purpose for this court to seek to achieve through appropriate purposive interpretation. We therefore think that the interpretation that we give to Article 34 should take into account this purpose of achieving an expansion of the range of enforceable human rights in Ghana. The doctrine of a living Constitution implies, as already pointed out above, that there is not a slavish adherence to the original subjective intent of the framers, but rather that the interpreter takes the constitutional text as is and interprets it in the light of the changing needs of the time. For instance, in the United States, the living Constitution approach to interpretation had a powerful influence during the period of President Roosevelt's New Deal in the 1930s when there was overwhelming public sentiment that the Constitution should be interpreted in the light of the needs of the time. Similarly, in the light of our history, culture and legal system, we consider the elaboration and enforcement of ESC human rights in Ghana as a need of our time. To the extent that the semantic possibilities of the text of Article 34 enable this need to be met, we think that this Court should fulfil that need."

Accordingly, the Supreme Court concluded as follows[99]:

"A presumption of justiciability in respect of Chapter 6 of the 1992 Constitution (dealing with the Directive Principles of State Policy) would strengthen the legal status of Economic, Social and Cultural Rights (ESC Human Rights) in the Ghanaian jurisdiction. Of course, there may be particular provisions in

---

97   [2008] SCGLR 1088

98   [2008] SCGLR 1088 at 1104-5

99   [2008] SCGLR 1088 at 1106

Chapter 6 which do not lend themselves to enforcement by a court. The very nature of such a particular provision would rebut the presumption of justiciability in relation to it. In the absence of a demonstration that a particular provision does not lend itself to enforcement by courts, however, the enforcement by this Court of the obligations imposed in Chapter 6 should be insisted upon and would be a way of deepening our democracy and the liberty under law that it entails."

Conclusion

This Chapter has shown that the Supreme Court of Ghana stands at the apex of a judicial system that enforces the human rights enshrined in the 1992 Constitution of Ghana. This system of justiciable human rights has underpinned the increasing strength of Ghanaian democracy[100]. Dialogue, such as undertaken at the First Summit, between high level judges from the international human rights community and a representative of the Ghanaian judiciary on comparative human rights insights, should be beneficial to the Ghanaian democratic cause.

---

100 For more information about this system, see Bimpong-Buta, S.Y.: *The Role of the Supreme Court in the Development of Constitutional Law in Ghana*, (Accra, Advanced Legal Publications, 200).
Committee of Experts, Proposals for a Draft Constitution of Ghana, Accra, 1992. Constitutional Commission, *The Proposals of the Constitutional Commission for a Constitution for Ghana*, Accra, 1968.
Date-Bah, S.K., On Law and Liberty in Contemporary Ghana (Accra, Ghana Academy of Arts and Sciences, 2008).

CHAPTER 8

THE INFLUENCE OF *RE AKOTO* ON THE SUPREME COURT'S PROTECTION OF LIBERTY IN GHANA TODAY[101]

Introduction

This Chapter discusses the influence of *Re Akoto*[102] on the Supreme Court's protection of liberty in Ghana today. I begin by recalling the famous passage by the late Chief Justice Sir Arku Korsah in that case which is the source of much of the debate associated with this case. I then cite some judicial remarks from the contemporary Supreme Court which show disapproval of the decision. I next outline the influence that the case had on the framers of the 1969 Constitution and has had on the judiciary since then. I conclude by affirming that *Re Akoto* has had an important influence on the ideology of the current Supreme Court Bench, a central theme of which is commitment to independence and protection of the liberty of the citizens and residents of Ghana.

Re Akoto and subsequent judicial reactions to the decision

It is worth recalling why *Re Akoto and 7 others* is famous. What was in issue in the case, of course, was the lawfulness of the preventive detention of Baffour Osei Akoto and seven others. Korsah CJ said in the case that[103]:

> "It is contended that the Preventive Detention Act is invalid because it is repugnant to the Constitution of the Republic of Ghana, 1960, as Article 13 (1) requires the President upon

---

101 I made the presentation on which this Chapter is based as the 11th Re Akoto Lecture, organised by the Student Representative Council of the Ghana School of Law in 2016, and attended by MPs and other politicians, judges, the members of Ghana Bar Association, Director and staff of the Ghana School of law and Chiefs.

102 [1961] 2 GLR 523.

103 *Ibid.* at 533- 534

assumption of office to declare his adherence to certain fundamental principles which are:

a. "That the powers of Government spring from the will of the people and should be exercised in accordance therewith.

b. That freedom and justice should be honoured and maintained.

c. That the union of Africa should be striven for by every lawful means and when attained, should be faithfully preserved.

d. That the Independence of Ghana should not be surrendered or diminished on any grounds other than the furtherance of African unity.

e. That no person should suffer discrimination on grounds of sex, race, tribe, religion or political belief.

f. That Chieftaincy in Ghana should be guaranteed and preserved.

g. That every citizen of Ghana should receive his fair share of the produce yielded by the development of the country.

h. That subject to such restriction as may be necessary for preserving public order, morality or health, no person should be deprived of freedom of religion, of speech, of the right to move and assemble without hindrance or of the right of access to courts of law."

This contention, however, is based on a misconception of the intent, purpose and effect of Article 13(1), the provisions of which are, in our view, similar to the Coronation Oath taken by the Queen of England during the Coronation Service. In the one case the President is required to make a solemn declaration, in the other the Queen is required to take a solemn oath. Neither the oath nor the declaration can be said to have a statutory effect of an enactment of Parliament. The suggestion that the declarations made by the President on assumption of office constitute a "Bill of Rights"in the sense in which the expression is understood under the Constitution of the United States of America is therefore untenable."

This passage has been the genesis of much disputation among law students and lawyers. Was it a missed opportunity and judicial pusillanimity or was it desirable judicial restraint from illegitimate law-making? The debate will continue. Although the 1960 Republican Constitution contained a gaping hole in that it had no express Bill of Rights embedded in it, optimistic human rights lawyers of the day, including Dr. J.B. Danquah, counsel for Baffour Osei Akoto, had hoped that the Supreme Court would seize the opportunity of this case to construe the President's declaration on assumption of office into the equivalent of a Bill of Rights. However, that was not to be.

Be that as it may, the contemporary bench seems to regard the *Re Akoto* case as a missed opportunity. Remarks in judgments of the Fourth Republic Supreme Court bench appear to express the view that the decision in *Re Akoto* did not advance the rule of law in our country. For instance, in *Amidu v President Kufuor*,[104] Justice Atuguba noted that:

> "I must confess that if it were open to me to be so bold, I would have eagerly held that the President could be sued in the performance or purported performance of his functions under the Constitution, since that would advance constitutionalism, the rule of law and the negation of the bemoaned days of *In re Akoto* [1961] 2GLR 523,SC. But as was aptly put by Smith J in *Balogun v Edusei* (1958) 3 WALR 547 at 553: "*The Courts of Justice exist to fulfil, not to destroy the law...*"

Also, Justice Kpegah in *Awuni v WAEC*[105] made the following observation:

> "The historical and political development of the country as demonstrated by the landmark case of *In re Akoto* [1961] GLR (Pt II) 523, SC not only made it paramount but inevitable that

---

104   [2001-2002] SCGLR 86 at 109
105   [2003-2005] SCGLR 381 at 399

the fundamental rights of the individual be enshrined and entrenched in the Constitution, 1992 but also desirable that a mechanism be provided for their enforcement. Therefore, in enacting the fundamental rights of the citizen in articles 12 to 32 of the Constitution, 1992 coupled with a provision in article 33(1) of the Constitution, 1992 empowering the High Court to enforce these rights, the framers of the Constitution, 1992 have not only demonstrated their resolve and determination to confer rights on the individual but also that these rights be enforceable as well. It may be that it is this mechanism that the framers of our Constitution, 1992 intended to use to avoid, in the future, a similar decision like the one in *In re Akoto*(supra)."

The learned judge was thus clearly indicating his disapproval of the decision in *Re Akoto*.

Speaking judicially in *Adofo v Attorney-General & Cocobod,*[106] I also said:

"The absence, though, of any meaningful Bill of Rights and the paucity of restraint on the power of the Parliament of the First Republic meant that judicial review did not loom large in the constitutional order established under that Constitution. Indeed,the contemporary formulation of the power of judicial review in force since 1969 was undoubtedly influenced by the perceived timorousness of the Supreme Court of the First Republic in the famous case of *ReAkoto* [1961] GLR 523. Since then, the Supreme Courts of the Second, Third and Fourth Republics have been clear about their power to strike down legislation in conflict with the Constitution."

Again in *Centre for Public Interest Law v Attorney-General,*[107] I expressed the following view:

"A range of opinions may validly be held about what is in the national interest or what promotes and protects the interest of Ghana. If the courts allow themselves to be drawn too easily

---

106   [2005-2006] SCGLR 42 at 49

107   [2012] 2 SCGLR 1261 at 1275-6.

into making judgments on these matters, they could be sucked into the zone of party political policymaking and competition. This would be invidious. On the other hand, the courts cannot completely wash their hands of making determinations on the basis of these criteria, where there is objective incontrovertible evidence on the basis of which a decision can be founded. Depending on the particularities of specific situations, the courts or the electorate may have a comparative advantage regarding reaching a judgment as to what is in the national interest or what promotes the interest of Ghana.

Judging the validity of the acts and contracts impugned by the plaintiff in this case raises this issue of comparative advantage. Should it be the Supreme Court or the electorate that determines whether the particular economic transaction entered into by the President is in the national interest and promotes the interest of Ghana? This, to my mind, is the central issue raised by this case. I am, however, in no way advocating a return to the nadir reached by the Supreme Court in *Re Akoto* [1961] GLR 523, when it said (*per* Korsah CJ,), in relation to the President's declarations, pursuant to Article 13 of the 1960 Constitution, on assumption of office, that: "The declarations however impose on every President a moral obligation, and provide a political yardstick by which the conduct of the Head of State can be measured by the electorate. The people's remedy for any departure from the principles of the declaration, is through the use of the ballot box, and not through the courts."

What is in the national interest or promotes the interest of Ghana is justiciable (and is not a matter of mere moral obligation). However, firm evidence has to be produced before this court can legitimately invalidate executive acts as being in breach of such broad norms. This Court would also do well to recognize that it is possible to have a range of legitimate views as to what is in the national interest."

These judicial views in the Fourth Republic clearly indicate an assumption of a bolder judicial role than that adopted in *Re Akoto*.

I have not found any judicial view expressed in the Supreme Court in favour of the *Re Akoto* decision.

The contemporary Judiciary owes much to the restructuring proposals made by the Constitutional Commission of 1968 on the basis of which the 1969 Constitution was formulated. Chapter 11 of the 1992 Constitution on the Judiciary continues to reflect the reforms proposed by the Commission. The Commission was acutely aware of the *Re Akoto* case and was clearly influenced by a desire to avoid similar judicial decisions. The Commission observed, in its Report,[108] that:

> "Our 1960 Constitution which claimed to be derived from the people was no more than an imposition upon the people of Ghana. Cases like *Baffuor Osei Akoto and Others v The Minister of the Interior and Another* (Civil Appeal No 42/61) show us how fraudulent it was even at its inception. There is no need to recite the consequences of that Constitution."

Influenced by this viewpoint, the Commission went on to propose provisions on the Judiciary which gave the Supreme Court an express power of judicial review over legislation. The courts were made the independent custodians of the liberty and dignity of Ghanaians. This new spirit of independence with which the Commission aimed to infuse the Judiciary has, to my mind, largely been transmitted intact to the Judiciary of today. Thus, I am arguing that *Re Akoto* has played a significant role in the achievement of the current judicial perspectives through which our courts perform their duties. This is not to say that there are no dissenters on the bench. But I am saying that a core element of the ideology of the contemporary bench is a determination to be independent and to uphold the Constitution.

---

108 At 20-21

Re Akoto's Legacy

In effect, it is contended that *Re Akoto's* legacy has been to strengthen constitutionalism and the rule of law in contemporary Ghana. Its influence on the 1969 constitutional dispensation has been of lasting benefit to the rule of law in Ghana subsequently. It strengthened the resolve of the legal community and many politically active citizens to secure a dispensation under which judges could be bold and give judgments upholding human rights. The current constitutional provisions on independence of the judiciary in Ghana (contained in Chapter 11 of the 1992 Constitution), which are traceable back to the 1969 Constitution, provide a solid basis for the institutional independence of the judiciary. Also, the code of conduct which has been put in place by the Ghana Judiciary is an important tool for buttressing the personal independence of judges. The judiciary has adequate institutional mechanisms in place for monitoring and sanctioning non-compliance with the code. In practice, however, stakeholders need to work constantly at it to ensure that the independence of the judiciary continues and flourishes further. Financial autonomy is an important element in judicial independence but constitutes an area that requires further work and improvement. Public feedback and engagement are also vital in policing the personal independence of judges. Vigilance is required of all the three branches of government and of the general public in order to ensure that the Ghana judiciary is and remains independent.

A second effect of *Re Akoto*, in my humble view, should be that the Supreme Court should eschew pedantic literalist interpretations in favour of the purposive. Without going into chapter and verse, I think that the contemporary Supreme Court has made considerable progress on this score as well. The case law within the past decade expressing a judicial preference for the purposive approach has been very encouraging. More generally, the *Re Akoto* decision has had a positive effect on the judicial philosophy of the contemporary bench, wittingly or unwittingly.

Conclusion

Though *Re Akoto* is regarded by many as a disappointing decision, it can be argued that its consequence has been to make subsequent Supreme Courts sensitive to the need to interpret the law purposively and liberally to protect the liberty of the citizen or resident in Ghana, even if this requires boldness in the face of ambiguity. In response to it, contemporary Supreme Court justices seem to have been emboldened to protect liberty within the territory of Ghana. Paradoxically, therefore, *Re Akoto* and the judicial behaviour it has induced are part of the legacy of freedom that infuses our current constitutional democratic dispensation.

CHAPTER 9

THE JUDGE IN GHANA: REMUNERATION SYSTEM AND PROMOTION POSSIBILITIES[109]

Introduction

The original title of the presentation on which his Chapter is based, proposed by the Konrad Adenauer Stiftung, was "The Civil Judge in Ghana: Remuneration System and Promotion Possibilities". In the context of Ghana, however, it does not really work, since all judges and magistrates in Ghana are both civil and criminal. The courts established by the Courts Act, 1993[110] and various Courts Acts dating back to 1960 and the First Republic have usually been vested with both criminal and civil jurisdictions. Under the current 1992 Constitution of the Fourth Republic of Ghana, only the Regional Tribunals, provided for under article 142 of the Constitution, have an exclusively criminal jurisdiction. These Tribunals in any case have become in practice obsolete. An examination of the remuneration system and promotion possibilities of judges in Ghana therefore inevitably has to apply to all judges in the country.

The law

This section provides an overview of the legal framework of the remuneration system for judges in Ghana. Article 71(1) of the 1992 Constitution provides that:

> "The salaries and allowances payable, and the facilities, and privileges available, to –
>
> a. ....

109　This Chapter is based on a paper delivered at the Second Conference on Current Challenges for an Independent and Effective Judiciary in West Africa, convened by the Konrad Adenauer Stiftung in Accra in February 2018.

110　Act 459

1. The Chief Justice and the other Justices of the Superior Court of Judicature;

2. ....

being expenditure charged on the Consolidated Fund, shall be determined by the President on the recommendations of a committee of not more than five persons appointed by the President, acting in accordance with the advice of the Council of State."

The purpose of this provision is to ensure independence in the determination of the salary and privileges of superior court Justices in Ghana. The remuneration, determined for superior court Justices, is safeguarded by article 127(5) which provides as follows:

"The salary, allowances, privileges and rights in respect of leave of absence, gratuity, pension and other conditions of service of a Justice of the Superior Court or any judicial officer or other person exercising judicial power, shall not be varied to his disadvantage."

Thus, the salary of a superior court Justice which has been independently recommended to the President and decided on by the President may not be diminished if a justice gives a judgment or order that displeases the Executive. Since the salary is charged on the Consolidated Fund, this implies that it does not need annual Parliamentary approval. There is constitutional authority for the payment of the salaries without such Parliamentary approval. The salaries of superior court Justices are therefore quite secure.

The convention has evolved, during the more than a quarter of a century of the Fourth Republic, for each President to appoint an article 71 Committee to make recommendations to him on the emoluments of Article 71 officeholders, including Justices of the Superior Courts. This, in brief, is the remuneration system that applies in Ghana to judges of the Superior Courts. According to article 126(1) of the 1992 Constitution, the Superior Courts consist of:

- The Supreme Court
- The Court of Appeal
- The High Court and Regional Tribunals.

In addition to these Justices of the Superior Courts, there are judges and magistrates of the lower courts. Lower court judges and magistrates are appointed by the Chief Justice, acting on the advice of the Judicial Council and subject to the approval of the President. (See article 148 of the 1993 Constitution). Lower court judges and magistrates receive salaries, allowances, facilities and privileges and other benefits determined by the President, acting on the advice of the Judicial Council. There tends to be more friction in the determination of the salaries and benefits of lower court judges and magistrates. These latter salaries and benefits are not charged on the Consolidated Fund and are therefore subject to Parliamentary appropriation. The process of arriving at the determination of remuneration for lower court judges and magistrates includes collective bargaining between the judicial administration and the professional body of judges in Ghana, namely the Association of Magistrates and Judges of Ghana ("AMJG").

Currently, the lower courts, as established by the Courts Act, 1993 (Act 459) are:
- The District Court (including the Juvenile Court); and
- The Circuit Court.

The District Courts are presided over by District Magistrates, while the Circuit Courts are presided over by Circuit Judges.

In addition to these regular courts which are classified as lower courts, the Courts Act, 1993 regards the Judicial Committees of the National House of Chiefs, the Regional Houses of Chiefs and of every Traditional Council as lower courts. They exercise an exclusive jurisdiction over causes or matters affecting chieftaincy. Accordingly, section 39 of the Courts Act, 1993 which establishes the lower courts reads as follows:

> "Pursuant to paragraph (b) of clause (1) of article 126 of the Constitution, the following are by this Act established as the lower courts:

a. Circuit Courts
b. District Courts
c. Juvenile Courts;and
d. the National House of Chiefs, Regional Houses of Chiefs and every Traditional Council, in respect of the jurisdiction of the House or Council to adjudicate over a cause or matter affecting chieftaincy."

Excluding the Judicial Committees of the traditional authorities which exercise a rather specialized jurisdiction and are not administered by the Chief Justice, the hierarchy of judges and magistrates in Ghana is as follows:

- Justice of the Supreme Court
- Justice of the Court of Appeal
- Justice of the High Court
- Circuit Judge
- District Magistrate (who also presides over the Juvenile Courts).

The opportunity for promotion up this hierarchy is examined next.

Promotion possibilities

Examples exist of judges who have been promoted up the judicial hierarchy after starting from the lowest rung. For instance, the retired Chief Justice, Justice Georgina Theodora Wood, began her career as a District Magistrate and served in every position in the judicial hierarchy before being appointed Chief Justice. In England and Wales, it is widely understood that if a lawyer is appointed to a lower court, there is no likelihood of his or her promotion to the more senior judicial positions. No equivalent understanding exists in Ghana. Accordingly, in Ghana, the possibility exists for promotion to be used as an instrument for rewarding efficient and independent decisions. There is, however, no evidence that this criterion exists as a conscious element in the existing promotion system. What this author knows from personal experience is that knowledge of the law and the absence of evidence impugning the probity of an applicant are what are determinative in applications for promotion.

The Judicial Council considers for appointments to senior judicial positions not only judges but also candidates other than serving judges. Accordingly, there is no automaticity in promotions for serving judges. Candidates can be and are sometimes appointed directly from the Bar to the High Court, Court of Appeal and Supreme Court. This competition between members of the Bar and serving judges is good for improving the quality of the pool from which senior judges are recruited[111]. Should reward for efficient and independent decision-making be a criterion for selection in this competition? That is a fertile question for debate.

What is critical is the provision of in-service training and continuing legal education for Magistrates and Judges. The Judiciary of Ghana has established a Judicial Training Institute. This Institute is responsible for the continuing capacity-building of judges and magistrates and has done commendable work in the area. It organises induction courses for newly-appointed judges and magistrates and convenes seminars on specific legal issues for serving judges and magistrates, sometimes with donor funding. It needs to be better resourced to provide more in-service judicial capacity building.

Conclusion

The account above has shown that the judge in Ghana has a settled framework of constitutional protection intended to enable him or her to exercise the duties of the office. The judge has good prospects of promotion if he or she is diligent and capable. In Ghana, the remuneration of the judge, compared to other positions in the public service, is competitive. However, private legal practice generates more remuneration than what judges are paid in the country.

---

111 For a discussion of this point, see Date-Bah, SK, *Reflections on the Supreme Court of Ghana* (Wildy, Simmonds & Hill, London, 2015)17

CHAPTER 10

THE IMPACT AND FUTURE OF THE COMMERCIAL COURT[112]

Introduction

This Chapter, which is based on an initial assessment of progress made by the Commercial Court a year after its establishment, begins with an extract from a Report submitted to the Ghana Government by a Commonwealth Secretariat team which I had the privilege of leading in 1995-1996[113]. The mission had been invited by the Government (through the Ministry of Finance and Economic Planning) to prepare a diagnostic survey of the Ghanaian legal system to identify impediments to the development of the private sector. It thus had a much broader focus than the judicial system. Nevertheless, the mission's report did have some observations relating to the courts. One of the problems identified by the team was that of delay in the dispute resolution process of Ghana. Thus, the mission made the following observations:

> "A.1 The time taken by judicial processes has been a source of complaint by business people in Ghana for a long time. The perception is not held by business people alone; it is found with persons from all walks of life who have sought the assistance of the courts in the resolution of their disputes.
>
> A.2 At the outset, it must be pointed out that the complaint is not directed at the intellectual content or correctness of judgments of the courts. No question has been raised about the basic fairness or justice of judicial decisions. The persistent complaint is over delays in the dispensation of justice. The causes of dissatisfaction are many and various: examples

---

112 This Chapter is based on a paper presented at a symposium on the impact and future of the Commercial Court held on Friday 7th April 2006. I was then Chairman of the Users Committee of the Commercial Court.

113 The team also included Justice ANE Amissah, a retired Justice of the Court of Appeal of Ghana.

are the operation (and, in some cases the substance) of the procedural rules, especially the opportunities they give for obstruction and adjournment; the inability of court bailiffs, sometimes in incredible circumstances, to serve writs or other court process on parties to court actions; the manual recording of court proceedings, especially the evidence at a hearing; the number of judicial officers staffing the courts; the lack of specialised knowledge by the judges of the world of business; judicial working hours and the length of the legal term; the time judges take over the writing of their judgments; the quality and numbers of support staff; and the lack of appropriate equipment and their users for expedition of the judicial process."

The need for a Commercial Court

It is very instructive to revisit the recommendations and conclusions reached by this Commonwealth mission in order to help us evaluate what progress the Ghanaian judicial process has made in the decade since that Report was prepared. To facilitate this, I set out below a summary of the Conclusions and Recommendations of the Commonwealth Secretariat team:

"F. Summary of Conclusions and Recommendations

F1   The main reason why business people wish to avoid the courts is the delay experienced in court actions. This delay is partly caused by the lack of facilities in the courts; a system of procedural rules which in some cases is out of date, and in other cases, gives opportunity for manipulation to the party who wants to stave off the action. But it is also due to some other practices of the court system outside these causes.

F2   That the NPART system has gained business approval is testimony to the fact that business people have no inherent objection to the judicial process, if it is operating efficiently. From its activities, the NPAR Tribunal has demonstrated that even with the same set of Rules of Court as apply in the courts today, it is possible for a determined tribunal to cut down the time taken by dispute resolution processes. Further, the constitution of the Tribunal should be considered with a view to applying its lessons to the courts dealing with commercial cases, where it would improve a court's understanding of specialised issues, and, as a consequence, reduce the delay which is otherwise caused. Ghana's financial and commercial institutions are becoming increasingly more sophisticated and complex. The introduction of the Stock Exchange and its attendant financial institutions; the use of new commercial and financial instruments, such as long term debt instruments, the introduction of privatisation and deregulation, create a commercial environment which requires dispute resolution systems which match the developments. Can the courts in their present state meet the new challenges? If not, there is a case for a re-examination of their skills, practices and procedures.

F3   The lack of equipment in the courts can be corrected by providing the necessary funds for them. World Bank funds are apparently available for equipment, but action has been delayed by a failure to arrive at a decision on the amount needed. The decision, if not yet taken, should be expedited. Further, improvement could be made by the training of staff to use the equipment and paying them an adequate wage to avoid the continuous haemorrhage to private business.

F4   The updating of the Rules of Court should address the problems not only of antiquated procedures but also try to reduce the opportunities for delay.

F5   The use of assessors in commercial cases should be encouraged, and should be made mandatory by the Rules upon the request of the parties, or even without such application, in specialised and complicated cases.

F6   A new law on the scope of declaratory actions and the judicial review of administrative action, regulating the procedures to be followed in such cases, and simplifying the law, is needed.

F7   The review power of the Supreme Court should be clarified by rules regulating more clearly the circumstances when a review could be held and matters related there to.

F8   Consideration should be given to the establishment of small claims courts to reduce the load of civil cases on the regular lower courts, to give access to those who would otherwise be denied justice, and to expedite the disposal of cases.

F9   Apart from the ordinary judicial process, arbitration is a practical recourse of business people in there solution of their differences. But the Ghana Arbitration Act needs to be updated. This should be undertaken as a matter of urgency. It is recommended that the UNCITRAL Model Law should be basis of there form.

F10   With regard to the complaint made against the Mortgages and Hire-Purchase Decrees, it is recommended that the exemption from the application of the provisions of the Mortgages Decree on the enforcement of rights through the courts which was granted by the Home Mortgage Finance Law, 1993 to financial institutions giving mortgage loans under the Act should be made to apply generally to all mortgages. It is not only the financial institutions identified by the Act which need the protection of the mortgage security. If the threshold for mandatory enforcement of a mortgagee's right through the courts should be 85%, it is more equitable to apply it across the board to all mortgages than to confine the privilege selectively to particular financial institutions. The same consideration could be given to seizures by sellers under hire-purchase arrangements. A fixed payment threshold of 85% of the purchase price after which the right to seize the goods must be exercised only through court action, applied generally, would encourage more investors into the hire-purchase business."

Progress made

Anyone who has followed developments in the judiciary and the courts system in Ghana in recent years will have observed that considerable progress has been made in addressing the problems identified in this passage from the Report of the Commonwealth team. However, there is still a long way to go, even if the reform process is definitely under way. The establishment of the Commercial Division of the High Court (now popularly known as "the Commercial Court") is definitely one of the milestones on the pathway to this reform . It is my opinion that the establishment and operation of the Commercial Court has contributed to making progress on the agenda for change set out in the passage above.

First, I consider the issue of assessors. The Commonwealth Report recommended the use of assessors in commercial cases and recommended changes in the Rules of Court to achieve this. Clearly, this recommended reform has now been achieved with the promulgation of Order 58 of the new High Court (Civil Procedure) Rules, 2004[114], rule 10 of which authorises the judges of the Commercial Court to appoint not more than two assessors to assist them in any particular case. The Commonwealth Secretariat's recommendation went a little further than the new rule, in that it proposed that the appointment of assessors should be mandatory, where the parties request it or, even without such application, in specialised and complicated cases. It may be that after the initial trial period of the system of assessors, the Judicial Service, or the Users Committee, can propose to expand the role of assessors along the lines of the Commonwealth Secretariat recommendation. Currently,the use of assessors is entirely dependent on the discretion of the judges of the Commercial Court.

---

114   CI 47

Secondly, the establishment of the Commercial Court is a further step in strengthening the process of automating the courts and training court officials to enable greater expedition in the judicial process. It is true that much still remains to be done. It should be reiterated that the majority of Ghanaian High Courts are still outside the fold of the Fast Track Courts and the Commercial Court. Nevertheless, the establishment of the Commercial Court is, as it were, an unwitting implementation of some of the main recommendations of the Commonwealth team. It will be recalled that the team urged a re-examination of the skills, practices and procedures of the courts, in the light of the increasing sophistication and complexity of Ghana's financial and commercial institutions. The team accordingly recommended that the Rules of Court be updated to deal not only with the problems of antiquated procedures but also to reduce the opportunities for delay. The team also urged the Judicial Service to get on with acquiring the needed equipment for modernisation and the attendant training of staff to use the equipment. This modernisation process will need to be maintained until it engulfs the whole of the judicial service.

Finally, one other aspect of the establishment and operation of the Commercial Court needs to be mentioned as it is a pleasing innovation which appears to be working. This is the Users Committee of the Court. The Users Committee consists of a Supreme Court Judge, representing the Chief Justice, who is the Chairman of it (I served in this position for several years); all the members of the Commercial Court; one representative from the Attorney-General's Office; one representative of the Ghana Bar Association; one representative of the Revenue Institutions in Ghana; one representative from the Ghana Investment Promotion Council; one representative from the Association of Non-Banking Financial Institutions; one representative of the Bank of Ghana; one representative of the Ghana Association of Bankers; one representative of the Ghana Manufacturers Association; three representatives of the private sector, nominated by the Private Enterprise Foundation; the Administrator of the Commercial Court; the Registrar of the Commercial Court; and the Director, Judicial Reform Programme of the Judiciary. The Committee is intended to operate as a watchdog of the Commercial Court and to liaise between the Court's Management Committee on the one hand and the Court's users and the general public on the other hand. It has been an interesting first year of operation for the Users' Committee which was inaugurated by His Lordship the Chief Justice on 20th April 2005. Since then, it has met once a month and succeeded in building bridges to the user community.

This institutional framework for a feedback on the work of the Commercial Court is an interesting model which may repay study for more general incorporation into the Judicial Service. It is, of course, not intended as a forum for redress or complaint on individual cases before the Court. There are other avenues in the Judicial Service for that. Rather, its task is to serve as a channel for mobilising the support of the commercial community and the general public in facilitating the activities of the Commercial Court, whilst at the same time ensuring that such community support does not infringe the independence of the judiciary and the impartiality of the learned Commercial Court judges. This task implies a role in providing feedback, to the administrators of the Commercial Court, of community impressions and reactions to the justice delivered by the Commercial Court. Reciprocally, the Users' Committee has a role in communicating, to the commercial community and the general public, the essence of the concept of a Commercial Division of the High Court and what may be expected of it and what may not be expected of it. There should thus be a two-way flow of communication between the Commercial Court and its stakeholders, with the Users' Committee, hopefully, facilitating this vital interactive process.

Conclusion

The establishment of the "Commercial Court" has been a positive development in the justice delivery landscape of Ghana. It is commendable that, following a diagnosis that delay in the dispute resolution process of Ghana was an impediment to the development of the private sector, steps have been taken by the judicial authorities to respond to this diagnosis. Judges of the Commercial Court will need to keep in mind, in their day to day decision-making, this objective of reducing delay in the dispute resolution process. It is noteworthy that the Commercial Court has made a considerable impact on the Ghanaian judicial scene. Since this Chapter is based on only one year of the Commercial Court's existence, it is hoped that the Judicial Service or some other institution will continue to carry out regular periodic assessments to document additional progress made since then for dissemination.

CHAPTER 11

A LIFE ON THE BENCH: THE CONTRIBUTION OF JUSTICE WILLIAM ATUGUBA TO CONSTITUTIONALISM AND THE RULE OF LAW IN GHANA[115]

Introduction

The Rule of Law and Constitutionalism are the bedrock on which our current system of governance is founded. Nobody is above the law and the responsibility is given to the courts to apply the law impartially to ensure that the law rules. Courts and judges are thus central to the constitutionalism and liberty currently enjoyed by Ghanaians.

Lord Bingham in his book, entitled *The Rule of Law,* captures the essence of the concept of the Rule of Law as follows[116]:

> "The core of the existing principle is, I suggest, that all persons and authorities within the state, whether public or private, should be bound by and entitled to the benefit of laws publicly made, taking effect (generally) in future and publicly administered in the courts."

To this definition, I would add an element identified by Lord Steyn of the United Kingdom House of Lords in *R(Alconbury Developments Ltd and Others) v Secretary of State for the Environment, Transport and the Regions,*[117] where he said: "...the rule of law enforces minimum standards of fairness, both substantive and procedural."

The Supreme Court of Ghana has rendered exemplary service to the people of Ghana in enforcing this essence of the Rule of Law. We

---

115 This was a Keynote Lecture, delivered on 30 July 2018, to honour Justice William Atuguba, on the occasion of his retirement from the Supreme Court.

116 Bingham, *The Rule of Law* (Allen Lane, London, 2010) 8

117 [2001] UKHL 23, [2003] 2 AC 295.

pay homage to one of its longest serving members, Justice William Atuguba. His contribution to the enforcement of the Rule of Law and Constitutionalism has been outstanding and exemplary.

Justice William Atuguba and Chief Justice Sophia Akuffo, were both appointed at relatively young ages to the Supreme Court and spent a large chunk of their adult life on the Supreme Court. I believe that they were jointly the longest serving Supreme Court Justices ever in our Republican history as at 1st July 2018. On that date, Justice Atuguba retired and therefore Chief Justice Akuffo, who retired in December 2019, became the longest serving Supreme Court Justice and Justice Atuguba the second longest serving Supreme Court Justice. They were both appointed in November 1995, well over two decades ago. As young Turks, they were not averse to breaking the mould on questions which came before them.

During the early years of his tenure, Justice Atuguba had occasion to express the following battling view:

> "In a compelling case, a court may take up judicial arms against an obvious injustice."[118]

This dictum was uttered by him in a 1997 case (*British Airways v Attorney-General*) in which he joined in the Supreme Court's decision that its supervisory jurisdiction was not limited to issuing prerogative writs but also extended to giving directions to the lower courts in appropriate cases.

The Court held that it was its duty, under its supervisory jurisdiction, to prevent or remedy breaches of the human rights of persons who complained of such breaches before the Court. Accordingly, whenever in the course of a matter before the Supreme Court, it found that a lower court was likely to commit an act of injustice or illegality, it was the duty of the Supreme Court to intervene immediately and issue such orders and directions as would avert the illegality or injustice. The lead judgment in the case, *British Airways v Attorney-General*[119], was read by Justice Bamford-Addo, but the

---

118 *British Airways v Attorney-General* [1997-98]1 GLR 55 at 74.

119 *British Airways v Attorney-General* [1997-98] 1 GLR 55

young Atuguba JSC, enthusiastically joined in with a concurring judgment. This case clearly contributed to the enforcement of the rule of law by directing the Circuit Court to discontinue the criminal trial of the plaintiffs in that case, whose trial was on criminal charges under a statute that had been repealed after the start of the trial.

The Chapter gives you a flavour of some of Justice Atuguba's judgments which have contributed to the Rule of Law in Ghana either by: (a) facilitating access to the courts; (b) subjecting the State to law; or (c) promoting the Independence of the Judiciary. By shining a light on these three facets of the Rule of Law, I hope to demonstrate to you some of the contributions to the Rule of Law and Constitutionalism in Ghana made by Atuguba JSC. I know that Justice Atuguba's role in the Presidential Election Petition Cases[120] of 2013 is what has made him most famous in Ghana. The Chapter will, however, not concentrate on that, but rather will attempt a broader, but short and selective, overview of his contribution to the Rule of Law in Ghana.

Facilitation of access to the courts

Justice Atuguba was part of the early judicial consensus in the Fourth Republic that enabled the doctrine of standing to be pushed aside when it comes to actions to enforce the Constitution of Ghana. In *New Patriotic Party v Attorney-General*,[121] he said:

> "It is axiomatic that a citizen of Ghana needs no locus standi to defend the Constitution,1992. But others that have done so cannot be called citizens and the present plaintiff is certainly not a citizen of Ghana. However, for the reasons I have earlier stated in this judgment and for the fact that most of the post Constitution, 1992 cases have entertained actions aforesaid expressly under article 2(1) of the Constitution, 1992, provided one is a person within the same, I would say that the old principle of standing has been discarded, though in *Bilson v Attorney-General* [[1993-94] 1 GLR 104, SC it was re-asserted.

---

120   *See In re Presidential Election Petition (Nos 1–4)* [2013] SCGLR (Special Edition)1.50, 61,73.
121   [1997-98] 1 GLR 378 at 440.

For these reasons, I resiled from the view I earlier held of this case, before writing this judgment, that the plaintiff lacks locus standi. I however lament that the departure from the old principle of locus standi has been effected, substantially, *sub silentio* and without the judicial ceremony befitting the status of the doctrine of stare decisis. Ceremony in this context requires an anxious and due consideration of the old principle and a reasoned indication of the need for departure from it."

This position was re-inforced in *Sam v Attorney-General(No2)*[122], where the Supreme Court reiterated its position that a citizen had a right to bring an action under article 2(1) of the 1992 Constitution of Ghana, irrespective of personal interest. The Court explicitly rejected the Attorney-General's preliminary objection that the plaintiff had no standing to bring the suit since he had no personal interest in the outcome of the case.

It will be recalled that in the *Sam* case, a citizen of Ghana had brought an action to invoke the original jurisdiction of the Supreme Court for a declaration that section 15 of the Divestiture of State Interests (Implementation) Law 1992 (PNDCL 326) was inconsistent with Articles 140(1) and 293(2) of the 1992 Constitution. Section 15 provides that:

> "No action shall be brought and no Court shall entertain any proceedings against the State, the Committee or any member or officer of the Committee in respect of any act or omission arising out of a disposal of any interest made or under consideration under this Law."

Thus, beyond ignoring the traditional rules on standing, the Supreme Court was called upon in this case to protect access to the courts. This it did in a forthright manner. The Court held that Article 140(1) of the 1992 Constitution conferred jurisdiction on the High Court in all matters, subject to the Constitution. Accordingly, unless the Constitution itself ousted or limited this jurisdiction by express and unambiguous words, no subordinate law could oust the jurisdiction of the High Court.

122   [1999-2000] 2 GLR 336

Justice Atuguba concurred in this decision of the Court. He concluded his concurring judgment as follows:[123]

> "I will therefore hold that in so far as the legality of, or acts done under PNDCL 326 during and for the period of the PNDC administration is or are concerned, section 34(3) debars this court from invalidating it or them. But in so far as the continued operation of PNDCL 326 is concerned and in respect of acts done under it as from 7 January 1993 when the Constitution, 1992 came into force, it is, as to section 15 there of and only that extent, null and void as being inconsistent with and in contravention of articles 32, 140(1) and 293(2) of the Constitution, 1992 since it disallows access to the courts even though permitted by those provisions."

So firm has Justice Atuguba's conviction been on the protection of access to the courts that he has espoused and vigorously defended a view on access to the Supreme Court with which I have disagreed. This disagreement relates to the interpretation of Article 130(1) of the 1992 Constitution, which reads as follows:

> "130.(1) Subject to the jurisdiction of the High Court in the enforcement of the Fundamental Human Rights and Freedoms as provided in article 33 of this Constitution, the Supreme Court shall have exclusive original jurisdiction in-
>
> a. all matters relating to the enforcement or interpretation of this Constitution; and
>
> b. all matters arising as to whether an enactment was made in excess of the powers conferred on Parliament or any other authority or person by law or under this Constitution."

Speaking for the majority of the Supreme Court in *Osei-Boateng v National Media Commission and Apenteng*[124] and following what I believed to be the wise precedent of our forebears, I held that ambiguity or imprecision or lack of clarity in a constitutional provision was a precondition to the exercise of the exclusive

---

123   [1999-2000] 2 GLR 336, at 367
124   [2012] SCGLR 1038

original jurisdiction of the Supreme Court under articles 2(1) and 130 of the 1992 Constitution. The language of article 130, which is taken almost word for word from the equivalent provision in the 1969 Constitution of the Second Republic, was given a purposive interpretation early in the life of the Second Republic that has been followed by Supreme Courts from then until now. This purposive interpretation allows courts other than the Supreme Court to interpret or enforce the Constitution, if the provision interpreted or applied is clear and unambiguous.

For instance, as far back as 1971, the Supreme Court, speaking through Chief Justice Bannerman, made the following statement in *Republic v Maikankan*[125]:

> "We wish to comment that a lower court is not bound to refer to the Supreme Court every submission alleging as an issue the determination of a question of interpretation of the Constitution or of any other matter contained in article 106 (1) (a) or (b). If in the opinion of the lower court the answer to a submission is clear and unambiguous on the face of the provisions of the Constitution or laws of Ghana, no reference need be made since no question of interpretation arises and a person who disagrees with or is aggrieved by the ruling of the lower court has his remedy by the normal way of appeal, if he so chooses. To interpret the provisions of article 106 (2) of the Constitution in any other way may entail and encourage references to the Supreme Court of frivolous submissions, some of which may be intended to stultify proceedings or the due process of law and may lead to delays such as may infact amount to denial of justice."

I think cases like *Republic v Maikankan* and *Ex parte Akosah*[126] are correct in saying that, where a constitutional provision is clear, the exclusive jurisdiction of the Supreme Court should not be exercised. This is because the exclusivity of the jurisdiction causes undesirable policy consequences, if it is exercised in relation to clear and unambiguous provisions in the Constitution. Where the Supreme

---

125 *Republic v Maikankan* [1971] 2 GLR 473 at 478.

126 [1980] GLR 592

Court exercises its exclusive jurisdiction, the High Court and all other courts are excluded from the exercise of their jurisdiction. The Supreme Court's rejection of jurisdiction in relation to clear provisions of the Constitution would not deny access to the courts, since the High Court would then exercise an enforcement jurisdiction. Thus, in my book *Reflections on the Supreme Court of Ghana*, I express the following view[127]:

> "The policy difficulty may be illustrated thus: why should a plaintiff from a distant regional capital, such as Bolga, who wants to enforce a clear provision of the Constitution, not be able to bring an action in the High Court at Bolga, but will have to resort to the Supreme Court in Accra, if *Sumaila Bielbiel*[128] is to be followed."

However, my brother Atuguba JSC was of a different view in the *Osei-Boateng* case where, after saying he agreed with the conclusion of the majority (expressed by me), he went on to say:

> "However, I perpetually disagree, with global respect to him, in so far as he holds that this court's enforcement jurisdiction does not arise unless an issue of interpretation arises. The original jurisdiction of this court stems from articles 2 and 130 of the Constitution. One of its most essential components is the enforcement of the Constitution as an item of jurisdiction in its own right and though it may arise jointly with an issue of interpretation its existence and invocation cannot be inextricably linked to the incidence of an interpretative issue, as a sine qua non prerequisite."

The view of Atuguba JSC expands access to the Supreme Court, but the view of the majority in *Osei-Boateng*, whilst it restricts access to the Supreme Court, does not restrict access to the courts, since the High Court is brought into play where the Supreme Court declines jurisdiction because of the clarity of the constitutional provision in question.

---

127 At 41

128 The full name of the case is *Adamu Daramani (No.2) v Sumaila Bielbiel & Attorney General (No. 2)[2011]2 SCGLR 611*

Justice Atuguba expressed his dissent in *Osei-Boateng* with his characteristic vigour as follows[129]:

> "The locus classicus of Anin J.A. (as he then was), in Republic *v. Special Tribunal, Ex parte Akorsah* [1980] GLR 592 at 605 summed up in his statement that *"there is no case of "enforcement or interpretation" where the language of the article of the Constitution is clear, precise and unambiguous"* needs restatement. It certainly cannot, with tremulous respect to him, be right to the extent that this court's enforcement jurisdiction only arises where the article that falls to be enforced is not devoid of ambiguity. No court other than the Supreme Court has jurisdiction to entertain an **ACTION to enforce any article of the Constitution even if its clarity is brighter than the strongest light. However, when an enforcement ISSUE coincidentally arises in any court and the article involved is crystal clear such court may apply the Constitution to it.**
>
> This means that for example if the President appoints a superior court judge of the High Court or Court of Appeal without the advice of the Judicial Council as required by article 144(3) of the Constitution he would have acted in clear breach of that provision. That provision is one of the clearest in the world and runs thus:
>
> > "144(3) Justices of the Court of Appeal and of the High Court and the Chairmen of Regional Tribunals *shall be appointed by the President acting on the advice of the Judicial Council."* (The emphasis is mine.)
>
> **An action to enforce the Constitution for the breach of this provision by way of declaration and ancillary reliefs can only be brought in the Supreme Court under articles 2 and 130 and in no other court."**

Justice Atuguba's dissent has now become law through the unanimous judgment of the Court in *Kor v Attorney-General &Justice Duose.*[130] The courts will thus have to work out the consequences for

---

129   [2012] 2 SCGLR 1038 at 1065-6
130   [2015-2016] 1 SCGLR 114

the lower courts, in terms of what enforcement of the Constitution is permitted for them, in view of the Supreme Court's assertion of its exclusive jurisdiction over enforcement of the Constitution.

To end this section on facilitating access to the Courts, I quote from a decision of the Supreme Court, presided over by Justice Atuguba. I spoke the words, but I spoke them on behalf of a unanimous Court.

The quotation is from *Adofo & Anor v Attorney-General:*[131]

> "The unimpeded access of individuals to the courts is a fundamental prerequisite to the full enjoyment of fundamental human rights. This Court has a responsibility to preserve this access in the interest of good governance and constitutionalism. Unhampered access to the courts is an important element of the rule of law to which the 1992 Constitution is clearly committed. Protection of the rule of law is an important obligation of this Court. Accordingly, we are willing to hold that, quite apart from the legal reasoning based on Article 140(1) of the Constitution, which is outlined later in this judgment, it is incompatible with the necessary intendment of Chapter 5 of the Constitution for a statute to provide for a total ouster of the jurisdiction of the courts in relation to rights which would otherwise be justiciable. This is an interpretation of the Constitution which is intended to reflect a core value of the Constitution, namely, public accountability of the government and its agencies in the interest of democracy."

Subjecting the Ghanaian State to law

The law to which the Ghanaian State was made subject during the military period was, of course, not in all respects the same as that which currently rules under the 1992 Constitution. The case of *Ellis v Attorney-General*[132] illustrates this difference. The legislation in issue in this case was the Hemang Lands (Acquisition and Compensation) Law, 1992[133]. Sections 1 and 2 of this statute provided that:

---

131   [2005-2006] SCGLR 42

132   [2000] SCGLR 24

133   PNDCL 294

"(1)Notwithstanding any law or any thing to the contrary,the lands specified in the Schedule to this Law are hereby vested in the Provisional National Defence Council, on behalf of the Republic, free from all encumbrances.

2(1) There shall be payable to the Ellis and Wood families a final and total compensation in the sum of two hundred million cedis in respect of the said land.

(2)The compensation specified in subsection(1) of this section shall be paid subject to the deduction therefrom of all taxes, rents and other charges payable and outstanding in respect of the said lands."

After the coming into force of the 1992 Constitution on 7th January 1993, the plaintiffs in this case brought action against the Attorney-General in the Supreme Court for a declaration under article 2 of the Constitution that PNDCL 294 was inconsistent with the Constitution and should be struck down.

The Supreme Court upheld a preliminary objection by the Attorney-General that the court lacked jurisdiction to declare PNDCL 294 a nullity because of section 34(3) of the Transitional Provisions appended to the 1992 Constitution. Concurring with the lead judgment by Adjabeng JSC, Justice Atuguba delivered himself of the following judicial observations:

"PNDCL 294 relates to matters concluded by it in terms of the vesting of the plaintiffs' lands in the PNDC on behalf of the Republic and as to the quantum of compensation for the same. *As these matters do not fall to be done on or after the coming into force of the 1992 Constitution, that Law, even if it be regarded as an operative existing law within the meaning of article 11(5) is incapable of infringing the 1992 Constitution...*[T}hough I accept the submission ... that article 11(5), relating to the operation of the existing law, is subject...to the provisions of the Constitution, inclusive of section 36(2) of the transitional provisions, yet the said 36(2) itself is subject to the principle of prospectivity of statutes...*Therefore, the consistency requirements of the said section 36(2) of the transitional provisions must relate to consistency with provisions of the Constitution directing something to be done or not to be done in a certain manner or otherwise governing a state of affairs in any respect, as from 7 January 1993 and not before that date...*

The pertinent question, therefore, is whether PNDCL 294, which expropriated the plaintiff's property, requires anything to be done which can affect the period commencing from 7 January 1993 (when the Constitution came into force), in a certain manner whereas a provision of the Constitution requires that very thing to be done as from 7 January 1993, in a different manner. The answer is clearly No!"

The position that Justice Atuguba was articulating here was that the Rule of Law before 7th January 1993 did not include the constitutional protections contained in the 1992 Constitution. This was a truism, but it still needed to be pronounced on authoritatively.

A case illustrating the Supreme Court's enforcement of the subjection of the State to law is *Republic v High Court (Fast Track Division) Accra; ex parte Attorney-General (Maud Nongo Interested Party).*[134] Justice Atuguba presided over a Supreme Court panel which in that case held unanimously in 2013 that, given the plain language of the provision in article 293(1) of the 1992 Constitution, the Court would hold that the State or the Republic is subject to execution of its funds. The Court so held since article 293 does not provide any legal impediment or defence, different from that available against private person, to any claim by any legal person against the State or Republic. Article 293(1) states that:

"Where a person has a claim against the Government, that claim may be enforced as of right by proceedings taken against the Government for that purpose...."

This case is a round affirmation of the Rule of Law and is a striking illustration of the subjection of the State to the law.

---

134   [2013-2014] 1 SCGLR 70

Promotion of the independence of the judiciary

A case that illustrates Justice Atuguba's commitment to judicial independence is *Ghana Bar Association v Attorney-General & Judicial Council* in which he read the lead judgment. This case in effect gave the Supreme Court's stamp of approval to the current practice regarding the selection and appointment of Supreme Court Justices. Although the President has the authority and power to nominate candidates for appointment as Supreme Court Justices to be approved and confirmed by Parliament, the Judicial Council has the exclusive prerogative to shortlist candidates for the President's consideration. Prior to the submission of the candidates to Parliament, the Council of State has to be consulted on them. This process may be contrasted with, for instance, the authority exercised by the President of the United States who does his own shortlisting and selection of nominees for confirmation by the Senate and may interview potential candidates.

The President of the USA thus has a completely free hand in nominating Justices of the Supreme Court. Of course, the nomination has to secure Senate's approval, but the President has untrammelled power to make the initial nomination. This is one end of the spectrum. Towards the other end of the spectrum is the contemporary United Kingdom regime for the appointment of senior judges. Judges used to be selected by the Lord Chancellor in England for appointment by the Queen. As is well known, prior to the Constitutional Reform Act, 2005, the Lord Chancellor was both the most senior judge in that jurisdiction, as well as a Cabinet Minister. He was also the Speaker of the House of Lords. He was thus in all three branches of the Government. The Constitutional Reform Act 2005 sought, among its various reforms, to remedy this historical anomaly. Among the reforms introduced by the Act was a new process for appointing senior judges which is in marked contrast to the US system. The Lord Chancellor's power to select judges was abolished. In its place was installed a new system which is more independent of the Executive than the contemporary Ghanaian system. For the limited purposes of this Chapter, it is not necessary to go into the details of the UK appointment system.

The Ghana Bar Association in *Ghana Bar Association & Ors v Attorney-General & Judicial Council*[135], sought a judicial interpretation that would have brought the Ghanaian system closer to the reformed UK system. In its view, the President should be bound by the advice given by the Judicial Council.

The Ghana Bar Association and its principal officers brought action against the Attorney-General and the Judicial Council for certain declarations. These were:

"1.   A declaration that upon a true and proper construction of Article 144 clauses (2) and (3) of the Constitution 1992 all appointments made by the President of the Republic of Ghana to the Superior Courts are valid only to the extent that such appointments are made in strict accordance with the advice of the 2nd Defendant herein, the Judicial Council.

2.   A declaration that upon a true and proper interpretation of Article 144 (2) and (3) of the Constitution 1992, a constitutional trust is created in the 2nd Defendant herein, the Judicial Council, to make nominations of persons best qualified to serve as Justices of the Superior Courts of Judicature, and the 2nd Defendant is required to ensurethat such nominations are actually submitted by the President to Parliament for approval after due consultations with the Council of State.

3.   A declaration that accordingly, upon a true and proper construction of article 144 clauses (2) and (3) of the Constitution 1992 the Judicial Council of the Republic of Ghana has a constitutional obligation to specifically advice the president of the Republic of Ghana as to which specific person(s) is/are suitable for appointment to serve as Justice(s) of the Superior Courts of the Judicature, in accordance with which advice the President is mandatorily required to exercise his powers of appointment.

---

135 [2015-2016] 2 SCGLR 872

4. A declaration that an appointment or non-appointment by the President of the Republic of Ghana of a Justice of the Superior Court in a manner out of accord with the advice of the Judicial Council is unconstitutional, null, void and of no effect."

The provision of the Constitution under interpretation therefore was on what "on the advice of" meant in relation to the Judicial Council.

In connection with "on the advice of" the Judicial Council, Atuguba JSC had this to say:[136]

"**ISSUE I**

(i) **Whether or not the constitutional requirement that the President of the Republic of Ghana must obtain the advice of the Judicial Council in the process of appointing Superior Court Justices means that the President is bound by the advice of the Judicial Council?**

This issue is the kernel of this action. The plaintiffs contend that to secure the independence and best quality of the Judiciary the advice of the Judicial Council on appointments to the Supreme Court should be binding on the President. They, inter alia, rely on paragraph 2.20 of the Memorandum on the Proposals for a Constitution for Ghana 1968 in which it was "**proposed that appointments to the Judiciary shall be by the President, and not on the advice of the Prime Minister**. It was noted that this proposal is"the most effective way of ensuring **that political considerations** and influences shall not be allowed to dictate these appointments.**"

They also rely on paragraph 123 of the *Proposals of the Constitutional Commission for a Constitution for the Establishment of a Transitional (interim) National Government for Ghana 1978* as follows;

---

136 [2015-2016] 2 SCGLR 872 at 880.

"123. One major limitation on the President's power is in the area of appointments to public offices. We concede and accept that the President should have some freedom in appointing the team with which to formulate and implement his programs and policies. *We feel, however, that this discretion should not be untrammelled, particularly in the appointment of persons to perform certain sensitive functions in which a degree of impartiality and independence from executive is considered essential...*"

Apart from these excerpts from the Proposals for the 1969 and 1979 Constitutions we have to bear in mind the recent history and realities concerning appointments to the superior courts, particularly the Supreme Court to ascertain further the spirit or core values that should inform our interpretation of article 144(2) and by extension clause 3 thereof, as counselled by *Tuffour v Attorney-General* (1980) GLR 634 C.A (sitting as the Supreme Court) and a plethora of well-known subsequent decisions of this court."

Justice Atuguba goes on later[137] to indicate the rationale of the phrase as follows:

"The involvement of the Judicial Council, the Council of State and Parliament are meant to be restraints on the appointing power of the President, see *Emmanuel Noble Kor v The Attorney-General and Justice Delali Duose*, Suit no. J1/16/2015 dated 10/3/2016, unreported, (4) The contrast between the expressions "shall...*acting on the advice of the* Judicial Council" and "*in consultation with the* Council of State, " shows that the restraining effect of the Judicial Council's recommendation on the President is greater than that of the Council of State. In other words if the recommendation of the Judicial Council cannot be flawed on the requirements of article 128(4) the consultation with the Council of State cannot warrant its rejection by the President. However if the President for the purposes of consulting the Council of State unearths information which he puts before the Council of State which

---

137   [2015-2016] 2 SCGLR 872 at 890

can unsettle the recommendation of the Judicial Council in terms of article 128(4) he can reject the recommendation of the Judicial Council even if the Council of State advises otherwise."

In effect then, the Supreme Court's interpretation of "on the advice of" is that it is not binding, within the context at least of Article 144(2). However, it does constrain the freedom of action of the President, in the sense that he may not appoint anybody whose name has not been communicated to him through the advice of the Judicial Council.

Although the Ghana Bar Association and others would have wished for more, this clarification of the law relating to the appointment of Supreme Court Justices is a meaningful contribution to the independence of the Judiciary in Ghana and it was achieved under the leadership of Justice Atuguba, as President of the Panel of the Supreme Court that heard the case.

During his long period of more than two decades on the bench, Justice Atuguba's judgments included many more materials than the few we have covered here to illustrate his contribution to the Rule of Law and Constitutionalism in Ghana. .

Conclusion

It is not only Justice Atuguba's judgments that provide evidence of his contribution to the Rule of Law and Constitutionalism. As his colleague on the bench for a decade, I observed that his contributions outside of the courtroom in such fora as the Judicial Council and the General Legal Council contributed to the strengthening of judicial independence and the rule of law. I commend him highly and congratulate him for his long service to the Judiciary. The quality of his judgments will be a lasting legacy of his time on the bench. I wish him happy retirement. He is, of course, a household name in Ghana because of the prominent role he played in the Presidential Election Petition cases in 2013. That case is too well known to require any extensive narration in this short piece. It is worth reminding ourselves that the case served to communicate to the general Ghanaian public, in an unprecedented manner, the role of the Supreme Court in the enforcement of the rule of law in Ghana.

To conclude, let me leave you with the words of Atuguba JSC from the Presidential Petition case for reflection and debate[138]:

"In modern times the courts do not apply or enforce the words of statutes but their objects purposes and spirit or core values. Our Constitution incorporates its spirit as shown for example, in article 17(4)(d). This means that it should not be applied to satisfy its letter where its spirit dissents from such an application."

---

138 *In re Presidential Election Petition (No.4)* [2013] SCGLR (Special Edition) 73 at 147

PART III:

HUMAN RIGHTS AND GOOD GOVERNANCE

BUILDING A ROBUST ETHICS INFRASTRUCTURE TO PROMOTE INTEGRITY IN GHANA[139]

Introduction

I begin with a brief clarification of concepts which will be used in this Chapter. "National integrity system" was, I believe, coined by one of my former colleagues at the Commonwealth Secretariat, Jeremy Pope, who later became one of the founders of Transparency International. It is virtually synonymous with a national ethics infrastructure. The expression "ethics infrastructure" was in its turn coined by the Organisation for Economic Cooperation and Development (OECD), in an Occasional Paper published in 1996, to refer to a set of rules, institutions and practices that are put in place to guide and enforce ethical conduct in the public sector. The Transparency International concept of a national integrity system embraces the key institutions needed to combat corruption. This brief clarification of concepts is helpful in addressing the theme of the National Integrity Conference, namely "Building a Robust Ethics Infrastructure to promote Integrity in Ghana". I see my task as discussing the central issue of how Ghana as a nation is to develop the standards, best practices and institutions to entrench honesty in its public service. That is a huge task and I, of course, can only nibble at the edges of this difficult and challenging theme.

According to one of the Directive Principles of State Policy, contained in Chapter 6 of the 1992 Constitution of Ghana (Article 35(8)): "The State shall take steps to eradicate corrupt practices and the abuse of power." Furthermore, this obligation to promote probity and integrity is reinforced by another of the directive principles of State

---

139 I gave the Key note Address on which this Chapter is based to the National Integrity Conference, held in October 2011, in Accra, and organised by the Commission on Human Rights and Administrative Justice("CHRAJ").

policy, contained in Article 37(1) of the same Constitution, which provides as follows:

> "The State shall endeavour to secure and protect a social order founded on the ideals and principles of freedom, equality, justice, *probity and accountability* as enshrined in Chapter 5 of this Constitution; and in particular, the State shall direct its policy towards ensuring that every citizen has equality of rights, obligations and opportunities before the law."
> (Emphasis supplied)

The Supreme Court has held that there is a presumption of justiciability that applies to these principles. Accordingly, the State is under a legally enforceable obligation to eradicate corrupt practices and abuse of power. These constitutional provisions are thus a point of departure from which we should explore the theme of building a robust ethics infrastructure for Ghana. Their net effect is that every government in Ghana has a constitutional obligation to have the political will to eradicate corruption.

Constructing an ethics infrastructure usually requires a two-pronged approach: a compliance orientation and an integrity-based approach. Compliance stresses adherence to strict rules intended to promote ethical standards, sanctions for breach of these rules and monitoring and control systems designed to ensure that the strict rules are obeyed. The compliance orientation aims to deter unethical behaviour through the fear of punishment. The integrity- based approach, on the other hand, lays emphasis on promoting ethical conduct and provides incentives for such conduct. The approach, which has also been called the "values approach", has the objective of increasing integrity and probity through promoting moral values and ethical principles. Both approaches need to be built into an ethics infrastructure.

In considering the building of a robust ethics infrastructure for Ghana, Ghana will need to enforce, or, where necessary, enact additional rules which are adequate for sanctioning unethical behaviour. Ethics infrastructure thus entails drawing coherently upon a range of legal and moral instruments, principles and standards to meet the ethical expectations of Ghanaian society. It implies identifying the most appropriate ways of achieving high ethical standards in public life. A high standard set in public life is likely to have a knock-on effect on the private sector.

During the first Integrity Conference, organized by the Commission for Human Rights and Administrative Justice (CHRAJ), held in Accra in October 1998, the CHRAJ Commissioner then, Mr. Emile Short, expressed the view that, given the limited success of attempts to combat corruption in Ghana based on legislation and prosecution, there was a need to establish a national integrity system with a primary focus on changing systems, rather than blaming individuals. In his view, a national integrity system would highlight preventive aspects in order to make corruption a high risk, low gain activity. In other words, he stressed the values approach, alongside the compliance approach. My focus in this Chapter on building a robust ethics infrastructure to promote integrity, will follow a similar approach. Although my own professional experience is at the compliance end of the ethics infrastructure continuum, I cannot stress enough the importance of the values approach to the building of an ethics infrastructure.

The values approach requires the establishment of a framework of moral values and ethical principles. What these values and principles are will be affected by the culture of particular societies. Accordingly, in Ghana we have to clarify our moral values and ethical principles by dialogue such as will take place at the Second Integrity Conference. The formulation of Codes of Conduct is very useful in crystallizing moral values and ethical principles. Effective measures have to be adopted for the diffusion of these moral values and ethical principles.

These introductory remarks are intended to set the scene for a review of: some of the measures Ghana has taken since 1998 in building a robust ethics infrastructure to promote integrity; and what further steps are required to ensure additional progress.

Elements of the national integrity system

In his Opening Statement at the 1998 CHRAJ-sponsored Conference with the theme of "Towards a Collective Plan of Action for the Creation of a National Integrity System", Commissioner Short indicated that the national integrity whose establishment he was advocating, was to be based on eight interdependent pillars. He identified them as:

1. "Development of public sector anti-corruption strategies

2. Establishment of independent anti-corruption agencies with adequate powers

3. An enhanced role for the media

4. Creation of greater public awareness about the cost of corruption in order to reduce tolerance levels

5. Active participation of civil society in the fight against the problem

6. Public participation in the democratic process

7. Accountability of the judiciary

8. International cooperation."

It would be useful to ascertain the degree of progress made in constructing these pillars in Ghana. One should also note that Commissioner Short made his remarks in 1998, before the launch, in March 1999, of the United Nation's Global Programme against Corruption. Since then, this Programme has contributed much to best practice in the fight against corruption. Nevertheless, Commissioner Short's summary of the pillars remains relevant and constitutes a good signpost to action in building an ethics infrastructure for promoting integrity in Ghana.

Role of the constitution

In discussing how Ghana is to achieve honesty in its public service, I inevitably have to highlight the role of the Constitution. As my colleague, Justice Sophia Akuffo said in a Supreme Court case which involved CHRAJ as a party[140]:

---

140 *Commission on Human Rights and Administrative Justice v Attorney-General & Kamara* [2011] 2 SCGLR 746 at 762

"... a national Constitution is a crucial and valuable tool for sound socio-economic development. It is for this reason that, in order to foster a well balanced society, the Constitution, whilst affording to the individual far-reaching rights and freedoms also imposes on the individual certain duties. Thus in Chapter 6, dealing with the Directive Principles of State Policy, the Constitution in article 37(1) declares certain social objectives which remain as fresh and pertinent as they did when they were first adopted,

...

The Constitution then proceeds, in article 41, to spell out, broadly, the concomitant duties of a citizen of Ghana, which include the duty:-

"to promote the prestige and good name of Ghana .... "to uphold and defend [the] Constitution and the law....

"to respect the rights, freedoms and legitimate interests of others, and generally refrain from doing acts detrimental to the welfare of other persons;

"to work conscientiously in his lawfully chosen occupation...."

Corruption is most inimical because it militates against the rights and freedoms of others and all sound principles of good governance. It is now generally considered, by all right thinking persons, to be a practice which raises serious moral and political concerns, undermines good governance and economic development, and distorts competitive conditions. On the part of participating citizens, it amounts to a dereliction of the above mentioned constitutional duties because it has a tendency to distort and even destroy the national potential for the realization of the ideals and principles declared in article

37. It is a real threat to the enjoyment of the wealth of the nation,by each citizen, in that it gives unfair advantage to the undeserving,whilst stultifying healthy competition. The high costs of public sector procurement of services, provisions and facilities are often the result of prices that have been inflated through corruption and corrupt practices.

171

It is in recognition of the nexus between transparency (honest dealing and ethical conduct) and the desired social order enshrined in the Constitution, that CHRAJ was established by the Constitution itself as one of the key institutional mechanisms for assuring a level playing field for all in the enjoyment of the benefits that would flow from a nation run on sound constitutional principles."

The 1992 Constitution covers the rule of law dimensions of the ethics infrastructure for promoting integrity in Ghana. Some of the pillars of the national integrity system, listed in 1998 by Commissioner Short, can be categorized under the rubric of "rule of law." Reference to the pillars is to be understood as pointing to either the key stakeholders or the key measures in the national integrity system, needed to deliver an effective anti-corruption framework. Among the pillars of the national integrity system that can be grouped under the role of the Constitution are: development of public sector anti-corruption strategies; establishment of independent anti-corruption agencies with adequate powers; enhanced role for the media; public participation in the democratic process; and accountability of the judiciary.

Development of public sector anti-corruption strategies and establishment of independent anti-corruption agencies

The 1992 Constitution provides a basis for the development of public sector anti-corruption strategies and the establishment of an independent anti-corruption agency. Chapter 24 of the Constitution provides for a Code of Conduct for public officers. It does this by prescribing that a public officer shall not put himself in a position where his personal interest conflicts or is likely to conflict with the performance of his office. Secondly, it provides that no person shall be appointed or act as the Chairman of the governing body of a public corporation or authority while he holds a position in the service of that corporation or authority. Thirdly, it requires specified holders of public office to submit a written declaration of their assets to the Auditor-General. Any allegation that a public officer has infringed any of the provisions of this Chapter of the Constitution on a Code of Conduct for Public Officers is to be made to the Commissioner for Human Rights and Administrative Justice and, in his or her case, to the Chief Justice. The CHRAJ Commissioner or the Chief Justice, as the case may be, is then authorized to investigate the allegation and to "take such action as he considers appropriate in respect of the results of the investigation."

These provisions of Chapter 24 of the Constitution lay a foundation for the construction of an edifice of public sector anti-corruption strategies. Indeed, CHRAJ has seized the opportunity provided by that Chapter to begin the construction of that edifice by elaborating, with the cooperation of the main stakeholders in the public sector, and publishing a Code of Conduct for Public Officers of Ghana. It has similarly promulgated Guidelines on Conflict of Interest to Assist Public Officials Identify, Manage and Resolve Conflicts of Interest. The Code of Conduct states its scope and purpose as follows:

> "This Code of Conduct (the Code) forms part of continuing efforts to develop systems and strategies to promote integrity, probity and accountability, dedicated and faithful service to the Republic of Ghana, as well as build and sustain public capacity to combat corruption and related misconduct.

> The Code is a generic one. Thus, it is developed to apply to all public agencies, bodies and institutions. It states the general principles only. Public agencies, bodies and other public institutions, using it as a **"minimum standard document"**, shall develop their in-house codes elaborating on the principles of this Code..."

The Code of Conduct establishes a National Ethics Advisory Committee to promote high ethical standards among public officers. The functions of the Committee are stated as including the following:

    a. "formulate a long-term plan for promoting high ethical standards in the public service;

    b. Monitor and evaluate the plan for promoting high ethical standards in the public service;

    c. Co-ordinate training programmes relating to the promotion of high ethical standards in public service;

    d. Review existing departmental measures relating to the promotion of high ethical standards, including the in-house codes, and

    e. Perform any other functions which are incidental to the objects of the Committee."

The flavour of the Code of Conduct presented in these quotations illustrates the fact that the Code addresses the "values" or "integrity-based" approach to the building of an ethics infrastructure. This is an important part of the task of building an ethics infrastructure. Without going into the specifics, it is worthwhile to highlight the main principles of the Code of Conduct. It sets out the following as its *General Principles and Values:*

1. Public officers shall honour and abide by the Constitution and laws of Ghana in the performance of their official duties with dignity, integrity, and professionalism.

2. Public officers shall perform their official duties with honesty and efficiency, adhering to appropriate standards.

3. Public officers shall not bring the public service into disrepute through their official or private activities.

4. Public officers shall not put themselves in positions where their personal interests conflict or are likely to conflict with the performance of the functions of their offices.

5. Public officers shall maintain political neutrality in the performance of their functions.

These are sound principles on which to found the building of an ethics infrastructure. They are intended to affect the culture of the public services in Ghana. Changing culture is an important ingredient in the anti-corruption campaign. The challenge is how to disseminate these values effectively to public servants and indeed to members of the public generally. The entrenchment of these values in the body politic will depend upon the continuing fashioning of more and more efficient mechanisms for their propagation to public servants and for making the general public aware of these obligations of public servants. An effective sanctioning process also has to be put in place to police breaches of the Code of Conduct. It is the expectation of CHRAJ that the generic Code of Conduct, fashioned by it, will be followed by customized codes of conduct devised by specific organizations and agencies to fit their individual circumstances.

Another technique set out in Chapter 24 of the 1992 Constitution, which buttresses the integrity-based approach, is that of the declaration of assets. The system, currently provided for in article 286 of the Constitution, is as follows: People holding specified public offices are to submit to the Auditor-General a written declaration "of all property or assets owned by, or liabilities owed by" them, directly or indirectly, before taking office. The same is to be done at the end of every four years; and at the end of their term of office. Failure to make this declaration or knowingly making a false declaration is a contravention of the Constitution and a complaint can be made to CHRAJ under article 287 in respect of this contravention. The specified public offices are: the President and Vice-President; the Speaker, Deputy Speakers and Members of Parliament; Ministers and Deputy Ministers of State; the Chief Justice, Justices of the Superior Courts of Judicature; Chairmen of Regional Tribunals, the Commissioner for Human Rights and Administrative Justice and his or her Deputies and all judicial officers; Ambassadors and High Commissioners; the Secretary to the Cabinet; Heads of Ministries or government departments or equivalent in the Civil Service; chairmen, managing directors, general managers and departmental heads of public corporations or companies in which the State has a controlling interest; and such officers in the public service and other public institutions as Parliament may prescribe.

This system of declarations has been criticized since the assets declaration forms are not accessible by the public. There are pros and cons to making the declaration forms accessible to the public. In building an ethics infrastructure, it is open to Parliament to expand and tighten this system through appropriate legislation.

The declarations could be made open to inspection by the public under specified conditions.

The second prong of the approach to the building of an ethics infrastructure is a heightened compliance orientation. This implies strengthening the rules proscribing corruption and reflecting best practice in this area. Ghana needs to do some more work in this field. Our legislation on corruption is relatively old and new legislation, embodying new ideas which have evolved in recent years, would be helpful in building a robust ethics infrastructure. For instance, the 2003 African Union Convention on Preventing and Combating Corruption should be studied by the relevant authorities with a view to embodying its more modern conception of what constitutes corruption in Ghanaian law. Article 4 of the AU Convention, in particular, merits consideration for adaptation and adoption. Ghana also ratified the 2003 United Nations Convention against Corruption in 2005. This UN Convention obliges its State parties to criminalise a wide range of acts regarded as corrupt, if those acts are not already proscribed as criminal under the domestic law of the State Party. This is further reason for the Attorney-General to carry out a systematic review of Ghana's Criminal Offences Act 1960 (Act 29) to bring it into conformity with Ghana's international obligations. It should be mentioned, however, that Ghana has, since the last CHRAJ Integrity Conference of 1998, enacted several pieces of legislation that are helpful in the fight against corruption. These include the Public Procurement Act, 2003 (Act 663) the Financial Administration Act, 2003 (Act 654), the Whistleblower Act, 2006 (Act 720) and the Anti-Money Laundering Act, 2008 (Act 749). Subsequent to the delivery of my keynote address upon which this Chapter is based, the Public Procurement (Amendment) Act 2016 (Act 914), The Office of the Special Prosecutor Act, 2017 (**Act** 959) and A Right to information Act, 2019 have been enacted.[141]

Commissioner Short's list emphasizes the establishment of independent anti-corruption agencies as one of the pillars of the national integrity system. It is good that in Ghana there is already an independent anti-corruption agency, namely CHRAJ. There is an

---

141   Act 989.

issue as to whether the anti-corruption Department within CHRAJ should be hived off into an independent agency outside CHRAJ or a fresh independent agency altogether should be established. This is an issue deserving of attention. I think allocating more resources to CHRAJ, the existing independent agency, is what is important. I will return to this theme when I later discuss the investigative function.

Enhanced role for the media and public participation in the democratic process

The 1992 Constitution provides for a framework that facilitates an enhanced role for the media and for public participation in the democratic process. Freedom of expression is at the heart of the constitutional regime introduced by this Constitution. It is unnecessary here to go into the chapter and verse supporting this proposition. However, one cannot resist referring to article 21(1)(a) which provides that:

> "All persons shall have the right to (a) freedom of speech and expression, which shall include freedom of the press and other media;.."

Also, Article 163 of the 1992 Constitution provides that:

> "All state-owned media shall afford fair opportunities and facilities for the presentation of divergent views and dissenting opinions."

Thus, the media, including the State and private media, have an opportunity to play an enhanced role in exposing corruption through the effective exercise of freedom of expression. In this regard, the abolition of criminal libel has had a liberating effect on the media. With this liberty has to come an enhanced moral obligation to conform to the tenets of responsible journalism. Stakeholders should do more to improve the capacity of the media to make use of the opportunity of free expression. Public education and awareness raising campaigns need to be pursued by the media. Accordingly, their owners and other stakeholders need to invest in building the capacity of journalists and other media practitioners to carry out such campaigns. In particular, the techniques of investigative journalism need to be better taught and disseminated to an ever wider web of journalists. Accordingly, training workshops on investigative journalism are, in my view, deserving of donor and government financial sponsorship. CHRAJ, in cooperation with mass media bodies, would do well to promote such a programme.

As to public participation in the democratic process, that is the central purpose of the 1992 Constitution and over the past two decades much has been achieved in this regard. The system of competitive multi-party politics now in place as a result of the 1992 Constitution is conducive to the exposure of corruption and the encouragement of public participation in the democratic process. Thus, my conclusion regarding an enhanced role for the media and public participation in the democratic process would be that there has been considerable success in this area. Every effort must be made to sustain this success.

Accountability of the Judiciary

Accountability of the Judiciary is one of the pillars of the national integrity system listed by Commissioner Short. In discussing it, it would be appropriate to begin with a quotation from the Latimer House Principles of the Commonwealth. These are principles adopted by member States of the Commonwealth and intended to embody best practice with regard to what the relationship ought to be between the Executive, the Legislature and the Judiciary. These Principles correctly identify under VII (Accountability Mechanisms) that "The principles of judicial accountability and independence underpin public confidence in the judicial system and the importance of the judiciary as one of the three pillars upon which a responsible government relies.[142]"

Judges in Ghana, and elsewhere in the Commonwealth, are not subject to the electoral accountability by which the Executive

---

142 The Principles were published by the Commonwealth Secretariat, the Commonwealth Parliamentary Association, the Commonwealth Legal Education Association, the Commonwealth Magistrates and Judges Association and the Commonwealth Lawyers Association in February 2009. See www.cpahq.org/cpa.hq/cpadocs/Commonwealth%20 Latimer%20Principles%20Web%20version.pdf

and the Legislature are bound in a democracy. This absence of electoral accountability for the judiciary does not, however, denote a lack of accountability. The accountability of the judiciary merely takes different forms, including: peer review by members of the profession; criticism, through the media, by lay members of the public and also by members of the Executive and the Legislature; and legislative reversal of judicial precedent or lines of development of case law disapproved of by the Legislature. The latter form is also referred to as parliamentary supremacy which, in Ghana, is subject to the supremacy of the written constitution. This implies that the provisions of the Constitution may restrain the will of Parliament.

Whilst the judiciary is not bound to follow the advice or prescriptions offered in criticisms by members of the profession or of the wider public, nor by strictures from the Executive or the Legislature, the exercise of the democratic right of free speech to scrutinise the judgments and conduct of judges, subject always to due compliance with the contempt of court laws, serves as an avenue for securing their accountability. The common law of contempt provides that one may not scandalise a judge. In other words, judges must not be so disparaged as to create an apprehension in the minds of the public as to whether they can rely upon the courts for the due administration of justice. It is not in the public interest to undermine, without justification, confidence in the administration of justice. The fundamental human right of freedom of expression is thus an important vehicle for securing the accountability of judges, although this right may on occasion be necessarily limited by the public interest requirements of the administration of justice. Much depends upon the facts of individual cases. The exercise of this freedom of expression by the Legislature and the Executive should not, however, be untrammelled and sometimes needs some constraints in the broader democratic interest.

The judiciary, under a written constitution, is usually given the role of a watchdog against abuse or excess of power by the Executive or the Legislature. As the Latimer House Principles put it: "Best democratic principles require that the actions of governments are open to scrutiny by the courts, to ensure that decisions taken comply with the Constitution, with relevant statutes and other law, including the law relating to the principles of natural justice.[143]" The Executive and the Legislature may therefore on occasion wish to react vigorously to the restraining action of the judiciary. However, because of the greater political power of the Executive and the Legislature, their unbridled attack on the judiciary can undermine the authority of the courts. Accordingly, particular national jurisdictions often develop conventions or law on how their Executive and Legislature may react to judicial decisions, without undermining the authority of the courts. For instance, Article 121 of the Indian Constitution reduces into black letter law what is a convention at Westminster, namely, that there should be no discussion in Parliament with reference to the conduct of any judge of the Supreme Court or of a High Court in the discharge of his or her duties except upon a motion for presenting an address to the President praying for the removal of that judge.

The fact that, subject to the relevant constitutional provisions, the legislature may decide to override the law developed in the courts is another manifestation of the accountability of judges. The Legislature, reflecting the will of the majority, to the extent that the relevant constitution does not limit the expression of that will, can stop a line of legal development that it disapproves of, as already pointed out, with appropriate legislation. Even if the change sought by the Legislature is constitutionally beyond its powers, it can, in association with the Executive, usually effect a constitutional amendment, in accordance with the appropriate procedure, which may include a referendum. All this means that judges cannot be a law unto themselves. The law that they interpret and apply must have the ultimate consent of the people. Without that, the Executive and the Legislature will collaborate to eliminate that law.

Finally, the fact that judges in Ghana, as in other jurisdictions, can be removed for stated misbehaviour represents another form of accountability. Indeed, the 1992 Constitution of Ghana has extended the scope of this form of accountability by adding "incompetence" as a ground for removal. Article 146(1) of the Constitution provides that:

---

143 *Ibid*

"A Justice of the Superior Court or a Chairman of the Regional Tribunal shall not be removed from office except for stated misbehaviour or incompetence or on ground of inability to perform the functions of his office arising from infirmity of body or mind."

For the forms of accountability outlined above to be effective, there must be certain institutional pre-conditions. First of all, there must be judicial independence. The judges must be accountable for their own decisions, freely and independently arrived at. They can hardly be made accountable for decisions which are not theirs, but, for instance, those of the Executive, for which they provide a front. This implies that there is a whole cluster of measures that have to be taken to protect the independence of judges and magistrates, including transparency in the appointment process and the independence of their appointing authority from the Legislature and the Executive. Chapter 11 of the 1992 Constitution, provides adequate measures which comply with this standard. After appointment, judges will need security of tenure to sustain their independence and thus the viability of their accountability. This implies that the mode of removal of judges has to be carefully regulated to ensure that they can only be removed for reasons of ill health or other incapacity or proven misbehaviour or incompetence, with the proof undertaken preferably before an independent tribunal. Additionally Article 146 of the Constitution, to which I have already referred, also measures up to this standard.

The judiciary should also be accorded financial independence and be well resourced, both at the general institutional level and at the level of personal remuneration and conditions of service. Indeed, the U N Basic Principles on the Independence of the Judiciary (endorsed by the General Assembly in 1985)[144] provides in its seventh Principle that:

"It is the duty of each Member State to provide adequate resources to enable the judiciary to properly perform its functions."

---

144   See United Nations General Assembly Resolution 40/32 and 40/46 of 1985

Continuing judicial education is also, to my mind, an essential element in sustaining judicial independence and judicial accountability. It also contributes to confidence building in both the judiciary itself and in the stakeholders of the justice delivery system. The judiciary in Ghana endeavours to meet this need through the activities of its Judicial Training Institute.

Secondly, there must be an effective system for the dissemination of the decisions of judges, particularly those of the superior courts, to the public and the profession. Peer review, criticism and observations or comments by the lay public are impossible, if the judgments delivered by the judges are not systematically, promptly and regularly reported. Peer review also implies that the profession needs to develop journals within which there can be systematic scrutiny of the judicial output. Such journals may be University based or published by a professional association, such as a bar association. The encouragement of the publication of such journals is an important part of the process of securing judicial accountability. Unfortunately, in Ghana in recent years, this peer review mechanism has receded. Judicial accountability in Ghana would be strengthened by a revival of the peer review journals,such as the University of Ghana Law Journal and the Review of Ghana Law, which, *interalia,* used to provide contemporary critiques of the judgments given in the superior courts or the establishment of new ones to carry out that task.

Thirdly, it is an institutional pre-condition to judicial accountability that the bar and the academic branch of the legal profession are independent and of good quality. Where judicial decisions are disseminated but there is an insufficient capacity within the jurisdiction to subject such decisions to rigorous analysis and comment, judicial accountability will fall short. This implies that the State and members of the profession should take effective steps to ensure a high quality in the initial training of members of the legal profession and institutional arrangements for continuing legal education of the profession. In my view, Ghana has a very good bar and academic branch of the legal profession.

Finally, the removal process for judges should be fair and must provide for impartial adjudication. The removal process must be predictable and institutionalised. Again, article 146 of the 1992 Constitution measures up to this standard.

Apart from judicial accountability for the quality of judgments, which is facilitated by the publication of law reports and law journals, there is the other side of judicial accountability: which is that judges have to be accountable for their integrity, comportment and decorum. There have to be institutional arrangements to check corruption and other inappropriate behaviour and to facilitate redress where there are complaints of corruption and improper conduct against judges. On this issue, it should be noted that the Ghana Judiciary has instituted a complaints procedure for tackling public dissatisfaction with any aspect of the service provided by the judiciary. The Ghana Judiciary has also formulated Codes of Conduct for its judges and magistrates, as well as for its supporting staff. The Judicial Council has established Ethics and Integrity Committees for Judges and Magistrates and for Judicial Service Staff to serve as a forum for the dissemination of the provisions of the Codes of Conduct and for the discussion of ethical matters. Quite apart from the impeachment process provided for in article 146 of the Constitution, the Judicial Council also has a Disciplinary Committee which investigates misconduct by judges and magistrates.

Role of other elements of the national integrity system

International cooperation

The fight against corruption has international dimensions and therefore international cooperation is needed to enhance its efficacy. For instance, in view of the close links between major corruption and money-laundering, a national integrity system has to provide for international arrangements to curb the opportunity for corrupt leaders to salt away the proceeds of corruption abroad in bank accounts and other investments. International arrangements need to be negotiated to enable the repatriation of illicit assets deposited abroad by corrupt leaders. International mutual assistance relationships and partnerships therefore need to be negotiated and implemented for the recovery of the proceeds of corruption.

CHRAJ also needs to maintain and increase its international cooperation relationships in order to keep up with best practice in the performance of its mission. It already has a good working relationship with the Malaysia Anti-Corruption Commission, the Botswana Directorate on Corruption and Economic Crime as well as other such counterparts. It is desirable for it to expand its network of cooperation. In this connection, the assistance given by the Danish Development Agency (DANIDA) to CHRAJ is acknowledged. The fight against corruption is one that other donor agencies would do well to target. The multiplier effect of success in this area would be inestimable. Cooperation in this sphere is also called for with the United Nations Office on Drugs and Crime (UNODC) and the World Bank. Cooperation between the Ghana Police and other Ghanaian investigative bodies with foreign world class national investigative agencies and organizations would also be useful.

Creation of greater public awareness about the cost of corruption to reduce tolerance levels

Inventiveness should be applied to the creation of public awareness of the cost of corruption. This is the kind of theme on which tax payers' money would be well-spent by the Information Services Division of the Ministry of Information and the National Commission forCivic Education. CHRAJ itself should organize fora for the discussion of the social, economic and political cost of corruption in order to reduce the public's tolerance of the phenomenon. The media also bear a heavy responsibility to help build an ethos that is hostile to corruption.

Active participation of civil society in the fight against corruption

The activities of the now famous Indian, Anna Hazare, the Gandhian campaigner, during the summer of 2011 in New Delhi testify to the galvanizing potential of civil society activists in the fight against corruption. The active participation of civil society in the fight against corruption is to be nurtured and encouraged. It is a healthy sign that, under the Fourth Republic of Ghana, civil society organizations have emerged which are actively engaged in the fight against corruption. The role that NGOs played in the planning of CHRAJ's national integrity Conference is ample testimony of their increasing engagement in the fight against corruption. This development is welcome and should be encouraged.

Role of the investigative function

Building up capacity for investigating corruption and abuse of power is one of the most important elements of a national integrity system. One may disseminate ethical principles and values as much as one likes, but if breaches of codes of conduct or of the Constitution or the law can be committed with impunity, the integrity system becomes meaningless. Well-trained and resourced investigators need, therefore, to be put into the mix to uncover acts of corruption and abuse of office so that appropriate sanctions can be meted out.

There can be a debate about the right institutional arrangements for carrying out such effective investigations. Some have argued for an independent anti-corruption agency in Ghana. There are pros and cons to this recommendation. As already pointed out, it can be argued that Ghana in fact already has an independent anti-corruption agency in CHRAJ. However, what the proponents for an anti-corruption agency are advocating for is a single purpose agency. CHRAJ has a triple purpose: Ombudsman, human rights agency and anti-corruption agency. Would the anti-corruption agenda be better served by a single-purpose agency? What is critical is that adequate resources are voted by the State to the investigative function, wherever it may be located. If the investigative function continues, as at present, to be located in several institutions, then there has to be effective coordination between these institutions.

Hong Kong provides an example of the success of its Independent Commission against Corruption, a single purpose anti-corruption agency. However, its success cannot be attributed only to its single purpose nature, but also to its effective autonomy from the existing power structures in HongKong and the budgetary largesse bestowed on it. It is virtually, I believe, allowed to determine its own budget. It was established in response to a police scandal in the 1970s which led to an erosion of public confidence in the willingness of the police to tackle corruption. The only way of satisfying public opinion in those circumstances was to create an institution independent of the law enforcement agencies that were believed to have been corrupted. What is important is that it was sufficiently well-resourced to enable it to achieve its mission.

Boosting capacity to detect corruption is to my mind the area where there is most room for improvement in the national integrity system of Ghana. Those given the responsibility of investigating allegations of corruption need to be much better resourced and trained. Judging by results, there is much still left for them to do. It has been said of the criminal law generally that the best deterrence to crime is not so much the severity of the penalty attached to the crime concerned, but the probability of detection of the crime. If a prospective criminal knows that it is highly probable that he or she will be caught, he or she will think twice before committing the crime. Accordingly, our governments, on a long-term basis, need to resource the detection of corruption adequately and provide for state-of-the art training of the personnel whose business it is to investigate corruption. The training capabilities of our police academies need to be upgraded. I recommend that they adopt international links with police academies in other countries with a better reputation for fighting corruption, if they do not already have such links, so as to learn from best practice elsewhere.

In particular, there should be more undercover "sting" operations to uncover corruption in those areas where there is widespread suspicion of corruption by the general public. Ghana's investigators need to be more proactive and adopt investigative techniques which yield results. If by their efforts they are able to establish a perception that those who engage in corruption are likely to be caught, there would be a sea change in the attitude of those who engage in this pernicious practice. The efficacy of investigation is thus perhaps the most important element in the anti-corruption campaign.

Recent Developments

Subsequent to the delivery of the paper upon which this Chapter is based, the Government of Ghana has set up the Office of the Special Prosecutor with a mandate to investigate and prosecute corruption offences. It was established by the Office of the Special Prosecutor Act, 2017 (Act 959). The object of this statute is to establish the Office of the Special Prosecutor to investigate specific cases of alleged or suspected corruption or corruption-related offences involving public officers and politically-exposed persons and also private persons involved in the commission of such alleged or suspected corruption or corruption-related offences. The Special Prosecutor is accorded a large measure of autonomy to prosecute such offences on the authority of the Attorney-General. A Special Prosecutor has been appointed and has commenced operations.

Conclusion: the way forward

This Chapter has endeavoured, in each section, to indicate what changes and further work are needed. What follows are overall concluding remarks on the way forward.

Public discussion of corruption is not taboo in Ghana. Ghanaians are quite willing to denounce corruption and to allege corruption, whenever there is a sniff of it. This is a healthy attitude. However, mere denunciation of corruption is not enough. The temptation of indulgent cathartic rhetoric which denounces corruption, without more should be resisted. There should be an endeavour to do more. Politicians, public servants and ordinary members of the public should all resolve to engage in concrete acts of resistance to the menace of corruption. This they can do by refusing to give and receive bribes and by playing appropriate roles in the national integrity system, aspects of which this Chapter has attempted to outline.

It sounds like a platitude, but the truth is that integrity is needed to fight corruption. Any government that wants to fight corruption in Ghana will therefore need to adopt measures intended to boost integrity in the country. Since the 1998 Conference, measures have been adopted in Ghana to shore up integrity. This should be a continuing process, going forward. The code of conduct process will continue to be an important element in this respect. A culture that is hostile to corruption needs to be established and maintained in the public sector.

The role of an independent judiciary will continue to be crucial in the national integrity system and government should endeavour to resource it adequately to enable it to fulfil its mission. Coupled with judicial independence, the mechanisms for ensuring the accountability of judges, which have already been outlined in this Chapter, should be vigorously applied.

The engagement of the general public in the fight against corruption will need to be reinvigorated through the media's dissemination activities. In this regard, as I have already stated, CHRAJ would be well advised to initiate and maintain a programme of relevant training workshops for journalists. CHRAJ itself, in co-ordination with the National Commission for Civic Education ("NCCE"), should systemise a programme of public education on the evils of corruption and its debilitating effect on the body politic.

To provide a sound empirical basis for discussions of corruption in Ghana, I think that the Government Statistician should give serious consideration to a periodic national survey, similar to the National Household Surveys that are conducted periodically, on the respondents' knowledge of corrupt acts. A statistically rigorous survey of actual corrupt acts that respondents have encountered would provide a better basis for national discussions than the current anecdotal evidence and perception surveys, such as those published by Transparency International.

After reviewing the measures that have been taken by Government, subsequent to the 1998 Integrity Conference, I have come to the conclusion that the area needing the most remedial action in our national integrity system is the investigative function, and, in particular, proactive investigation of areas of national life where there is widespread suspicion of corruption. The Executive Branch of Government needs to signal to the established investigative agencies, like the Police, particularly the Criminal Investigations Department, the Bureau of National Investigations, where appropriate, the Economic and Organised Crime Office, and last, but not the least, CHRAJ, that they have political backing to embark on a strategy of proactive investigation of corruption. Beyond such signal, Government must allocate these agencies adequate resources to enable them to carry out their work in this area. A sustained investigative effort in this direction is bound to yield results. Furthermore, the knowledge by the public and public officials that such an investigative strategy is in place is bound to have a chilling effect on corruption. A realistic prospect of being found out is a factor that will exert a powerful effect on the behaviour of public servants. This policy deserves to be given a high priority in the public interest.

To recapitulate the message of the Chapter, it is that to fight a successful campaign against corruption in Ghana, we need to strengthen the moral fibre of the public services, alongside enforcing the law against corruption, which ought to be modernized. The State's capacity to detect acts of corruption needs to be enhanced significantly. Resources for law enforcement, particularly against corruption, should be boosted and the accountability of law enforcement agencies placed on a firm footing. Finally, the State needs to court the cooperation of other stakeholders in the fight against corruption, such as the media, civil society and the general public. All these basic well-known ideas should feature in our national integrity system. These elements and more are to be found in the *National Anti-Corruption Action Plan (2012–2021)*, a draft of which was placed before the National Integrity Conference. The National Anti - Corruption Action Plan reflects current international wisdom to the effect that corruption is best fought through a coordinated and comprehensive approach. It therefore offers, following a painstaking consultation process , a ten year framework for making progress towards the eradication of corruption through such a holistic approach.

EMERGENCY POWERS IN EMERGING DEMOCRACIES: THE CASE OF GHANA[145]

Introduction

Constitutionalism in emerging democracies is vital. This implies that the powers of a State's organs, and in particular of the Executive, are limited and there are effective mechanisms for ensuring that they stay within those limits. However, from time to time, States encounter extraordinary circumstances which require the use of extraordinary powers. It is crucial for all democracies and, in particular, emerging democracies, that in such circumstances care is taken to ensure that the use of such extraordinary powers does not compromise the democratic process and democratic rights and obligations[146]. The public interest in the preservation of democracy has to be balanced against the need to provide security in times of crises. That balance should be struck in a manner that does not impair, at least in the medium term, the constitutional arrangements that have been put in place to ensure that the democratic rights of the people prevail.

This Chapter outlines Ghana's constitutional provisions on emergency powers and assesses to what extent they conform to the prescription of not compromising democratic governance and processes. Ghana is treated here as a microcosm of emerging democracies. Unfortunately, from the point of view of data on precedents, but fortunately, from the point of view of residents in Ghana, the constitutional provisions on Emergency Powers

---

145 This Chapter is based on a paper that I delivered at a Conference of the Commonwealth Lawyers Association held at Livingstone, Zambia, in April 2019.

146 On the need to ensure that emergency powers do not compromise democracies, see Bryan A Rooney, *Emergency Powers in Democratic States and the Outbreak of Conflict*, Ph.D. dissertation submitted to the Graduate School of Vanderbilt University, Nashville, Tennessee, 2017

have never been invoked since the coming into force of the 1992 Constitution of Ghana.

Article 31 of the 1992 Constitution makes provision for Emergency Powers. It comes immediately after the Bill of Rights provisions in the Constitution and is clearly a derogation from them. However, before discussing Article 31, it is necessary to set its context and outline Ghana's credentials as an emerging democracy.

Ghana as an Emergent Democracy

Ghana's emergence as a democratic State has taken quite a while. During the Fourth Republic (which commenced on 7th January 1993), there have been three peaceful changes of government from an incumbent government to the opposition. Prior to the Fourth Republic, changes in government had been by coups d'état. The Fourth Republic has had a vigorous judiciary which has endeavoured to protect the rule of law and human rights. Competitive multiparty politics is now firmly ensconced in the Ghanaian body politic. Civil society groups such as think tanks and religious groups have manifested their commitment to the evolving democratic system. The mass media have found their voice and vigorously use it. The law of criminal libel has been abolished and there are specific provisions in the 1992 Constitution aimed at protecting the freedom and independence of the media.[147]

Ghana has operated its current 1992 Constitution for over a quarter of a century. It is a Constitution that has been described as a hybrid, combining elements of the United States constitutional model with the Westminster model. It was adopted in 1992 after an initial draft of it was put together by a Committee of Experts appointed by the country's last military Government, the Provisional National Defence Council (PNDC). The Report of the Committee of Experts was put before a Consultative Assembly which formulated a draft Constitution based on it. This was in turn put before the people in a national referendum. After it was approved by the referendum,the Constitution entered into force on 7th January1993.

---

147   See Chapter 12 of the 1992 Constitution.

A prominent feature of the Committee of Experts' report was a commitment in it to preserve tried and tested constitutional provisions that had worked during previous periods of constitutional rule in Ghana. The Committee of Experts mined the previous Republican Constitutions (that is the 1969 and 1979 Constitutions) for relevant provisions. In its Report, the Committee said[148]:

> "The Committee operated on the cardinal principle that we should not re-invent the wheel. Accordingly wherever we found previous constitutional arrangements appropriate, we built on them. In this connection, with appropriate modifications, we relied substantially on some of the provisions of the 1969 and 1979 Constitutions of Ghana to the extent that they are relevant to the general constitutional structure proposed in this report."

Thus, though Ghana's emergence as a democracy had been interrupted by military interventions, the Committee drew on the past periods of constitutional rule to establish the foundation for the current period of constitutional rule, including the provisions on emergency powers.

Emergency Powers under the 1992 Constitution of Ghana

Article 31(1) of the 1992 Constitution of Ghana provides that the President of Ghana may, acting in accordance with the advice of the Council of State, by Proclamation, published in the *Gazette*, declare that a state of emergency exists in Ghana or in any part of it for the purposes of the provisions of the Constitution. Accordingly, although the declaration of the state of emergency is by the President, he has to do so on the advice of the Council of State. The phrase "on the advice of", in relation to the Council of State in this Article, is commonly understood to mean that, without that advice, the state of emergency cannot be declared. The Council of State is, under the 1992 Constitution, an advisory body to the President and is distinct from Cabinet. It was first introduced into Ghanaian constitutional

---

148   Committee of Experts, *Proposals for a Draft Constitution of Ghana*, Accra, 1992. Para. 3

law by the 1969 Constitution of the Second Republic,where its function was stated as "to aid and counsel the President". The President under that 1969 Constitution was a ceremonial one, with the head of government being the Prime Minister. The institution of the Council of State was retained, with a different membership,in the next two Constitutions of Ghana which however had executive Presidents. Article 89(1) of the 1992 Constitution provides that: "There shall be a Council of State to counsel the President in the performance of his functions." The current Council of State consists partly of elected representatives of the regions of the country and appointees of the President. Its role, in my view, is to give advice to the President which is more detached (that is, less partisan) than what would come from his Cabinet.

When a state of emergency is declared by the President, on the advice of the Council of State, he is obliged by Article 31(2) of the Constitution to place immediately before Parliament the facts and circumstances leading to the declaration of that state of emergency. Parliament then has a duty to decide within 72 hours whether the Proclamation should remain in force or it should be revoked. The President is bound by the decision of Parliament. If the proclamation of the state of emergency is approved by Parliament, then it shall continue in force for three months or until an earlier date specified in Parliament's resolution. Subsequently, Parliament may,by a resolution passed by a majority of its members, extend its approval of the declaration of the state of emergency for periods not exceeding one month at a time. Parliament may also, by a resolution of a majority of its members, revoke the state of emergency.

The 1992 Constitution expressly specifies that among the circumstances justifying the declaration of a state of emergency are[149]:

- a natural disaster;
- a situation in which action has been taken or threatened to be taken by anyone which is calculated or likely to deprive the community of the essentials of life;

---

149 Article 31(9)

- a situation in which action has been taken or threatened to be taken by any one which renders necessary the taking of measures necessary to secure the public safety, the defence of Ghana and the maintenance of public order and of supplies and services essential to the life of the community.

The permitted derogation from the normal rule of law that a state of emergency allows is contained in the following language from the 1992Constitution[150]:

> "Nothing in, or done under the authority of an Act of Parliament shall be held to be inconsistent with, or in contravention of, articles 12 to 30 of the Constitution to the extent that the Act in question authorises the taking, during any period when a state of emergency is in force of measures that are reasonably justifiable for the purpose of dealing with the situation that exists during that period."

This provision means that any derogation from the Bill of Rights (Articles 12 to 30 of the Constitution contain the Bill of Rights) has to be by legislation. The mere fact of the declaration of a state of emergency does not automatically authorise conduct in breach of the Bill of Rights. The state of emergency, rather, authorises Parliament to enact or the Executive to apply legislation containing measures reasonably justifiable for the purposes of dealing with the situation which has resulted in the state of emergency, even if such measures are inconsistent with, or in contravention of, the Bill of Rights provisions in the 1992 Constitution.

It is in this light that Parliament has enacted the Emergency Powers Act, 1994.[151] This Act sets out the consequential powers of the President, following the declaration of a state of emergency. During a state of emergency, the President may order[152]:

- The detention of persons or the restriction of the movement of persons

---

150 Article 31(10)

151 Act 472

152 See s. 5 of the Act.

- The deportation and expulsion from Ghana of a person who is not a citizen

- The taking, possession or control of a property on behalf of the Republic

- The acquisition of property

- The searching of premises without a warrant

- The payment of compensation to a person affected by an action taken under the emergency

- The arrest, trial and punishment of a person for breach of an instrument, order or a declaration related to the state of emergency;

- The suspension of operation of a law

- The removal of a person from the emergency area, where the emergency relates only to a part of the Republic.

Article 32 of the 1992 Constitution deals with the rights of persons detained under a state of emergency. It provides that where a person is restricted or detained "by virtue of a law made pursuant to a declaration of a state of emergency", he is to be furnished no later than 24 hours after commencement of his restriction or detention with a written statement of the grounds on which he has been restricted or detained. The spouse, parent, child or other available next of kin is to be informed within 24 hours of the commencement of the restriction or detention. Not more than 10 days after the commencement of a person's restriction or detention, there shall be published a notice in the *Gazette* and in the media stating that he or she has been restricted or detained and giving particulars of the provision of law under which his restriction or detention is authorised and the grounds for it. Furthermore, not more than ten days after the commencement of the restriction or detention, the case of the restricted or detained person shall be reviewed by a tribunal composed of not less than three Justices of the Superior Court of Judicature, appointed by the Chief Justice. After this initial review, there shall be regular reviews at intervals of not more than three months of the case. The same tribunal is prohibited from reviewing a case more than once. The restricted or detained person is entitled to consult a lawyer of his or her choice and to be represented at the hearing by a lawyer of his or her choice.

However, there has never been a declaration of a state of emergency under the 1992 Constitution. Rather, the special powers that have been deployed periodically by the Government have been under relevant public order legislation.

The Public Order Act, 1994 (Act 491)

The Public Order Act's effect does not depend upon the declaration of a state of emergency. Nonetheless, a particular provision in it has been deployed repeatedly by the Ghanaian Government in its effort to control situations of local emergency which fall short of the need to declare a state of emergency. It is the power to impose a curfew. The Act provides that[153] where the Minister of the Interior considers that it is reasonably required in the interest of public defence, public safety, public health, the running of essential services or the protection of the rights and freedoms of any other person, he or she may impose a curfew in a part of Ghana. The Act does not give authority to impose a curfew on the whole of Ghana.

Ministers of Interior have exercised this power on many occasions to help quell the outbreak of civil disorder in particular localities. Although the exercise of the power is a derogation from the freedom of movement entrenched under the 1992 Constitution, it probably comes within the public interest exception to the enforcement of the fundamental human rights contained in the Bill of Rights (Chapter 5 of the 1992 Constitution). Article 12(2) provides as follows:

> "Every person in Ghana, whatever his race, place of origin, political opinion, colour, religion, creed or gender shall be entitled to the fundamental human rights and freedoms of the individual contained in this Chapter but subject to respect for the rights and freedoms of others and for the public interest."

---

153 See s.4

This provision has been interpreted by the Ghanaian Supreme Court as placing limitations that are reasonably required for the protection of the rights of other persons and in the public interest on the fundamental freedoms in the Bill of Rights[154].

The Imposition of Restrictions Act, 2020 (Act1012)

It will be recalled that in Chapter 1, it was explained that the Government of Ghana enacted the Imposition of Restrictions Act, 2020 to give the President authority to deal with the health emergency arising from the Covid-19 pandemic, by imposing restrictions on the human rights specified in Article 21 of the 1992 Constitution. Article 21, by its own terms, allows derogations from the human rights conferred by it, to the extent that a thing done under the authority of a derogating statute is shown to be reasonably justifiable in terms of the spirit of the Constitution[155]. This was the option chosen by the Government, instead of invoking Article 31. Under the Imposition of Restrictions Act, 2020, among the specific restrictions imposed were: the closing of Ghana's borders to both foreign and local nationals; the lockdown of the Greater Accra and Kumasi Metropolitan Areas in Ghana for weeks, under which residents of these areas were required to stay at home and only leave home for essentials. Although there has been some criticism of this approach, on the ground that the statutory derogation from the rights conferred by Article 21 lacks the institutional scrutiny and accountability embodied in Article 31, so far there has not been a successful challenge of the Imposition of Restrictions Act, 2020.

Conclusion

Because of an undesirable experience with preventive detention under Ghana's Independence Constitution and the First Republican Constitution, it is obvious that the framers of the 1992 Constitution did not want to confer unbridled power on the Executive and the Legislature even in a state of emergency. Thus, those detained and restricted in a state of emergency are given the rights outlined

154 *Republic v Tommy Thompson Books Ltd, Quarcoo & Coomson* [1996-97] SCGLR 804.
155 See Article 21(4) of the 1992 Constitution.

earlier. The declaration and maintenance of a state of emergency are also not left to the whims of the Executive alone. No Ghanaian Government has yet found it necessary to declare a state of emergency under the 1992 Constitution. Nevertheless, provisions do exist under the Constitution for such a declaration under appropriate circumstances. Those provisions reflect Ghana's history. The Ghanaian provisions thus endeavour to strike a balance between security and democratic rights. The current situation may be contrasted with the consequences of the failure of the Supreme Court of Ghana to assert itself in the infamous case of *Re Akoto,*[156] where the court upheld a statute[157] which allowed the Government, without a declaration of a state of emergency, to determine, subjectively, that particular people were acting in a manner prejudicial to the security of the State and could thus be preventively detained.

---

156 [1961] GLR 523

157 The Preventive Detention Act, 1958 (No 17 of 1958)

CHAPTER 14

RELIGION, HUMAN RIGHTS AND DEMOCRACY IN THE GHANAIAN CONTEXT[158]

Introduction

After a relatively chequered earlier history, the Republic of Ghana has now settled down as a thriving representative democracy. It has a Bill of Rights entrenched in its current 1992 Republican Constitution. The provisions in it are entrenched in the sense that they cannot be amended except through a special procedure including a national referendum. The Bill of Rights contains a provision on freedom of religion. Thus freedom of religion is a fundamental human right in the Ghanaian legal regime.

Article 21(1((c) of the 1992 Constitution contains the specific provision on freedom of religion that states:

> "**21.**
>
> (1) All persons shall have the right to-
>
>   (a) ...
>
>   (b) ...
>
>   (c) freedom to practise any religion and to manifest such practice;..."

This entrenched provision in the Constitution has been part of the various Constitutions of Ghana since 1969. It is thus a settled fundamental human right which has in the main been respected by successive governments.

In January 2010, a Presidential Commission of Enquiry was established to consult with the Ghanaian people on the operation to it. Some of the submissions received by this Constitutional Review

---

158 This Chapter is based on a paper I prepared for a Law and Religion Symposium at Bringham Young University, Provo, Utah, USA in October 2013.

Commission were on the religious freedom embodied in Article 21. These submissions are considered in the next section.

Proposals on religious freedom to the constitutional review commission

The Constitutional Review Commission ('CRC') summarised the submissions it received as follows:

a. "The Constitution must contain express provisions on the freedom of religion so that citizens will respect each other's religion.

b. The part of the Constitution which states that there is the freedom of worship should be emphasised and elaborated.

c. A total number of seven days must be made available for the celebration of Moslem festivals. Three days before the celebration begins and four days for the celebration.

d. Article 21(c) on the freedom to practise any religion and to manifest any religion should be reviewed. Religion has been used as a tool to destroy a nation; not all religions should be allowed to exist because some religions are not religions at all.

e. Regulation of religion should not be brought under state control; the *status quo* should be maintained.

f. Religious bodies should be made to cater for their members rather than exploit them. Some people join churches only to realise that they have been making others rich.

g. Religion should be sanitised; what is happening elsewhere must not happen in Ghana.

h. There has to be a church formation regulatory body to grant permit to individuals who want to build churches. This is because churches have a great impact on society and must be carefully regulated.

i. The law on the right to religion should be enforced to stop the infringement of the right to practice religion in schools or educational institutions.

j. There should be a mosque in every second cycle school to ensure freedom of religion.

k. The law should ensure that spiritualists are not licensed because they are behind all evil activities taking place in the country.

l. Churches should be mandated by law to pay tax on the monies donated to them by their congregations so that their contributions can help in national development. This will also reduce the number of churches being established as well.

m. The law should tax the collection/offertory and tithes of churches because they make a lot of revenue and taxing them will enable the government raise a lot of revenue.

n. Government should set up a Ministry of Religious Affairs to govern churches because there are a lot of churches being set up. This ministry would regulate the activities of churches and allow the nation to benefit from the revenue of the churches."[159]

These submissions can be taken as reflecting contemporary issues relating to religious freedom that are of concern to the Ghanaian public. This short Chapter discusses a number of the policy issues arising from the submissions made to the Constitutional Review Commission, namely:

1. Is it legitimate to assert that "not all religions should be allowed to exist because some religions are not religions at all"?

2. Should a regulatory body or a dedicated Ministry of the Government be established to decide on the formation of churches and to regulate the activities of churches, thus allowing the nation to benefit from the revenue of the churches?

---

159 Report of the Constitutional Review Commission: *From a Political to a Developmental Constitution* (Accra, 20th December, 2011) 697-8.

3. Should mosques be established in all secondary schools to facilitate the practice of freedom of religion? (The proponents probably assume that all secondary schools have Christian chapels).

4. Should the law ensure that spiritualists (by which is usually meant, in Ghana, practitioners of African traditional religion) are not licensed because they are behind all evil activities taking place in the country?

5. Should churches pay tax on the donations made to them?

6. Should the *status quo* on religious freedom be maintained?

The Constitutional Review Commission reached the following conclusions on these questions[160]:

> "313. The Commission finds that to ensure national unity and cohesion the *status quo* regarding religious rights should be maintained.
>
> The Commission observes that in Botswana, the law ensures that in every community where there is a church, the church funds the building of schools and other amenities for the use of the community.
>
> The Commission finds the recent spate of inimical practices of the heads of some religious bodies is not in the public interest. While some of them are in jail for their nefarious activities, others are battling their cases in court or are being investigated by the law enforcement agencies on suspicion of having committed various crimes.
>
> The Commission observes that the freedom to practice any religion and to manifest such practice is not absolute and that it is subject to the public interest.
>
> The Commission endorses the current state of the law which allows the imposition of reasonable restrictions on

---

160   *Ibid.* 698-9

fundamental freedoms but does not deny the citizen those freedoms to which he was entitled.

E. RECOMMENDATIONS
RECOMMENDATIONS FOR CONSTITUTIONAL CHANGE

1. The Commission recommends that Article 21(4) (c) should be amended to include in the list of criteria that may lead to restrictions in the exercise of rights, the words "public order" and "public morality".

RECOMMENDATIONS FOR ADMINISTRATIVE ACTION

1. The Commission recommends that the relevant regulatory authorities work with the various religious associations to abate, if not eliminate, the many inimical practices some religious groups and their officers engage in, and which were the subject of many submissions to the Commission."

Observations

The above conclusions of the Commission reflect the fact that Ghanaians are probably quite satisfied with the *status quo* on religious freedom which confers a large degree of freedom on individuals and groups to practise whatever religion they choose, but which imposes some limits on this freedom. The main restriction is that provided for in relation to all the fundamental human rights and freedoms contained in Ghana's Bill of Rights. Article 12(2) of Ghana's 1992 Constitution provides that:

> "(2)Every person in Ghana, whatever his race, place of origin, political opinion, colour, religion, creed or gender shall be entitled to the fundamental human rights and freedoms of the individual contained in this Chapter but subject to respect for the rights and freedoms of others and for the public interest."

To my mind, the principle of freedom of religion embodied in article 21 of the 1992 Constitution and the exception to it in Article 12(2) *(supra)* are sufficient conceptual tools for tackling issues relating to religious freedom in Ghana. They provide the doctrinal means of dealing with, for instance, the issues arising from the submissions made to the Constitutional Review Commission. The doctrine that a person, exercising his or her religious freedom, has to respect the rights and freedoms of others and the public interest, is a considerable limitation and can be deployed to suppress the perceived ill consequences of religious freedom that some of those who made submissions to the Commission complained of.

Thus, using the doctrinal tools identified above, it would be illegitimate for the State to assert that "not all religions should be allowed to exist because some religions are not religions at all". That would constitute a central attack on religious freedom. Individuals and groups should be free to practise what they consider to be a religion, even if others think that they are wrongheaded to pursue that particular religion. However, if in the course of practising their religion, these individuals break the criminal or other law, law enforcers should be free to apply the law to them. Religion should not provide an escape route from compliance with the law.

Secondly, there is no need for a dedicated Ministry to deal with only the formation of churches and their activities. The range of Government Ministries dealing with the relevant subject matters should apply law and policy to religious bodies in the same way as they do in relation to other persons. In my opinion, the State should not exercise a right to control entry into the religious "market". In other words, it is not for the State to decide who should or should not form a church or other religious body or be a spiritualist. The submissions to the CRC seeking such control are unacceptable and in conflict with the right to practise religion freely, contained in article 21(1) of the 1992 Constitution. They are thus in conflict with the simple but clear doctrinal basis for action in this area, contained in the Constitution, namely: persons within the Ghanaian jurisdiction are free to practise any religion and to manifest it, so long as they respect the rights and freedoms of others and the public interest.

With regard to whether churches or other religious bodies should pay tax on donations made to them, it could be observed that this is a policy issue for determination by the Government of the day. The Government, however, clearly has the authority to levy such tax through appropriate legislation, if it so decided. This is achievable within the existing constitutional arrangements in Ghana.

Finally, a few comments about the practice of religion in State-owned secondary schools. It is demonstrable that the practice of religion is encouraged in Ghanaian State schools. In some other jurisdiction, it might be plausibly argued that this is not a sufficient separation of the State from religion. However, the Ghanaian Constitution has to be interpreted in its social context. Ghanaians are a very religious people. Indeed the Preamble to the country's 1992 Constitution invokes the name of the Almighty God as the ultimate source of its authority. It proclaims as follows:

"IN THE NAME OF THE ALMIGHTY GOD

We the People of Ghana,

IN EXERCISE of our natural and inalienable right to establish a framework of government which shall secure for ourselves and posterity the blessings of liberty, equality of opportunity and prosperity;

IN A SPIRIT of friendship and peace with all peoples of the world;

AND IN SOLEMN declaration and affirmation of our commitment to;

Freedom, Justice, Probity and Accountability;

The Principle that all powers of Government spring from the Sovereign Will of the People;

The Principle of Universal Adult Suffrage; The Rule of Law;

The protection and preservation of Fundamental Human

Rights and Freedoms, Unity and Stability for our Nation;

DO HEREBY ADOPT, ENACT AND GIVE TO OURSELVES THIS CONSTITUTION".

The God who is invoked is, however, not linked to any particular religion. He can thus be viewed equally as the God of the Christians,

Muslims and adherents of traditional African religion, the three main faiths followed in Ghana.

It is probably correct, therefore, to assert that the practice of religion in State secondary schools is in consonance with the *volksgeist* of Ghana, if it is possible to determine this. There is, however, a complication arising from this proposition, which is pointed out in some of the submissions to the CRC, namely: logically, equal facilities and opportunities should be accorded for the practice of all faiths. Historically, it cannot be said that this has happened in Ghana. The Christian faith has probably been favoured in most State schools and, accordingly, the educational authorities need to work towards achieving more equality in opportunity for other faiths.

Conclusion

The basic legal architecture for the practice of religious freedom in Ghana is in place. However, there has been hardly any litigation on this theme and therefore the case law in the area is under developed. Nevertheless, the conclusion reached by the Constitutional Review Commission is right that the constitutional *status quo* provides an adequate basis for reconciling freedom of religion with the needs of the public interest. The proposal made by the Commission for a minor constitutional amendment is probably unnecessary, in the light of my view of article 12(2) of the 1992 Constitution. In short, freedom of religion is alive and well in Ghana. This is good for the democratic health of the country, since freedom of religion is an important index of the extent of general toleration of different views in a society. Tolerance is, undoubtedly, an essential element in a democratic culture.

CHAPTER 15

THE CONSTITUTIONAL MANDATE OF THE COUNCIL OF STATE ("ON THE ADVICE OF" AND "IN CONSULTATION WITH")[161]

Introduction

The two phrases in the subject of this Chapter, namely "on the advice of" and "in consultation with", occur in Article 91 (1) of the 1992 Constitution which provides as follows:

> "The Council of State shall consider and advise the President or any other authority in respect of any appointment which is required by this Constitution or any other law to be made in accordance with the advice of, or in consultation with, the Council of State."

What do the above phrases from the 1992 Constitution mean and what is required of the Council of State in relation to them? These are questions that will be explored in this Chapter. The various constitutional provisions will be enumerated first and then those that relate to appointments will be discussed. Next will be a discussion of the phrases in contexts that do not relate to appointments.

Enumeration of relevant constitutional provisions

Before discussing the issues raised by the phrases referred to above, it would be helpful to enumerate the specific provisions in the Constitution where they occur.

* All Article 70 appointments, with the exception of the Chairman, Deputy Chairmen and other members of the Electoral Commission, are to be made by the President: "acting in consultation with the Council of State";

---

161 This Chapter is based on a paper which I presented to the Council of State in March 2018.

- By Article 70(2), the Chairman, Deputy Chairmen and other members of the Electoral Commission are to be appointed by the President, acting on the advice of the Council of State;

- The President's power to appoint Ambassadors and High Commissioners and other persons to represent Ghana abroad is to be exercised, "acting in consultation with the Council of State", according to Article 74(1);

Specifically, the Council of State's advice or consultation is required as follows under the 1992 Constitution:

- Under article 44(6), if a member of the Electoral Commission is absent or dies, the Commission is to continue its work until the President, "acting on the advice of the Council of State, appoints a qualified person to fill the vacancy";

- The President's power to appoint the Chairman of the National Development Planning Commission is to be exercised, "in consultation with the Council of State", according to Article 86(2);

- Under article 144(1), provision is made for the Chief Justice to be appointed by the President, "acting in consultation with the Council of State and with the approval of Parliament";

- Under article 144(2), Justices of the Supreme Court are to be appointed by the President, "acting on the advice of the Judicial Council, in consultation with the Council of State and with the approval of Parliament";

- Under article 146(4) relating to the establishment of a Committee by the Chief Justice to consider a petition for the removal of a Justice of a Superior Court, provision is made for members of the Committee to include two members to be appointed by the Chief Justice "on the advice of the Council of State".

- Under Article 146(6), the President's power to appoint a Committee to consider a petition for the removal of a Chief Justice is to be exercised, "acting in consultation with the Council of State". The Council of State's function in this respect has been expanded by judicial decision to include assessing whether a *prima facie* case has been established against the Chief Justice.

- According to Article 183(4), the Governor of the Bank of Ghana is to be appointed by the President, "acting in consultation with the Council of State for periods of four years each";

- According to Article 185(3), the Government Statistician is to be appointed by the President, "in consultation with the Council of State";

- Under Article 186(1), the Chairman and five other members of the Statistical Service Board are to be appointed by the President "in consultation with the Council of State";

- Under Article 189(1), the Chairman and four other members of the Audit Service Board are to be appointed by the President, "acting in consultation with the Council of State";

- In relation to the Police Council, Article 201 gives the President power to appoint two members of the Police Service to serve on the Council, but such appointment is to be made "in consultation with the Council of State";

- The Inspector-General of Police is required to be appointed, "in consultation with the Council of State", by Article 202(1);

- By Article 206, the President is to appoint to the Prisons Service Council a representative of religious bodies and two members of the Prison Service, "in consultation with the Council of State";

- By Article 207, the Director-General of the Prisons Service is to be appointed by the President "acting in consultation with the Council of State";

- By articles 211 and 212, two members of the Armed Forces Council, the Chief of Defence Staff of the Armed Forces and the Service Chiefs are to be appointed by the President "in consultation with the Council of State";

- Under Article 232(2), members of the National Commission for Civic Education are to be appointed by the President "acting on the advice of the Council of State";

The article 70 appointments, referred to earlier in the first bullet point, comprise the following:

> "1. The President shall, acting in consultation with the Council of State, appoint-
>
>   a. the Commissioner for Human Right sand Administrative Justice and his Deputies;
>
>   b. the Auditor-General;
>
>   c. the District Assemblies Common Fund Administrator;
>
>   d. the Chairmen and other members of-
>   i. the Public Services Commission;
>   ii. the Lands Commission;
>   iii. the governing bodies of public corporations;
>   iv. a National Council for Higher Education howsoever described; and
>
>   e. the holders of such other offices as may be prescribed by this Constitution or by any other law not inconsistent with this Constitution."

However, it is not only in relation to appointments that the Constitution makes provision for the advice of the Council of State to be sought. The phrase "on the advice of" also appears in Article 5 of the Constitution on the creation, alteration or merger of Regions. The Article provides as follows:

> "5.
>
> 1. Subject to the provisions of this article, the President may, by constitutional instrument-
>   a. create a new region;
>   b. alter the boundaries of a region;or
>   c. provide for the merger of two or more regions.
>
> 2. If the President, upon a petition being presented to him and, on the advice of the Council of State, is satisfied that there is substantial demand for-

a.   the creation of a new region;

b.   the alteration of the boundaries of a region, whether or not the alteration involves the creation of a new region; or

c.   the merger of any two or more regions; he shall, acting in accordance with the advice of the Council of State, appoint a commission of inquiry to inquire into the demand and to make recommendations on all the factors involved in the creation, alteration or merger.

3.   If, notwithstanding that a petition has not been presented to him, the President is, on the advice of the Council of State, satisfied that the need has arisen for taking any of the steps referred to in paragraphs (a), (b) and (c) of clause (1) of this article, he may, acting in accordance with the advice of the Council of State, appoint a commission of inquiry to inquire into the need and to make recommendations on all the factors involved in the creation, alteration or merger."

The President is also required to act, "in consultation with the Council of State" in the exercise of the prerogative of mercy. Article 72 of the Constitution provides that:

"72.

1.   The President may, acting in consultation with the Council of State-

a.   grant to a person convicted of an offence a pardon either free or subject to lawful conditions; or

b.   grant to a person a respite, either indefinite or for a specified period, from the execution of punishment imposed on him for an offence; or

c.   substitute a less severe form of punishment for a punishment imposed on a person for an offence; or

d.   remit the whole or part of a punishment imposed on a person or of a penalty or forfeiture otherwise due to Government on account of any offence."

Consultation and advice in relation to appointments

The above enumeration of the various provisions requiring consultation or advice in relation to appointments illustrates the policy objective of the provisions. Clearly, the framers of the Constitution wanted to constrain the absolute freedom of the President to appoint as he wishes and to oblige him to take into account the views of the Council of State in the exercise of his discretion.

Before discussing the one decided case in Ghana which considers the meaning of "on the advice of", let me illustrate the issue posed by looking at two contrasting paradigms for the exercise of the executive power to appoint senior judges, namely in the United Kingdom and the United States of America.

Comparative material

Article II section 2(2) of the Constitution of the United States provides, in relation to the President, that:

> "He shall have Power, by and with the Advice and Consent of the Senate, to make Treaties,...and by and with the Advice and Consent of the Senate, shall appoint Ambassadors, other public Ministers and Consuls, Judges of the supreme Court, and all other Officers of the United States, whose Appointments are not herein otherwise provided for, and which shall be established by Law;..."

[Some of the points made below have also been made in Chapter 11 of this volume]

Thus, pursuant to this power, the President of the US has a completely free hand in nominating Justices of the Supreme Court. Of course, the nomination has to secure the approval of the Senate, but he has untrammelled power to make the initial nomination. The other end of the spectrum is the contemporary United Kingdom regime for the appointment of senior judges. Judges used to be selected by the Lord Chancellor in England for appointment by the Queen. As is well known, the Lord Chancellor was both the most senior judge in that jurisdiction, as well as a Cabinet Minister. He was also the Speaker of the House of Lords. He was thus in all three branches of the Government. The Constitutional Reform Act 2005 sought, among its various reforms, to remedy this historical anomaly. Among the reforms introduced by the Act was a new process for appointing senior judges which is in marked contrast to the US system just cited above. The Lord Chancellor's power to select judges was abolished. In its place was installed a new system which is more independent of the Executive than the contemporary Ghanaian system. I will briefly describe it to inject a comparative perspective into our discussion.

Since 3rd April 2006, most senior judges in England have been selected by the independent Judicial Appointments Commission (or JAC). The JAC recommends to the Queen for appointment all the judicial offices listed in Schedule 14 of the Constitutional Reform Act 2005, which does not include Supreme Court Judges and Heads of Divisions of the Judiciary. It also assists with the selection of Heads of Divisions, including the Lord Chief Justice, the Master of the Rolls, President of the Queen's Bench Division, President of the Family Division etc. It does not, however, undertake the selection of judges for the Supreme Court.

The Judicial Appointments Commission was established by section 61 of the Constitutional Reform Act 2005. It is a very interesting institution. Through it the influence of the Executive branch of Government on the selection of judges has been diminished. The JAC is described as an executive non-departmental public body sponsored by the Ministry of Justice. It comprises 15 Commissioners. Under the Constitutional Reform Act, the JAC's statutory duties are to

- Select candidates solely on merit;
- Select only people of good character; and
- Have regard to the need to encourage diversity in the range of persons available for judicial selection.

Schedule 12 of the Constitutional Reform Act 2005, which deals with the Judicial Appointments Commission, provides that a person must not be appointed as a Commissioner if he is employed in the civil service of the State. Also the number of Commissioners who are holders of judicial office must be less than the number of Commissioners who are not holders of judicial office. There are 15 Commissioners, 12 of whom (including the Chairman) are appointed through open competition. The other 3 are selected by the Judges' Council. The Chairman has to be a lay member. If an appropriate authority declines to accept a selection made by the JAC, that authority has to provide written reasons for its rejection of the selection.

I have given the above information about the JAC of the UK in order to illustrate an approach to tackling the issue that is addressed in the 1992 Constitution of Ghana by providing for advice from, or consultation with, the Council of State. The issue is how to diminish the influence of the Executive Branch of Government in relation to some public offices whose holders should be encouraged to act independently. Incidentally, it is noteworthy that the UK system does not provide for Parliamentary confirmation of any judges whatsoever.

Under the Ghanaian Constitution, appointments to most significant public offices are by the President. However, the Constitution seeks to depart from the US paradigm where, as earlier noted, the President has untrammelled power when nominating, subject only to the Senate's confirmation in appropriate cases. In Ghana, the President is required to consider the views of the Council of State in the enumerated cases before making an appointment.

The meaning of "on the advice of"

In the Supreme Court case of *Ghana Bar Association & Ors v Attorney-General & Judicial Council, consolidated with Sky v Attorney-General and Danso-Akyeampong v Attorney - General*[162], the Supreme Court had occasion to consider the meaning of the phrase "on the advice of". The Ghana Bar Association and its principal officers brought action against the Attorney-General and the Judicial Council for certain declarations. These were:

---

162   [2015-2016] 2 SCGLR 871

"1. A declaration that upon a true and proper construction of Article 144 clauses (2) and (3) of the Constitution 1992 all appointments made by the President of the Republic of Ghana to the Superior Courts are valid only to the extent that such appointments are made in strict accordance with the advice of the 2nd Defendant herein, the Judicial Council.

2. A declaration that upon a true and proper interpretation of Article 144 (2) and (3) of the Constitution 1992, a constitutional trust is created in the 2nd Defendant herein, the Judicial Council, to make nominations of persons best qualified to serve as Justices of the Superior Courts of Judicature, and the 2nd Defendant is required to ensure that such nominations are actually submitted by the President to Parliament for approval after due consultations with the Council of State.

3. A declaration that accordingly, upon a true and proper construction of article 144 clauses (2) and (3) of the Constitution 1992 the Judicial Council of the Republic of Ghana has a constitutional obligation to specifically advice the president of the Republic of Ghana as to which specific person(s) is/are suitable for appointment to serve as Justice(s) of the Superior Courts of the Judicature, in accordance with which advice the President is mandatorily required to exercise his powers of appointment.

4. A declaration that an appointment or non-appointment by the President of the Republic of Ghana of a Justice of the Superior Court in a manner out of accord with the advice of the Judicial Council is unconstitutional, null, void and of no effect."

The provision of the Constitution under interpretation therefore was on what "on the advice of" meant in relation to the Judicial Council. But elucidation of that meaning is relevant also to the Council of State. Although one of the consolidated suits in this action was aimed at the Council of State and its advice, in relation to the Electoral Commission, the Supreme Court refused to decide that issue, since the relevant Writ had not made any allegation of any breach or threatened breach of any constitutional provision. The Court therefore reached the conclusion that the Plaintiffs, in relation to the Electoral Commission, were seeking an advisory opinion. This is not permitted and it was thus dismissed.

In relation to the advice of the Judicial Council, Atuguba JSC had this to say[163]:

> **"ISSUE I**
>
> (i) **Whether or not the constitutional requirement that the President of the Republic of Ghana must obtain the advice of the Judicial Council in the process of appointing Superior Court Justices means that the President is bound by the advice of the Judicial Council?**
>
> This issue is the kernel of this action. The plaintiffs contend that to secure the independence and best quality of the Judiciary the advice of the Judicial Council on appointments to the Supreme Court should be binding on the President. They inter alia, rely on paragraph 2.20 of the Memorandum on the Proposals for a Constitution for Ghana 1968 in which it was "**proposed that appointments to the Judiciary shall be by the President, and not on the advice of the Prime Minister.** It was noted that this proposal is "the most effective way of ensuring **that political considerations** and influences **shall not be allowed to dictate these appointments.**"

They also rely on paragraph 123 of the *Proposals of the Constitutional Commission for a Constitution for the Establishment of a Transitional (interim) National Government for Ghana 1978* as follows;

> "123. One major limitation on the President's power is in the area of appointments to public offices. We concede and accept that the President should have some freedom in appointing the team with which to formulate and implement his programs

---

163   At 879.

and policies. We feel, however,that this discretion should not be untrammelled, particularly in the appointment of persons to perform certain sensitive functions in which a degree of impartiality and independence from executive is considered essential..."

Apart from these excerpts from the Proposals for the 1969 and 1979 Constitutions we have to bear in mind the recent history and realities concerning appointments to the superior courts,particularly the Supreme Court to ascertain further the spirit or core values that should inform our interpretation of article 144(2) and by extension clause 3 thereof, as counselled by *Tuffour v Attorney-General* (1980) GLR 634 C.A (sitting as the Supreme Court) and a plethora of well-known subsequent decisions of this court."

Justice Atuguba goes on later[164] to indicate the rationale of the phrase as follows:

"The involvement of the Judicial Council, the Council of State and Parliament are meant to be restraints on the appointing power of the President, see *Emmanuel Noble Kor v The Attorney-General and Justice Delali Duose*, Suit no. J1/16/2015 dated 10/3/2016, unreported, (4) The contrast between the expressions"shall...*acting on the advice of the* Judicial Council" and *"in consultation with the* Council of State,*"* shows that the restraining effect of the Judicial Council's recommendation on the President is greater than that of the Council of State. In other words if the recommendation of the Judicial Council cannot be flawed on the requirements of article 128(4) the consultation with the Council of State cannot warrant its rejection by the President. However if the President for the purposes of consulting the Council of State unearths information which he puts before the Council of State which can unsettle the recommendation of the Judicial Council in terms of article 128(4) he can reject the recommendation of the Judicial Council even if the Council of State advises otherwise."

---

164 At 889

The view of Justice Dotse expressed in his concurring opinion, with which Sophia Akuffo JSC agreed, was that:

> "In all these, what is clear is that, *"in consultation with the Council of State"* connotes that, before the Justices of the Supreme Court for example are appointed, the President must have consultations with the Council of State on the nominees being considered for such appointment.
>
> It is therefore right and or correct to state that, whilst the President is mandated by the express provisions of the Constitution in articles 144(2) and (3) to seek the advice of the Judicial Council before appointments to the Supreme Court and Court of Appeal are made, and similarly consult with the Council of State on the appointment process of the Supreme Court Judges, he is nonetheless not bound by the advice or opinion of these bodies. My understanding however is that, if these bodies did not recommend a particular candidate or nominee, the President cannot go behind that advice to appoint someone else. It also follows that, if the Judicial Council recommends a particular person and the President does not feel obliged to appoint that person, there is in fact no obligation on the President to have that person appointed.
>
> As a matter of fact, the President is not bound by any such advice. The only thing is that, the President can also not go outside the names or lists of persons recommended to him by these bodies."

In effect then, the judicial interpretation of "on the advice of" is that it is not binding, within the context at least of Article 144(2). However, it does constrain the freedom of action of the President, in the sense that he may not appoint anybody whose name has not been communicated to him through the advice of the Judicial Council. Although the Supreme Court declined to decide the issue, on the facts of the case, one can reasonably deduce that a similar interpretation is to be applied to the advice of the Council of State, under Article 70(2) in relation to the Chairman, Deputy Chairmen and other members of the Electoral Commission.

Meaning of "in consultation with" in relation to appointments

Consultation is even less binding. Once the details of the proposed appointee are placed before the Council of State for discussion, the requirement is probably satisfied. It depends upon how thorough the work of the Council of State is in finding a flaw with a particular candidate.

"On the advice of" outside of the appointment process

It will be recalled that Article 5(2) provides as follows:

> "(2) If the President, upon a petition being presented to him and, on the advice of the Council of State, is satisfied that there is substantial demand for-
>
> a. the creation of a new region;
> b. the alteration of the boundaries of a region, whether or not the alteration involves the creation of a new region; or
> c. the merger of any two or more regions;
>
> he shall, acting in accordance with the advice of the Council of State, appoint a commission of inquiry to inquire into the demand and to make recommendations on all the factors involved in the creation, alteration or merger."

In the context of Article 5, is the advice of the Council of State binding? If the Council of State determines that a Commission of Enquiry is not needed to inquire into the demand made in a petition for the creation of a new region, would that strip the President of authority to set up such a Commission? The Supreme Court decision in *Ghana Bar Association & Ors v Attorney-General & Anor* does not cover this issue and therefore it is open for discussion.

In consultation with, outside the appointment process

It will be recalled that Article 72 on the Prerogative of Mercy requires consultation with the Council of State as follows:

"(1) The President may, acting in consultation with the Council of State-

a. grant to a person convicted of an offence a pardon either free or subject to lawful conditions; or

b. grant to a person a respite, either indefinite or for a specified period, from the execution of punishment imposed on him for an offence;or

c. substitute a less severe form of punishment for a punishment imposed on a person for an offence;or

d. remit the whole or part of a punishment imposed on a person or of a penalty or forfeiture otherwise due to Government on account of any offence."

Although there is no judicial decision on the issue, this probably means that if the President exercises his prerogative of mercy without consulting the Council of State, it is invalid. However, he is not bound by any advice that the Council of State may offer him in relation to an intended exercise of the prerogative of mercy.

The extent of the obligation imposed on the Council of State when it is required to be consulted or to give advice to the President

The Constitution does not expressly spell out the extent of due diligence to be carried out by the Council of State when the President consults it or receives advice from it. That, I think, is a matter for the self-regulation of the Council. As a matter of common sense, however,one would expect greater diligence and meticulousness in relation to advice that the President is under a greater obligation to take than as regards a consultation.

Wider advisory role of the Council of State

At this juncture, I would like to say a few words about the wider advisory role given to the Council of State by Article 91(3) of the 1992 Constitution. These then are *obiter dicta* by the author.

Article 91(3) provides as follows:

> "The Council of State may, upon request or on its own initiative, consider and make recommendations on any matter being considered or dealt with by the President, a Minister of State, Parliament or any other authority established by this Constitution except that the President, Minister of State, Parliament or other authority shall not be required to act in accordance with any recommendation made by the Council of State under this clause."

The authority conferred by Article 91(3) is thus to make non-binding recommendations, upon request by the President, a Minister, Parliament or any other authority, or on the initiative of the Council of State itself. The recommendation may be on any matter being considered or dealt with by the President, a Minister of State, Parliament or any authority established by the Constitution. This is a useful advisory role that the Council of State could deploy to the benefit of the State, if resorted to strategically. It is, of course, beyond the requirement that the President should act either on the Council of State's advice or in consultation with the Council of State, which has occupied the bulk of this presentation.

Conclusion

I would end by saying that **COGENCY** is what counts. Whether the outcome of the deliberations of the Council of State is advice to the President or a response to his consultation or it is a recommendation to him or to any other constitutionally established authority, what counts is how persuasive the opinion of the Council of State is. If the Council of State's argument is persuasive, the President or other authority will find it hard to ignore, whether it is contained in an advice, a response to a consultation or recommendation.

PARLIAMENT'S CONSTITUTIONAL MANDATE TO APPROVE INTERNATIONAL BUSINESS AGREEMENTS MADE BY THE GOVERNMENT: RELEVANT SUPREME COURT DECISIONS[165]

Introduction

Parliament has a constitutional obligation, under Article 181(5) of the 1992 Constitution of Ghana, to consider and decide whether to approve international business agreements entered into by the Executive Branch of Government. This is a powerful tool for injecting transparency into the Government's international business transactions. The obligation has been articulated and explained in a series of Supreme Court decisions. It is the purpose of this Chapter to elucidate the extent of Parliament's obligation, drawing liberally from relevant Supreme Court judgments. It, therefore, uses the actual language of Supreme Court judgments to explain the meaning of article 181(5) to show Parliament what its responsibility is.

The clear obligation of Parliament, under article 181(5) of the 1992 Constitution, unfortunately, remained unenforced until the case of *Attorney-General v Faroe Atlantic Co. Ltd*[166] in 2005, more than a decade into the Fourth Republic. *Faroe Atlantic* is thus the starting point of this exposition.

Attorney-General v Faroe Atlantic Co. Ltd: Interpretation of Article 181(5) of the 1992 Constitution

The Plaintiffs in *Faroe Atlantic* sued for breach of a Power Purchase Agreement ("PPA") that they had entered into with the Government of Ghana, acting through the Ministry of Mines and Energy. They sought the reliefs of specific performance or, in the alternative,

---

165 This Chapter is based on a presentation that I made at a Capacity Building Workshop for Members of Parliament held in Koforidua, Ghana, in October 2019.

166 [2005-2006] SCGLR 271

damages for breach and payment of interest on the assessed damages. Summary judgment was entered for the plaintiffs in the High Court on these reliefs. The Government appealed to the Court of Appeal. When the appeal was dismissed, it appealed again, to the Supreme Court. At the Supreme Court, the Government raised the issue of the constitutional validity of the PPA, because of its non-compliance with article 181(5) of the 1992 Constitution. That was how the Supreme Court came to consider this issue for the first time.

At the Supreme Court, Dr. Justice Twum, allowed the appeal,using contract and civil procedure grounds. I, however, decided the case by reference to the impact of article 181(5) of the 1992 Constitution. Article 181 of the Constitution reads as follows:

1. "Parliament may, by a resolution supported by the votes of a majority of all the members of Parliament, authorise the Government to enter into an agreement for the granting of a loan out of any public fund or public account.

2. An agreement entered into under clause (1) of this article shall be laid before Parliament and shall not come into operation unless it is approved by a resolution of Parliament.

3. No loan shall be raised by the Government on behalf of itself or any other public institution or authority otherwise than by or under the authority of an Act of Parliament.

4. An Act of Parliament enacted in accordance with clause (3) of this article shall provide–

   a. That the terms and conditions of a loan shall be laid before Parliament and shall not come into operation unless they have been approved by a resolution of Parliament; and

   b. That any moneys received in respect of that loan shall be paid into the Consolidated Fund and form part of that Fund or into some other public fund of Ghana either existing or created for the purposes of the loan.

5. This article shall, with the necessary modifications by Parliament, apply to an international business or economic transaction to which the Government is a party as it applies to a loan."

I said, in the *Faroe Atlantic* case, that[167]:

"The plain meaning of article 181(5) would appear to be that where the Government of Ghana enters into"an international business or economic transaction" it must comply with the requirements, *mutatis mutandis*, imposed by article 181 of the Constitution. Those requirements clearly include the laying of the relevant agreement before Parliament. The agreement is not to come in to operation unless it is approved by a resolution of Parliament. On the facts of this case, since the Respondent neither pleaded nor proved any such Parliamentary approval, this provision would be fatal to their claim in this action, unless an examination of this issue is foreclosed by *res judicata*."

The origin of the current article 181 of the 1992 Constitution is article 133 of the 1969 Constitution. The latter provision dealt exclusively with loans and made no reference to international business or economic transactions. As I pointed out in the *Faroe Atlantic* case[168]:

"These original provisions of the 1969 Constitution were maintained unchanged in the 1979 Constitution as article 144. It is in the 1992 Constitution that this long-standing provision on the giving and raising of loans is modified to include another category of contract, namely"an international business or economic transaction to which the Government is a party"."

I then proceeded to interpret Article 181(5) as follows[169]:

"My interpretation of this proposal, which was, in substance, adopted by the Consultative Assembly which deliberated on the proposals formulated by the Experts and is embodied in

---

167 [2005-2006] SCGLR 271 at 294 - 295

168 *Ibid at* 296

169 *Ibid.* at 297

article 181 of the current Constitution, is that international business or economic transactions are to be treated, *mutatis mutandis*, the same as loan agreements, from the point of view of the requirements contained in article 181. This, to my mind, means that an international business transaction or international economic transaction to which the Government is a party must be submitted to Parliament for approval, even though the nature of the obligation embodied in such transaction is not one of debt."

Justice Sophia Akuffo agreed with this interpretation and reprimanded the Court of Appeal for not taking seriously enough its obligation to enforce the Constitution. She said[170]:

"It is my respectful view that the manner in which the learned Justices of the Court of Appeal dealt with such an important issue relating to the need for Parliamentary approval in terms of article 181(5) of the 1992 Constitution left a lot to be desired. The 1992 Constitution is the supreme law of the land and article 1(1) makes it clear that:

"*...the powers of government are to be exercised in the manner and within the limits laid down in this Constitution.*" (My emphasis). As the supreme law of the land, the Constitution is applicable at all times and all acts and things, particularly those done for and on behalf of the Republic of Ghana, must always be tested against its provisions. In the course of judicial proceedings, it is incumbent upon every judge to keep its provisions in mind to assure compliance, not only by the parties before it, but also by the court itself."

Justice Georgina Wood also agreed, saying[171]:

"I agree with him that this particular transaction, even if viewed from the plaintiffs' angle, that it is merely a contract for the supply of electric power, and not a loan, it is an international

---

170   *Ibid* at 304
171   *Ibid.* at 308

business or economic transaction to which the Government of Ghana is a party, which given the unambiguous provisions of article 181(5), needed parliamentary approval."

Attorney-General v Balkan Energy Ghana Ltd & Ors[172] : further elaboration of the scope and meaning of Article 181 (5)

The task of the Supreme Court in *Attorney-General v Balkan Energy Ghana Ltd & Ors* was to interpret the phrase or term "international business or economic transaction to which the Government is a party" as it is used in article 181(5) of the 1992 Constitution. The case was a reference from the High Court for constitutional interpretation. The Supreme Court had, unusually, referred the case to itself, exercising the powers of the High Court, which it is entitled to do. The trial High Court had decided not to refer the case to the Supreme Court, but the Supreme Court quashed that decision in *Republic v High Court (Commercial Court Division, Accra) Ex Parte Attorney-General (Balkan Energy Ghana Ltd & Ors Interested Parties).*[173]

The facts of the case were as follows: Mr. Elders, a businessman resident in Texas, USA, identified a business opportunity in Ghana and persuaded the owner of the second defendant to invest in it. The Government of Ghana wanted to generate electricity urgently from a power barge located in the Western Region of the country. The barge needed rehabilitation and the Government wanted to negotiate with a private investor to achieve this and bring its generating capacity urgently on stream. Balkan Energy LLC, a US entity, the second defendant, entered into a Memorandum of Understanding("MOU") with the Government of Ghana on 16th May 2007. This was to enable the second Defendant to take advantage of the business opportunity identified by Mr. Elders, the third Defendant. Because of advice given to Mr. Elders, the investors in the business opportunity decided to incorporate the first defendant in Ghana and to make it the party to a Power Purchase Agreement ("PPA").

---

172   [2012] 2 SCGLR 998
173   See [2011] 2 SCGLR 1181

The main issue in this case was whether the PPA between the first Defendant, a Ghanaian Company, and the Government was an agreement within the scope of Article 181(5). On 27th July 2007, Balkan Energy (Ghana) Limited, the first defendant, which had been incorporated in Ghana 11 days previously, entered into a PPA with the Government of Ghana. A dispute arose under the PPA. The Government of Ghana claimed that the second and third defendants had misrepresented to it that they could make the power barge operational within 90 working days and that it was on the basis of this misrepresentation that it had entered into the MOU and the PPA. However, they had failed to do this.

The first Defendant, on 23rd December 2010, initiated arbitration proceedings against the Government of Ghana under the auspices of the Permanent Court of Arbitration at the Hague. At these proceedings, the Ghana Government raised the point that the PPA needed Parliamentary approval under article 181(5) of the 1992 Constitution, but that this approval had not been sought and therefore the PPA was invalid, as having been executed in breach of a constitutional provision. The Government of Ghana argued before the arbitration tribunal that non-compliance with the constitutional provision made the PPA invalid, including its arbitration clause, and consequently the arbitral tribunal had no jurisdiction over the dispute before it. The Arbitral Tribunal, however, held that it had jurisdiction. The Tribunal expressed a willingness to take account of the Supreme Court's interpretation of the constitutional provision in question. However, ultimately, after the delivery of the Supreme Court's judgment, the Arbitral Tribunal refused to accept the Court's interpretation of Ghanaian law.[174]

The Attorney-General had, in June 2010, issued a Writ of Summons in the Commercial Division of the High Court, Accra, claiming a declaration that the PPA is an international business transaction that needed Parliamentary approval and was unenforceable because it did not have such approval. The plaintiff also claimed that the

---

174 See *Balkan Energy (Ghana) Ltd. V Republic of Ghana* PCA Case no 2010-7, para 388 of the Final Award, where the Tribunal stated that: "At this point and with due deference and respect, after having considered the Supreme Court judgment in detail, the Tribunal must depart from the conclusion reached by that Court."

arbitration agreement contained in the PPA was an international business transaction and was also in breach of article 181(5) and therefore unenforceable. After the institution of the suit, the plaintiff, that is, the Attorney-General, applied to the High Court to refer to the Supreme Court for interpretation the following two questions:

"Whether or not the Power Purchase Agreement dated 27th July 2007 between the Government of Ghana and Balkan Energy (Ghana) Limited constitutes an international business transaction within the meaning of Article 181(5) of the Constitution.

Whether or not the arbitration provisions contained in clause 22.2 of the Power Purchase Agreement dated 27th July 2007 between the Government of Ghana and Balkan Energy(Ghana) Limited constitutes an international business transaction within the meaning of Article 181(5) of the Constitution."

The High Court refused to refer the questions. Accordingly, the Attorney-General applied to the Supreme Court to exercise its supervisory jurisdiction over the High Court to quash its decision not to refer. In a Ruling of 2nd November, 2011, the Supreme Court did indeed quash the decision of the learned High Court judge. It then referred the two questions set out above to itself. Prior to the oral argument on the two questions before the Supreme Court, the Court requested counsel for the parties to address in their Statements of Case the following issues which are relevant for the determination of the two principal questions posed above:

The definition of an international business transaction within the meaning and context of Article 181(5) of the Constitution.

Can a Government of Ghana contract with a Ghanaian legal person or entity ever be an international business transaction?

If so, how are we to distinguish an international business transaction of a Ghanaian legal person from its other contracts with the Government of Ghana? Are you able to formulate any clear indices or criteria?

The Supreme Court said that the phrase "international business or economic transaction to which the Government is a party", if purposively construed, should not lead necessarily to the result that only agreements between entities resident abroad and the Ghana Government can be embraced within the meaning of the term. Given the complexity of contemporary international business transactions, there will be transactions of such a clear international nature that they should come within any reasonable definition of an international business transaction, but which may have been concluded with the Ghana Government by an entity resident in Ghana. In such a situation, the Supreme Court's view was that the substance, rather than the form, should prevail[175]. The Supreme Court also said[176]:

> "What we have just said begs the question of what "international" means. In this connection, we think that there is the need to combine both the *nature of the business or economic transaction* criterion and the *parties* criterion proposed by the plaintiff in his submission, in order to formulate a test for determining what transactions come within the ambit of article 181(5) of the 1992 Constitution."

It went on later to state that[177]:

> "In our view, to give effect to the framers' purpose, there is need to imply into article 181(5) an understanding that only **major** international business or economic transactions are to be subject to its provisions. We do, however, agree with the defendants that Parliament needs to exercise its legislative power in relation to article 181(5) in order to clarify which transactions are to be viewed as major."

---

175 *Ibid* at 1029
176 *Ibid.* at 1029
177 *Ibid.* at 1032

Duty of Parliament in relation to definition of "international"

The Supreme Court was clear that[178]:

> "Because of the practical consequences of determining that a transaction comes within the scope of article 181(5), an interpretation of the provision needs to result in practical guidance to the Executive, Parliament and parties to transactions with government to enable them to apply the constitutional vision of the framers. It is therefore imperative that Parliament takes up early the challenge of framing the modifications to article 181 needed to give greater certainty and clarity as to what categories of international business or economic transactions to which the Government is a party come within the ambit of article 181(5)."

The Supreme Court proceeded to pronounce authoritatively that[179]:

> "We think that a business transaction is"international"within the context of article 181(5) where the nature of the business which is the subject-matter of the transaction is international in the sense of having a significant foreign element or the parties to the transaction (other than the Government) have a foreign nationality or reside in different countries or, in the case of companies, the place of their central management and control is outside Ghana.
>
> The word"significant"is used in the above definition to denote the fact that the foreign elements or contacts that lead to a judgment of internationality in relation to a transaction have to be subjected to a qualitative assessment before reaching that judgment. The significance is in relation to the purpose of article 181(5). Thus, for instance, the example given in the defendant's Statement of Case "that every contract that the Government enters into for the supply of vehicles is an "international economic or business transaction" because "it is a notorious fact that nearly all the cars plying our roads are imported"would not necessarily be correct because the fact

---

178 *Ibid.* at 1033-1034
179 *Ibid.* at 1034

only of the importation of the vehicles would not be significant enough in relation to the purpose of article 181 (5) to justify the transaction being characterized as an international business transaction.

The sale of cars domestically to the government would not be an international trade transaction, in spite of the incidental fact that the cars sold were imported. The fact of their importation, when qualitatively assessed by a court, may well result in a decision by the court that their importation is not a significant foreign element in the transaction in question. This qualitative assessment is important in separating business transactions which are international within the meaning of article 181(5) from those that are not. The defendants' hypotheticals are only a sample of many other transactions which could literally be brought under the semantic umbrella of an "international business transaction", but which should not be so construed for the purposes of article 181(5). Examples would be documentary letters of credit and contracts for the international sale of ordinary goods or for the carriage of goods by sea".

The meaning of "business" in the context of Article 181(5) of the 1992 Constitution

The Supreme Court expressed itself on the meaning of "business" in the following terms[180]:

> "As to the meaning of business, we are willing to accept the defendants' interpretation of it that "where a transaction is commercial in nature, or pertains to or impacts on the wealth and resources of the country, it would be a "business or economic transaction" and a subject of interest in any examination of Article 181(5)."

---

180   *Ibid* at 1035

The Martin Amidu cases: Further elaboration of the scope of Article181(5):

Amidu (no.2) v Attorney-General, Isofoton SA & Forson (no1)[181]

In this case, Mr. Martin Amidu, a former Attorney-General, brought action in the Supreme Court in his personal capacity against 3 defendants: the first was the incumbent Attorney-General; the second was Isofoton SA, a foreign company registered in Spain;and the third was an agent or attorney of the second defendant. The suit sought the following declarations:

"i) A declaration that:

On a true and proper interpretation of Article 181 (3) (4) and section 7 of the Loans Act, (Act 335) the laying before and approval on 1st August 2005 of the terms and conditions of the Second Financial Protocol between the Republic of Ghana and the Kingdom of Spain for an amount of sixty-five million Euro (€65,000,000) for the implementation of various development projects and programmes in Ghana did not nullify the effect of Article 181 (5) of the 1992 Constitution that mandates further laying before and approval of any specific international business or economic transaction to which the Government is a party even if payment had to be made from the said loan approved by Parliament.

The Agreement between Isofoton S. A of Montalban 9th 28014, Madrid Spain, a foreign registered company and the Ministry of Food and Agriculture of the Government of Ghana dated 22nd September 2005 for the execution of a project designated as "Solar PV Powered Water Pumping and Irrigation Systems in Remote Rural Areas of Ghana" is an international business or economic transaction within the meaning of Article 181(5) of the 1992 Constitution and never became operative because it was not laid before and approved by Parliament and is accordingly null, void and without effect whatsoever.

---

181   [2013-2014] 1 SCGLR 167

The Agreement between Isofoton S. A. of Montalban 9, 28014, Madrid Spain, a foreign registered company and the Ministry of Energy of the Government of Ghana in 2001 for the execution of the "Solar Electrification Project in Ghana Phase II" is an international business or economic transaction within the meaning of Article 181 (5) of the 1992 Constitution and never became operative because it was not laid before and approved by Parliament and is accordingly null, void and without effect whatsoever.

The conduct of the 2nd Defendant in suing for breaches of the said Agreements through his lawful Attorney the 3rd Defendant when he knew that the Agreements were international business or economic transactions which had never been laid before and approved by Parliament is inconsistent with and in violation of the Articles 2 and 181 (5) of the Constitution.

The conduct of the 3rd Defendant, a Ghanaian citizen, in holding himself out as an Attorney to sue in the Courts of Ghana on behalf of the 2nd Defendant for damages in an international business transaction which had not been laid before and approved by Parliament is also inconsistent with Articles 2 and 181 (5) of the Constitution.

The conduct of the 1st Defendant accepting the claims of the 2nd and 3rd defendants and purporting to settle same for entry in the High Court as a consent judgment when the 1st Defendant knew the said two Agreements between the 2nd Defendant, a foreign registered and resident company, and the Government of Ghana constituted an international business or economic transaction which had to be laid before and approved by Parliament to become operative is inconsistent with and in violation of Articles 2 and 181 (5) of the 1992 Constitution.

The High Court which heard and granted reliefs in two actions commenced by the 3rd Defendant on behalf of the 2nd Defendant in Consolidated Suit Nos. BC23/2008 and BC24/2008 pursuant to the said international business or economic transaction which had not become operative under Article 181 (5) of the 1992 Constitution had acted without jurisdiction and is amenable to the supervisory jurisdiction of this Honourable Court under Article 132 of the 1992 Constitution for orders and directions to comply with the Constitution.

The High Court, Accra, acted without jurisdiction and usurped the exclusive and original jurisdiction of this Honourable Court in its ruling dated 24th April 2012 on an application for declaration of nullity when it purported to interpret Article 181 (3) (4) and (5) of the 1992 Constitution to mean that the approval of the terms and conditions of the Second Spanish Financial Protocol loan aforementioned in relief (1) above by Parliament automatically excluded the further laying before and approval by Parliament of subsequent international business or economic transactions arising out of the said terms and conditions of the loan to which the Government is a party as mandated by Article 181 (5) of the Constitution."

The main facts on which the plaintiff based his cause of action were that the second defendant entered into two international business agreements with the Republic of Ghana, which were not laid before Parliament for the approval of Parliament. There was an agreement concluded with the Minister for Food and Agriculture on 22nd September 2005 for "Solar PV Powered Water Pumping and Irrigation Systems in Remote Rural Areas in Ghana" and another one concluded in 2001 with the Minister of Energy for "Solar Electrification in Ghana Phase II." The Plaintiff contended that these agreements were international business or economic transactions to which the Government is a party, within the meaning of Article 181(5) of the Constitution. Accordingly, not having been laid before Parliament and approved by Parliament, they were void.

The Supreme Court held that[182]:

"It is evident that this purpose of ensuring transparency, openness and Parliamentary consent in relation to international business transactions or international economic transactions to which the Government is a party deserves to

---

182 *Ibid.* at 185

be applied as much in relation to the so-called implementation agreements as to project loan agreements. In other words, the purposive approach insisted upon by the 2nd Defendant, when reasonably applied, should lead to the conclusion that an international business or economic transaction to which the Government of Ghana is a party should not cease to be treated as such, under article 181(5), simply because activities under it are to be financed under a loan agreement that has already been approved by Parliament."

Amidu (no 1) v Attorney-General, Waterville Holdings (BVI) Ltd & Woyome[183]

This case also illustrates the scope of Art 181(5). On 26th April, 2006, the Government of Ghana signed two separate but similar agreements with the second defendant for the rehabilitation of the Ohene Djan and El Wak stadia in Accra and the Baba Yara stadium in Kumasi, respectively. The agreements were not sent to Parliament for approval. Also, specified conditions precedent in them were not fulfilled. In spite of this, the second Defendant was given access to the contractual sites and it began work on the project, demolishing structures and clearing the sites.

On 1st August 2006, the Attorney-General terminated the agreements, claiming that "since the contracts did not receive approval from Cabinet in accordance with Clause 17 of the Contracts, the Contracts have never become effective." In spite of this, on 9th March, 2009, the second defendant wrote relying, on a clause in the 26th April 2006 contracts, to claim fees and pre-financing costs for the initial construction works from the Government.

To cut a long story short, the third Defendant brought action against the Attorney-General for alleged breach of contract and secured a settlement of his claim. Payments were made by the Government of Ghana, pursuant to the settlement agreement.

---

183   [2013-2014] 1 SCGLR 112

Outraged by this turn of events, the former Attorney-General, Martin Amidu, brought action in his personal capacity against the 3 defendants seeking the following declarations:

"A declaration that the Agreement entitled "Contract for the Rehabilitation (Design, Construction, Fixtures, Fittings and Equipment) of a 40,000 seating Capacity Baba Yara Sports Stadium in Kumasi, Ghana" entered into on 26th April 2006 between the Republic of Ghana and Waterville Holdings (BVI) Limited of P. O. Box 3444 Road Town Tortola, British Virgin Islands is an international business or economic transaction under Article 181 (5) of the 1992 Constitution that could only have become operative and binding on the Government of Ghana after being laid before and approved by Parliament."

"A declaration that the Agreement entitled "Contract for the Rehabilitation (Design, Construction, Fixtures, Fittings and Equipment) of a 40,000 Seating Capacity Ohene Djan Sports Stadium and the Upgrading of the El Wak Stadium in Accra, Ghana" entered into on 26th April 2006 between the Republic of Ghana and Waterville Holdings (BVI) Limited of P. O. Box 3444 Road Town, Tortola, British Virgin Islands is an international business or economic transaction under Article 181 (5) of the 1992 Constitution that could only have become operative and binding on the Government of Ghana after being laid before and approved by Parliament".

A declaration that the two Agreements each dated 26th April 2006 as stated in reliefs (1) and (2) herein not having been laid before and approved by Parliament pursuant to Article 181 (5) of the 1992 Constitution is each inconsistent with and in contravention of the said Article 181 (5) of the Constitution and consequently null, void and without operative effect whatsoever.

A declaration that a bridge financing agreement arising between the Republic of Ghana and the 2nd defendant, (Waterville Holding (BVI) Limited), pursuant to the two Agreements each dated 26th April 2006 is each a loan transaction within the meaning of Article 181 (3), (4) and (6) of the 1992 Constitution whose terms and conditions had to be further laid before Parliament and approved by a resolution of Parliament to be operative and binding on the Republic of Ghana.

A declaration that the conduct of the 1st Defendant in paying sums of money in Euros to the 2nd Defendant in purported pursuance of claims by the 2nd Defendant arising out of the said two Agreements each dated 26th April 2006 as stated in reliefs (1) and (2) herein is inconsistent with and in contravention of the letter and spirit of the 1992 Constitution, particularly Article 181 (5) thereof and is each accordingly null, void, and without effect whatsoever.

A declaration that all transactions and claims by the 3rd Defendant a Ghanaian citizen with one Austro-Invest Management of CH-6302 ZUG Untermuhli 6, Switzerland, (a foreign registered and wholly owned company liquidated on 26th July 2011) premised upon the said two Agreements between the Republic of Ghana and the 2nd Defendant, Waterville Holdings (BVI) Limited, constitute international business transactions within the meaning of Article 181(5) of the 1992 Constitution to be laid before and approved by Parliament to become operative and binding on the Republic of Ghana.

A declaration that the transactions or any purported transaction between the 2nd Defendant, Waterville Holding (BVI) Limited, (a foreign registered and resident company), 3rd Defendant, a Ghanaian citizen, with Austro-Invest Management Limited (also a foreign registered and wholly owned company now liquidated), and the Government of Ghana to syndicate foreign loans and other financial assistances from foreign financial institutions and sources that financially encumbers the Republic of Ghana for the stadia projects, the subject matter of the two Agreements each dated 26th April 2006 aforementioned constitute an international business or economic transaction within the meaning of Article 181 (5)of the 1992 Constitution for the purpose of the operability of the transactions.

A declaration that on a true and proper interpretation of Articles 181 (3), (4), (5), and (6) and the spirit of the 1992 Constitution the Republic of Ghana cannot incur liability for any foreign or international loan or expenses incidental to such foreign or international loan transactions without parliamentary approval of the transaction for it to be operative and binding on the Republic of Ghana.

A declaration that conduct of the 1st Defendant in paying or ordering the payment by the Republic of Ghana of claims raised by the 3rd Defendant with the said Austro-Invest premised upon a purported foreign or international financial engineering agreement arising out of the said afore mentioned two Agreements of 26th April 2006 and/or any other international business Agreement with the Government of Ghana which were never laid before or approved by Parliament is inconsistent with and in contravention of the letter and spirit of the Constitution, particularly Articles 181 (3), (4), (5), and (6) of the 1992 constitution thereof and are accordingly null, void and without effect whatsoever".

There were other declarations sought by the Plaintiff, which need not be set out here. The declarations already set out give a flavour of the role that Art 181(5) played in the litigation. In short, the Plaintiff claimed that the agreements under which the second and third Defendants claimed were unconstitutional and therefore null and void and could not serve as a legal basis for the payment of any monetary claims. Accordingly, any payments made to the second and third Defendants should be refunded, even if made pursuant to the settlement agreement.

In June 2013, the Supreme Court upheld the action by Mr. Amidu and held that the stadia contracts and the settlement agreement were null and void. It further ordered the second and third defendants to refund all payments made to them by the Ghana Government.

The effect of non-compliance with Article 181(5) of the 1992 Constitution

The exact effect of non-compliance with Article 181(5) of the 1992 Constitution has been spelt out by the Supreme Court. In *Amidu (no 1) v Attorney-General, Waterville Holdings (BVI) Ltd & Woyome*, it stated that[184]:

> "A contract which breaches article 181(5) of the Constitution is null and void and therefore creates no rights. (See *The Attorney-General v Faroe Atlantic Co. Ltd.* [2005-2006] SCGLR 271 and *The Attorney-General v Balkan Energy Ghana Ltd. 2 ors.* Unreported, 16ᵗʰ May, 2012.) It should not be legitimate to evade this nullity by the grant of a restitutionary remedy. Although one accepts the cogency of the argument that there is need to avoid unjust enrichment to the State through its receipt of benefits it has not paid for, there is the higher order countervailing argument that the enforcement of the Constitution should not be undermined by allowing the State and its partners an avenue or opportunity for doing indirectly what it is constitutionally prohibited from doing directly. The supremacy of the Constitution in the hierarchy of legal norms in the legal system has to be preserved and jealously guarded".

Arbitration

On 10 October 2014, Waterville initiated arbitration proceedings against Ghana's Attorney-General in London. The parties to those proceedings agreed to address, as a preliminary issue, whether the Tribunal, established under the International Chamber of Commerce Rules, had jurisdiction to decide on the claims brought by the Claimant. The Claimant averred that the Respondent (the Attorney-General) was not entitled to any repayment and that the Respondent was not entitled to pursue claims against the Claimant except under arbitration pursuant to arbitration clauses contained in the Stadia Agreements. The ICC Tribunal held that the law governing the

---

184   [2013-2014] SCGLR 112 at 141

arbitration agreements contained in the Stadia Agreements was the law of Ghana[185]. The Tribunal held that the arbitration agreements were separable from the Stadia Agreements which had been held to be unconstitutional. Accordingly, the Claimant's right to commence arbitration under the arbitration agreements had not been extinguished by the settlement agreement. However, the Tribunal acknowledged that the Supreme Court of Ghana was vested with exclusive jurisdiction to deal with constitutional or "public interest" matters. Such matters were therefore beyond the jurisdiction of the Tribunal. The Tribunal therefore held that other aspects of the Parties' disputes which did not involve an issue of interpretation of the Ghanaian Constitution would be arbitrable.

Accordingly, the Tribunal held that it had no jurisdiction to declare that the Stadia Agreements or the subsequent Settlement Agreement were valid and enforceable because this question had been decided by the Supreme Court and was within the Court's exclusive jurisdiction. The Supreme Court had jurisdiction under Article 2 of the 1992 Constitution to make the order compelling Waterville to refund "all monies" paid to it. The Supreme Court was entitled to deny Waterville's *quantum meruit* claim in order to give effect to the "penumbra effect" of Article181.

"The penumbra effect[186]"

The Supreme Court has explained the "penumbra effect" as follows:

> "In this context, an issue that emerges strikingly for constitutional interpretation is the extent to which the nullity of international business or economic transactions in consequence of their non-compliance with article 181(5) of the 1992 Constitution affects restitutionary rights under the common law. To put the issue another way: if an agreement to perform certain acts comes within article 181(5), but has not

---

185 See *Waterville Holdings v Attorney-General*, PARTIAL AWARD ON JURISDICTION, 20 MARCH 2017. This Award may be contrasted with that in the *Balkan Energy* arbitration where the Tribunal refused to accept the law as laid down by the Supreme Court, although the proper law of the PPA was Ghanaian law.

186 [2013-2014] SCGLR 136-7

yet been submitted to Parliament for its approval, is it lawful for the Executive to bypass the obligation of article 181(5) by requesting the acts contemplated under the contract to be performed by its partner anyway and then make payment to the partner under claims for restitution? In principle, it would appear to be clearly against public policy to allow such evasion by the Executive of its constitutional duty. Article 181(5) thus needs to be construed purposively to invalidate claims to restitution in such situations.

This dimension of this case is what brings it within the exclusive jurisdiction of this court under article 130 of the 1992 Constitution. The 2nd and 3rd defendants argue in their Statements of Case that since this Court has already interpreted article 181(5) of the 1992 Constitution in *The Attorney-General v Faroe Atlantic Co. Ltd.* [2005-2006] SCGLR 271 and *The Attorney-General v Balkan Energy Ghana Ltd. 2 ors.* Unreported, 16th May, 2012, it is unnecessary for it to assume jurisdiction in this case. They contend therefore that the right forum for this case is the High Court for it to apply the interpretation already put on the provision by the Supreme Court. However, it is clear from the facts set out above that the 3rd defendant does not admit to relying on any contractual provision in the two terminated contracts. So *Faroe Atlantic* and *Balkan Energy* are not directly in point. What is in issue is whether there is a penumbra effect of article 181(5) such that rights and obligations which are devised to enable an evasion of the provision's duty can equally be nullified. This is a task of constitutional interpretation for this court and not for the High Court."

Does Article 181(5) apply to statutory corporations?

The issue of whether Article 181(5) of the 1992 Constitution applies to statutory corporations fell for consideration before the Supreme Court in *Klomega (No. 2) v Attorney-General & Ghana Ports and Harbours Authority & Others (No. 2).*[187] The Court there said:

---

187 [2013-2014] 1 SCGLR 581.

"The cumulative points made by the defendants above amount to an irresistible case that in the context of article 181(5) and the facts of this case, the 2nd defendant is not to be regarded as coming within the meaning of "Government". As pointed out by the defendants, to subject statutory corporations with commercial functions to the Parliamentary approval process prescribed in article 181(5) would probably increase the weight of Parliament's responsibilities in this regard to an unsustainable level. Accordingly, it is reasonable to infer that the framers of the 1992 Constitution did not intend such a result.

Thus, in our view, "Government" in the context of article181(5) should mean, ordinarily, the central government and not operationally autonomous agencies of government. Where an agency has a separate legal personality distinct from central government, it usually comes under sectoral ministerial supervision. The Board of the corporation and the appropriate Ministry should then exercise oversight over its international business or economic agreements. That oversight should be exercised within the context of the procurement laws of this country. Parliament would be sucked into unnecessary minutiae if it were to have the function of approving the international business or economic agreements of statutory corporations. That is why "Government", in the context of article 181(5), should be interpreted purposively to exclude corporations such as the 2nd defendant."

Conclusion

The line of Supreme Court decisions discussed above has put flesh on the bare bones of Article 181(5). It deserves to be known better by lawmakers, policymakers and actors in government. The result of these judicial decisions has been to produce unprecedented transparency in the transnational transactions of the Executive through Parliamentary scrutiny of the international business transactions of the Executive. Parliament, however, needs to do more by enacting the legislation contemplated by the framers of the

Constitution, to give statutory force to the"necessary modifications" to article 181. It is hoped that Parliament will take the necessary action and also carry out its scrutiny responsibilities with diligence.

PART IV:

BUSINESS LAW

REFLECTIONS ON THE EVOLUTION OF BUSINESS LAW IN GHANA SINCE INDEPENDENCE[188]

Introduction

Business law is not a subject which is taught as such in the Law Faculties and Law Schools of Ghana. It may be taught perhaps in Business Schools. This is principally because it covers too extensive an area. Unlike Constitutional Law, which is a recognised subject taught by Law Faculties/Law Schools in Universities, business law encompasses a wide range of legal subjects which impinge on the doing of business. This could mean virtually the whole legal system. Accordingly, I have been selective in choosing the particular areas of law whose evolution is considered in this Chapter. It concentrates on the law of contract and of business units.

The law of contract constitutes the substrate of much of business law and is thus a primary candidate for attention in any discussion of business law. Companies, partnerships and sole proprietorships (whether with registered business names or not) are also fundamental to business law since they are the means through which business people participate in the economy and run their enterprises. Larger enterprises tend to be companies. The significance of such enterprises to the economy explains my selection of company law alongside the law of incorporated private partnerships for special focus. The development of the concept of the incorporated private partnership was an innovative initiative by Professor Gower to fashion a vehicle for the development of small and medium-sized Ghanaian enterprises. The concept has, however, not met with the success that he would have wished for. Of Professor Gower, more hereafter.

---

188 The lecture, on which this Chapter is based,was given on 5th November 2018 as the second of the Annual Legon Law Lectures Series of the University of Ghana School of Law. The first was by Nana Dr. S.K.B. Asante and was on constitutional law.

While considering the evolution of the law of contract in Ghana, it should, of course, be remembered that specialised contracts are governed by the general principles embodied in general contract law. Examples of specialised contracts would be those for the sale of goods, carriage of goods, insurance, bills of exchange and similar transactions.

The evolution of the law of contract and of business units that will be analysed and discussed here is what has occurred through statutory reform and case law.

State of business law at Ghana's independence

The business law that the sovereign new State of Ghana inherited at Independence, on 6th March 1957, was based on the received English law. As is well-known, the reception statute which introduced that English law was the Supreme Court Ordinance of 1876, section 14 of which provided that:

> "The common law, the doctrines of equity, and the statutes of general application which were in force in England at the date when the Colony obtained a local legislature, that is to say on the 24th day of July 1874, shall be in force within the jurisdiction of the court."

At independence, therefore, Ghana received the business law contained in the common law, the doctrines of equity and the statutes of general application which were in force in England on 24th July 1874. The law at Independence also embodied, of course, the statutes enacted by the colonial legislature, including notably the Companies Ordinance 1907. The courts in Ghana, and indeed in the Gold Coast, have always regarded it as their mandate to apply contemporary English case law, where needed, rather than any fossilised or antiquated English law, prevalent in England in 1874. Accordingly, the law available to our courts at Independence to govern business transactions was in broad terms fit for purpose since it was the same law that underpinned business transactions in England and in other Commonwealth jurisdictions. It,however, needed to be customised by Ghanaian courts and the Ghanaian legislature to specific Ghanaian needs and aspirations. This Chapter's brief account of the evolution of Ghanaian business law in the areas I have selected will, hopefully, illuminate the extent to which our courts and legislature have succeeded in this task of adaptation.

The law reform movement after Independence

The first years of Independence and of the First Republic were characterised by a burst of law reform activity under the leadership of Geoffrey Bing QC, the expatriate Attorney-General. He was appointed Attorney-General in September 1957 by Osagyefo Dr. Kwame Nkrumah, when the position was a civil service post of non-Ministerial status. He was a former left-wing Labour Member of Parliament at Westminster, who became the Constitutional Adviser to the Prime Minister in the last days of the Gold Coast. After his appointment as Attorney-General, a position he occupied for four years till October 1961, he brought into the Attorney-General's Department, alongside the Ghanaian legal talent he attracted, an assortment of excellent expatriate lawyers who, among other duties, worked on law reform.

In his book, *Reap the Whirlwind: An account of Kwame Nkrumah's Ghana from 1950 to 1966*[189], Bing gives a fascinating account of how he secured the recruitment of Francis Bennion, Patrick Atiyah and Professor L.C.B. Gower, among several other lawyers, to make progress with the agenda of the Attorney-General's Department. Professor Gower was never an employee of the Attorney-General's Department, but was retained as a consultant to produce Ghana's Companies Code 1963, as is well known. Patrick Atiyah,[190] who had by then already written his well-known treatise on the Sale of Goods, was recruited from the University of Khartoum, Sudan, and employed at the Attorney-General's Department. He worked, among other duties, on the Contracts Act 1960. Francis Bennion was seconded from the Parliamentary Counsel Office of the U.K. House of Commons to serve as a Parliamentary draftsman at the Attorney-

189 MacGibbon & Kee, 1968, London. Chapter9.
190 *Ibid* at 320

General's Department[191]. Other recruited expatriate lawyers included[192]: A N Stainton, also of the Parliamentary Counsel Office of the House of Commons, a leading draftsman; S. Simasivayam of Ceylon, an experienced draftsman from the civil service of Ceylon (Sri Lanka); Pauli Murray, an African-American female lawyer and civil rights activist who was recruited to teach at the Ghana School of Law and whose distinguished career subsequent to leaving Ghana has led to a Hall of Residence being named after her at Yale University; and Vincent Grogan, previously Director of Statute Law Revision in the Irish Republic.

Bing offers the following explanation for his success in recruiting such abundant talent to Ghana[193]:

> "In those days Ghana presented opportunity for people of ability who for some reason or another were thwarted in their own country, to carry out abroad the work they had hoped to do at home. For example, we were able to get a foremost expert on English Company Law, Professor L.C.B. Gower, then Cassel Professor of Commercial Law at London University and who is now one of the Law Commissioners, to come to Ghana to work on that type of progressive Corporation legislation which he had been unable to persuade those in authority to accept in England."

The Ghanaian legal talent Mr. Bing recruited included Nana Dr. S K B Asante, the 2017 lecturer in this series of lectures of the School of Law of the University of Ghana. The story of his recruitment is illustrative of the drive with which Bing ran his Department. After Nana Dr S K B Asante's qualification as a solicitor in England, the plan in Government was to deploy him to the Lands Department, but the Attorney-General intercepted him and persuaded the stakeholders that it would be a better plan for the young Asante to join a commercial unit that he was setting up within his Chambers. In the *Festschrift* in his honour, Nana himself documents this phase of his career under Bing as follows:

---

191   *Ibid* at 320.

192   *Ibid* at 320 *et seq.*

193   *Ibid* at 322.

"In 1960, I returned to Ghana and spent one year at the Attorney-General's Department. That period saw the establishment of the legal infrastructure of an independent Ghana spearheaded by Geoffrey Bing who is generally remembered for his role in the notorious Preventive Detention Act, 1958. On the other hand, he recruited Professor LCB Gower of LSE to draft a new and imaginative Companies Code for Ghana and the brilliant PS Atiyah, now a Professor at Oxford, to work on the Contract Act of Ghana. Other experts I met there were AR Bennion, Parliamentary Counsel, F Glasgow of the West Indies and Ghanaian senior colleagues like ANE Amissah, Mills-Odoi and VCRAC Crabbe. They gave me valuable guidance."[194]

The reforms in contract law and company law, referred to by Nana Dr S K B Asante, have been the foundation for the evolution of a modern business law in Ghana. I will spend some time discussing them below. The efforts of Professors Gower and Atiyah resulted in the Companies Code 1963[195] and the Contracts Act 1960[196], respectively.

The Contracts Act 1960 and the Evolution of Contract Doctrine in Ghana

The enforcement of contracts is, of course, recognised widely as the foundation of modern business law. It was thus visionary for the Nkrumah Government under the legal leadership of the Attorney-General of the day, Geoffrey Bing, to seek to sort out certain perceived defects in the received common law of contract in order to make the common law doctrine of contract then prevalent in Ghana more fit for purpose. It was the young Patrick Atiyah, later to become a Professor of English Law at Oxford University (from 1977 to 1988), who spearheaded this reform endeavour. He served

---

194 See Asante, "Actors in the Transition from an African Village to the Global Village and Back: Reflections and Words of Appreciation" in Oppong and Agyebeng, *A Commitment to Law, Development and Public Policy: A Festschrift in Honour of Nana Dr SKB Asante* 683 at 689.

195 Act 179

196 Act 25

in the Attorney-General's Department from 1959 to 1961[197]. His classic book, *Introduction to the Law of Contract*, was published in 1961, whilst serving in Accra. He developed into a huge figure in the common law world after leaving Ghana. On his death in May 2018, an Obituary in the Telegraph (the English newspaper) described him as "one of the most important legal scholars of his generation in the common-law world"[198]. His work on the Contracts Bill contributed significantly to the evolution of contract law in Ghana.

Some of the reforms effected by the Contracts Act 1960 will be discussed next. Let us begin with an analysis of the modification of contracts[199]. The doctrine of consideration in its classical configuration was an impediment to the effective modification of contracts. The classical doctrine required contracts to be supported by consideration not only when a contract was originally formed, but also when modifying a pre-existing contract. For instance, in the West African Court of Appeal case of *Union Trading Company Ltd. v Hauri*,[200] the Court held that the performance by the Appellants of a pre-existing contractual obligation to the Respondent was not sufficient consideration to support the agreement sued on.

The intended purpose of applying the doctrine of consideration to the modification of existing contractual relationships is to prevent economic blackmail and duress. It has been considered undesirable, in policy terms, to enable promisors to break or threaten to break contracts in order to secure acts or promises additional to those which the other contracting party is under an obligation to perform. However, consideration is not the doctrine best suited for achieving this social policy objective.

UTC v Hauri, the case cited earlier, is an application of the principle enunciated in the old English case of *Stilk v Myrick*.[201] That case has been widely understood as asserting that a promisor cannot improve his or her position under a contract by securing concessions from a

---

197 The Telegraph, 30 April 2018, Obituaries.

198 *Ibid.*

199 See Date-Bah, "*The Doctrine of Consideration and the Modification of Contracts*" (1973) 5 RGL 10.

200 (1940) 6 WACA 148

201 (1809) 2 Camp. 317

promisee, so long as the original contract remains binding on him or her. This principle covers most agreements to amend an existing contract, since, almost invariably, agreements to amend are made with the purpose of securing a concession from the promisee or making the promisee renounce a legal right. The law's insistence on the necessity for consideration, when contracts are modified, however, amounts to denying enforceability to an important category of promises, namely, those that enable business people to make a "re-adjustment of a going business deal", to use the words of Karl Llewellyn, the famous American lawyer.[202]

The law needs to give business people some flexibility in this area, in the interest of smooth business dealing. Once the original agreement has satisfied the classical requirements of consideration, the parties should be allowed the liberty to re-adjust their relations with flexibility, unimpeded by technical consideration requirements. By satisfying the consideration test when a contract is made, that contract transaction passes into the category of consensual transactions thought worthy of enforcement. Once the parties' agreement has passed this threshold requirement, there is no further need for consideration, when the terms of the original bargain are sought to be modified. A doctrine of public policy that requires the invalidation of modification agreements induced by economic duress would better fulfil the social policy objectives in this particular area of contract law.

The young Atiyah was no doubt persuaded by these considerations to propose the abolition of consideration in the modification of contracts. His proposal was accepted and finds expression in section 9 of the Contracts Act 1960[203] as follows:

> "The performance of an act or the promise to perform an act may be sufficient consideration for another promise notwithstanding that the performance of that act may already be enjoined by some legal duty, whether enforceable by the other party or not."

---

202 Karl Llewellyn, "Common Law Reform of Consideration. Are there measures?"(1941) 41 Col. L. Rev. 863 at 867.

203 Act 25

Accordingly, contemporary Ghanaian law on the modification of contracts is that, so long as the original contract was supported by consideration, that consideration must, as it were, be imported into any subsequent modification agreement, which is therefore enforceable. This is a desirable evolution of Ghanaian contract doctrine, achieved by legislative intervention.

Another aspect of the doctrine of consideration which is modified by the Contracts Act, 1960 is the refusal to enforce agreements to waive or forego a debt or to pay only part of a debt. All first year students of contract law in Ghana know, or should know, as the rule in *Pinnel's Case*[204], this principle reformed by the Contracts Act 1960. In that case, an English court held in the Seventeenth Century that payment of a lesser sum in satisfaction of a larger debt would not be recognised as discharging the obligation of the debtor. An argument that the plaintiff in the case had accepted part payment of a debt owed to him in satisfaction of the whole debt was rejected by the Court, with Lord Coke declaring:

> "Payment of a lesser sum on the day in satisfaction of a greater sum cannot be any satisfaction of the whole... but the gift of a horse, hawk, or robe etc. in satisfaction is good. For it shall be intended that a hawk, horse, or robe, etc. might be more beneficial to the plaintiff than the money.[205]"

Overcoming the rule in *Pinnel's Case* is an aspect of ensuring the enforceability of modification agreements. Accordingly, section 8(2) of the Contracts Act 1960 reforms the law by providing that:

> "A promise to waive the payment of a debt or part of a debt or the performance of some other contractual or legal obligation shall not be invalid as a contract by reason only of the absence of any consideration therefor."

The intervention, described above, of the Ghanaian legislature in 1960 can be interpreted as an endeavour to reinforce commercial morality and to prevent the law thwarting the reasonable expectations of business people, on whose activity depends much

---

204   (1602) 5 Co.Rep 117a.

205   *Ibid*

that is vital to the process of development. In a similar vein, the Contracts Act 1960 reformed two other aspects of the doctrine of consideration. First, under the classical doctrine of consideration, a promise to keep an offer open for acceptance, often referred to as a firm offer, is not binding. This is because it is not supported by consideration. However, section 8(1) of the Contracts Act 1960 now provides as follows:

> "A promise to keep an offer open for acceptance for a specified time shall not be invalid as a contract by reason only of the absence of any consideration therefor."

Also, the Contracts Act 1960 abolished the English law rule that consideration must move from the promisee[206]. This aspect of the doctrine of consideration needed to be reformed to enable the modernisation of the law on privity of contract and the enforcement of third party contractual rights for which the Contracts Act 1960 also provided. (We will consider next in more detail the reform of the law on third party contractual rights effected by the Contracts Act.) With these reforms to the doctrine of consideration, modern Ghanaian contract law has come close to the goal of enforcing most commercially significant promises. The extent of enforceable agreements has been expanded. The non-enforcement of gratuitous options (or firm offers), modification agreements and third party contractual rights was a commercially inconvenient restriction on the enforceability of promises. The Contracts Act 1960 removed that restriction.

The gratuitous (or gift) promise remains, however, unenforceable. There has been no pressure by the courts to change the rule on the non-enforceability of gratuitous promises. I once wrote a review[207] (in 1969) of the High Court case of *Tsede v Nubuasa,*[208] in which I concluded as follows:

> "The law must lend its weight to the enforcement of commercial morality and business probity in order to sustain

---

206　See section 10 of the Contracts Act 1960.

207　See Date-Bah, "*Tsede v Nubuasa: A Welcome Inroad into the Doctrine of Consideration*" (1969) 6 UGLJ 60.

208　[1962] GLR 338

the confidence of the business community in the security of commercial transactions into which its members enter. Such confidence is necessary in this community, if Ghana is to be able to keep up the process of commercial expansion and investment which is of vital importance for its general process of economic development.

It is for these reasons that the decision of Prempeh J in *Tsede and Others v Nubuasa and Another* is to be welcomed. It is submitted that this decision brings the Ghanaian law near to making the principle of promissory estoppel a sword and not a mere shield. In the United States of America, the principle of promissory estoppel based on a promisee's reasonable reliance to his detriment on a deliberate promise given him has become recognised as a basis of liability. It is believed that Prempeh J's judgment in the instant case has, perhaps unwittingly, brought the Ghanaian law near to the adoption of such a basis of promissory liability."

The direction of travel hinted at, probably unwittingly, in this case was, however, never followed up in subsequent cases and thus the gratuitous promise remains unenforceable even when it has been reasonably relied on. In general, therefore, what the courts in Ghana will enforce are bargains (broadly conceived), rather than promises, as such. This does not, however, derogate from the fitness for purpose of our law since the gratuitous promise does not play a significant role in business transactions.

Sections 5 and 6 of the Contracts Act 1960 provide for the enforcement of third party contractual rights in Ghana. Section 5 states that a provision in a contract which purports to confer a benefit on a person who is not a party to the contract may, subject to the provisions of the statute, be enforced or relied on by that third party as though he were a party to the contract. Section 6(b) of the Contracts Act 1960 clarifies the derivative nature of the rights of third parties by making them subject to the equities. It is not necessary here to go into an in-depth analysis of third party contractual rights. In my youth, I wrote an article, published in the

University of Ghana Law Journal, on that subject[209]. For the purpose of this lecture, suffice it to declare that Ghanaian law was put ahead of English law by the proposals of Atiyah which were accepted and enacted by the Ghanaian authorities then.

Apart from modernising the doctrine of consideration and the enforcement of third party contractual rights, the Contracts Act 1960 reformed another pocket of the law of contract that needed review. The classical effect of the doctrine of frustration on contracts could be quite unpredictable and capricious. The event causing the frustration was treated by the common law like a guillotine which severed the contractual relationship at the time of the occurrence of the frustrating event. Obligations arising before the event remained in force, whilst those due to arise after the event fell away. The parties' rights therefore depended, as it were, on the luck of the draw. Sections 1 to 3 of the Contracts Act 1960 inject more rationality into the mix by providing for the discharge of both parties to the contract from further performance of the contract[210], when a frustrating event occurs. Furthermore, all sums paid to any party under the contract before the frustrating event may be recovered by the party who paid them[211]. All sums payable to any party before the frustrating event cease to be payable[212]. However, if a party has spent money on the performance of the contract before the frustrating event, that party can recover from the other party an amount equivalent to his expenses so long as these do not exceed the total sum payable under the contract[213]. Thus in this area also, the Contracts Act 1960 has played a role in modernising the general law of contract in Ghana and making it fit for modern business purposes.

The overall effect of the Contracts Act 1960 has been to assist the evolution of general contract law in Ghana and to make it a more fit instrument to underpin the development of business law in the country. Contract law is the foundation of business law. Together with ideas from the law of equity, it provides the building blocks

---

209   Date-Bah,"*The Enforcement of Third Party Contractual Rights in Ghana*"(1971)8 UGLJ 76
210   See section 1(1) of the Act.
211   See section 1(2).
212   See section 1(2).
213   See section 1(3).

for company law and all the other specialised areas of business law. Of course, legislative intervention is called for in some of the specialized areas, such as banking and insurance, particularly in relation to the regulatory framework. However, the common law underlay will usually be found in the law of contract. The Contracts Act 1960 has thus served this economy well by reforming those aspects of the law of contract that needed reform and making the law functional. On the whole, the general contract law of Ghana is fit for purpose, except in the area of unfair contract terms. This latter area needs attention and the Law Reform Commission is currently working on it.

Evolution of Contract Law through Case Law not Based on the Contract Act 1960.

Decisions of Ghanaian courts on contracts have generally reflected decisions of the English courts, although they are not bound by them. Thus, there have not been significant doctrinal departures from orthodox English contract doctrine. In a sense, this has served a useful purpose, since predictability and certainty are advantageous attributes of any system of contract law. Innovation by judges, if it creates uncertainty, is generally not appreciated by business people. Nevertheless, some adaptation of English doctrine to the circumstances of Ghana is called for from time to time and there has been some. I will here give a couple of illustrations of such innovation.

First, I will consider resort by Ghanaian courts to the doctrine of unconscionable contracts (underutilised in England but offering a potential for good in a jurisdiction such as Ghana) to achieve a just result in the circumstances of our country. Setting contracts aside on account of their unconscionable nature is not a doctrine that has been emphasised or often resorted to by the English courts. However, given the social circumstances of Ghana, the equitable doctrine of unconscionable bargain is one that can usefully be pressed into use here. The Supreme Court invoked the doctrine in

CFC Construction Co. (W.A.) Ltd, Rita Read v Attisogbe.[214] In this case, the Supreme Court observed, in relation to the equitable doctrine of unconscionable bargain, that:

> "Although there have been a few recent cases applying this doctrine of unconscionable bargain in the English jurisdiction, the English courts have tended to rely more on the doctrine of undue influence rather than on the unconscionability doctrine. Australian and Canadian courts have, on the other hand, applied the doctrine more often."

The Supreme Court went on to hold that:

> "In our view, this is a line of precedent which deserves further development in the Ghanaian jurisdiction. It gives an opportunity to the courts to protect the vulnerable from being taken advantage of."

The doctrine of unconscionable bargain was then adopted, adapted and applied by the Supreme Court in the following terms:

> "Thus on the facts of this case, the second plaintiff's old age is a circumstance that could be construed as a disability justifying the invocation of the doctrine of unconscionable bargain. Whether, on the evidence, the invocation of the doctrine is appropriate is a question that we will shortly be addressing. Another of the circumstances listed by him is "illiteracy or lack of education". [Him here refers to Fullagar J., the Australian judge in the case relied on by the Supreme Court.] This circumstance affords an opportunity to the courts to intervene to protect illiterate parties from being taken advantage of. It will be recalled that this was the circumstance which impelled King-Farlow J. to invoke the doctrine in *Acquaye & Ors. v Halm* (supra). It is an unfortunate fact that, close to a century after the judgment by King-Farlow J., illiteracy remains a widespread phenomenon in Ghana. It is a fact of which judicial notice may legitimately be taken. This fact needs to be taken into account in the courts' development of doctrine. Even though the facts of the present case do not raise illiteracy as a special

---

214 [2005-2006] SCGLR 858.

disability in relation to the doctrine under discussion, the fact that the doctrine lays a foundation that will enable the courts to remedy serious disadvantage to illiterate and other disadvantaged persons through the application of equitable principles commends the doctrine to us.

In our opinion, therefore, the courts in Ghana have the right to set aside as unconscionable any dealing, whether by contract or by gift, where on account of the special disability of one of the parties, he or she is placed at a serious disadvantage in relation to the other. The categories of special disability should not be regarded as closed."

Another case in which the Supreme Court demonstrated doctrinal innovation in the law of contract is *City & Country Waste Ltd v Accra Metropolitan Assembly.*[215] The Supreme Court had to determine the legal consequences of an illegal contract in this case. It identified the issue to be resolved as follows:

"The common law doctrine of illegality of contract is complex and its effect often unjust. Consequently, some common law jurisdictions (such as New Zealand, through its Illegal Contracts Act 1970) have undertaken legislative reform of the effects of the doctrine. The facts of this case pose the issue whether this Court should, in this jurisdiction, wait for such legislative reform or whether it would be appropriate for this final Court to take a decision which constitutes a step in a stepwise judicial reform of the law to achieve a just result on the facts of this case. The doctrine of illegality of contract offers a defence against the enforcement of the obligations of a contract. This proposition is often expressed in the Latin maxims: *ex turpi causa non oritur actio;* and *in pari delicto potior est conditio defendentis.* However, the rules relating to when a claim of illegality will be upheld by the courts as such a defence are complicated and confusing. The particular sub-set of these rules on illegality which are relevant to this case are those concerning contracts rendered unenforceable by statute. These rules, in short, prescribe that a contract that is

---

215   [2007-2008] SCGLR 409

expressly or impliedly proscribed by statute is illegal. These rules are in fact not as difficult as some of the other rules in the general area of illegality of contract. On the facts of this case, what is difficult is not the determination of whether the contract sued on was illegal or not. Rather, the difficulty is with determining the legal consequences of such determination. It is with regard to the effect of a determination of illegality that this Court will need to be creative in order to serve the needs of justice."

It was in furtherance of this need to be creative that the Court reached the following conclusion:

"The critical issue is whether this Court is entitled to grant the Plaintiff restitutionary relief in respect of the services actually rendered the Defendant or whether the illegality of the contract is also a defence to the restitutionary claim. It is open to this Court to base an alternative restitutionary claim on the Plaintiff's claim for the recovery of the value of its services, indorsed on its Writ, although the Plaintiff's intent was to found that claim on the contract that we have held to be illegal. The Plaintiff can legitimately argue that a restitutionary claim by it is not equivalent to enforcing the illegal contract. The Plaintiff is bound by the unenforceability of the illegal contract. Nevertheless, in the interest of justice, it is reasonable for the Plaintiff to seek to reverse the unjust enrichment of the Defendant through its retention of the benefit of the Plaintiff's services without any payment for them at a reasonable rate, not necessarily coincident with the contract rate negotiated under the illegal contract. In the English case law, the illegality of a contract has been held to be an effective defence to even a restitutionary claim, unless the parties are not *in pari delicto* (or equally at fault).

The next issue arising therefore is whether the Plaintiff is not *in pari delicto* with the Defendant according to the orthodox English authorities on the issue. A review of the English case law reveals that, in assessing the fault of the parties, the law adopts a rather technical approach, according to which

263

recovery is allowed only where a Plaintiff can demonstrate that he or she was induced to enter into the illegal contract by the fraud, duress or oppression of the other party; or that he or she was ignorant of a fact that rendered the contract illegal; or that he or she belonged to a vulnerable class protected by statute. By way of illustrating the last category, the words of Lord Mansfield in *Browning v Morris* (1778) 2 Cowp. 790 at 792, may be quoted:

> "Where contracts or transactions are prohibited by positive statutes,for the sake of protecting one set of men from another set of men; the one, from their situation and condition being liable to be oppressed and imposed upon by the other; there, the parties are not *in pari delicto* and in furtherance of these statutes, the person injured after the transaction is finished and completed, may bring his action and defeat the contract."

We do not think that we ought in this Court to be constrained excessively by the weight of the English case law in finding a just outcome in this case. Rather, we are encouraged to develop Ghanaian law in this area by some of the ideas contained in the English Law Commission's Consultation Paper No. 154 on *Illegal Transactions: The Effect of Illegalityon Contracts and Trusts*. This Consultative Paper, after an extensive and erudite review of the complex English law in the area, concludes as follows (at p.91):

"We have said that we believe that there is a continued need for some doctrine of illegality in relation to illegal contracts and that, in certain circumstances, it is right that the law should deny the plaintiff his or her standard rights and remedies. However, we have also explained how, in some situations, we believe that the plaintiff is being unduly penalized by the present rules. This injustice would seem to be the inevitable result of the application of a strict set of rules to a wide variety of circumstances, including cases where the illegality involved may be minor, may be wholly or largely the fault of the defendant, or may be merely incidental to the contract in question. We consider that the best means of overcoming this injustice is to replace the present strict rules with a discretionary approach under which the courts would be able to take into account such relevant issues as the seriousness of the illegality involved, whether the plaintiff was aware of the illegality, and the purpose of the rule which renders the contract illegal. The adoption of some type of discretionary approach has the support of the vast majority of academic commentators in this area; and it is the approach which has been followed in those jurisdictions where legislation has been implemented. Moreover, we have not been able to devise a new enlightened regime of "rules" that would provide satisfactory answers to all disputes involving illegal contracts. In our view, a balancing of various factors is required so that, put quite simply, the law on illegal contracts does not lend itself to a regime of rules."

We have decided to adopt this structured discretionary approach to the resolution of issues arising from illegality of contracts. The approach is to be fleshed out on a case by case basis. On the facts of the present case, balancing the need to deny enforceability to the contract sued on by the Plaintiff against the need to prevent the unjust enrichment of the Defendant, and, considering that in relation to the Defendant's non-compliance with the statutory provisions binding on it, the Plaintiff was not *in pari delicto* in a broad sense, we have come to the conclusion that the Plaintiff must be paid reasonable compensation for the services it rendered to the Defendant."

I have quoted this long passage from the judgment of the Supreme Court to demonstrate the Court's willingness to innovate in appropriate cases to achieve a just result. Such innovation, of course, contributes to the evolution of Ghanaian contract law.

Evolution of company law since independence: selective observations

At Independence, the statute governing the registration of companies was the Companies Ordinance 1907. It was largely a re-enactment of the English Companies Act of 1862. Professor Gower described it as "nearly 50 years behind the times when enacted".[216] At Independence, therefore, it was nearly a century out of date and in crying need of reform.

It was thus not surprising that one of the earliest efforts of the Independence Government at law reform was in relation to the existing companies' legislation. On 25th August 1958, the Governor-General of Ghana appointed Professor L C B Gower as a Commissioner under the Commissions of Enquiry Ordinance[217] to enquire into the working and administration of the existing company law of Ghana and to make recommendations for the amendment of the Companies Ordinance and any other laws of Ghana which the Commissioner considered necessary in the light of his conclusions after his enquiry. The Commissioner was directed to take into account and examine the laws of such other African States as he considered appropriate. In framing his recommendations,the Commissioner was required by his terms of reference to take into account the need for encouraging African enterprise in Ghana and also encouraging foreign investment.

A few years prior to the appointment of Professor Gower, the Government, through the Minister of Commerce and Industry,had appointed a Working Party to review the Companies Ordinance 1907. The Working Party reached the inevitable conclusion that the Companies Ordinance was "nothing but a snare by reason of its omissions and ambiguities."[218] It accordingly formulated a new draft Ordinance based on the English Companies Act 1948. That was then the most recent consolidated English legislation on companies available. This draft Ordinance was, however, never

---

216 *Final Report of the Commission of Enquiry into the Working and Administration of the Present Company Law of Ghana* (1961) 2 (Here in after referred to as "*The Final Report*".

217 Cap 249

218 *Ibid.* at 4.

enacted, since the Government took the view that it did not suit Ghanaian conditions.[219]

Gower's proposals were thus to be practically the first reform of the company law regime in Ghana since the enactment of the outmoded Companies Ordinance 1907. In the light of his Terms of Reference, Professor Gower considered that he had three options:

1. To recommend the adoption of a law enacted by or proposed to be enacted by another African State;

2. To recommend the adoption, with modifications, of the English Act of 1948; or

3. To recommend a new approach.

He decided to adopt the last option. He explained that[220]:

> "[His] aim has been to try and produce a Code which, starting from the fundamental principles of English law, yet borrows ideas from other systems when these can been grafted without distortion. Not only has there been grafting, there has been pruning – and ruthless pruning of rules which seem to me to be bad, obsolete or unsuitable to Ghanaian conditions.
>
> Nor are the ideas embodied in the Code merely the result of borrowings from elsewhere; some are entirely novel. An attempt has been made to give Ghana an up-to-date streamlined system of company law modelled to her requirements and better than that prevailing anywhere else."

Some of the innovations that Gower introduced into Ghanaian law can be summarised as follows:

- the law expressed in a Code, absorbing much of the case-law;
- introduction of the single-document constitution replacing the memorandum and articles;
- abolition of the ultra vires doctrine(at least of its worst aspects);
- the single-member company;

---

219 *Ibid*

220 *Ibid* at 4. Para. 18.

- compulsory no-par-value shares and the abolition of authorised capital;
- rationalisation of the law on pre-incorporation contracts;
- permitted re-purchase of shares;
- abolition of the doctrine of constructive notice of registered documents;
- a statutory statement of directors' duties;
- dissolution without going through the full winding up procedure.

These innovations resulted in a companies' statute for Ghana which was well ahead of its time, when it was enacted, and has stood the country in good stead for more than half a century. A Bill was, however, under consideration by Parliament, at the time when the Lecture on which this Chapter is based was given. The Bill was subsequently enacted in 2019 as the Companies Act 2019[221]. It revised and updated some of the provisions of the 1963 Act.

In this short Chapter, it is impossible to explore fully the rich tapestry of the reforms introduced by Professor Gower. I therefore select only a couple of topics for discussion below and also explore the further evolution of the law brought about by the Companies Act 2019.

Before proceeding with this exercise, however, I should give you the background to the Companies Act 2019. A Business Law Reform Committee of Experts was established in April 2008 by the then Attorney-General, Honourable Joe Ghartey, as part of the Business Law Reform Project of the Ministry of Justice and Attorney-General's Department. The theme for the Business Law Reform Project was: "Improving the Ease of Doing Business".

This was the context within which the Committee of Experts carried out its mandate. That mandate was to consider what reform to the existing company law regime was needed, taking into account views from the business community, the legal community and interested

---

221   Act 992

members of the general public in Ghana and from reputable company law experts.

The Committee, which I had the privilege of chairing, was originally an independent one in the sense that its membership was drawn from outside the Attorney-General's Office and indeed was from outside the Executive branch of government. However, the Committee was later expanded by the next Attorney-General, Honourable Betty Mould-Iddrisu, to bring in members of the Attorney-General's Office, including from the Registrar-General's Office. The proposals for a Companies Bill that were recommended by the Committee to the Attorney-General were thus the product of the deliberations of members from both without and within Government. The proposals were also subjected to an extensive consultation process. The Bill was considered by the last Parliament, but it could not go through all the Parliamentary processes for enactment before the dissolution of that Parliament. The Bill was, however, enriched by the amendments proposed to it by that Parliament. Subsequently, the current Attorney-General, Honourable Gloria Akuffo, guided it through Cabinet again for it to be passed by Parliament and assented to by the President in 2019.

Abolition of the Worst Parts of the Ultra Vires Doctrine

Before the Companies Act 1963, a doctrine of *ultra vires* was applied in Ghana. Companies had to be incorporated with an objects clause. If the directors, after a company's incorporation, sought to carry out any activity outside its mandate, any transaction implementing the activity would be considered invalid and unenforceable. This doctrine occasioned much hardship to third parties who contracted with companies, not knowing of the limitations placed on a particular company's capacity to contract. The Cohen Committee established in England to review English company law had reached the conclusion that the doctrine of *ultra vires* had become "an illusory protection for the shareholders and yet may be a pitfall for third parties dealing with the company."[222] Professor Gower decided to adopt and adapt the recommendation made by the

---

222 The Report of the Cohen Committee, Cmd 6659 para. 12, quoted in *The Final Report* 42.

Cohen Committee to modify the *ultra vires* doctrine, although it had not yet been implemented in England at the time of his Report.

This led to the enactment of section 25 of the Companies Act 1963, which provides that a company incorporated under the Act has the same capacity and powers as an individual *vis a vis* third parties, but that an objects clause should continue to bind a company and its members in relation to the powers of its directors. Thus, although the Companies Act, 1963 abolished the worst aspects of the doctrine of *ultra vires*, it in fact retained the *ultra vires* rule in a restricted form. Whilst transactions in breach of an objects clause were valid in relation to third parties, members or debenture holders of the company concerned had the right to bring an action against the company to restrain its breach of the objects clause and the High Court had the discretion to halt the breach, if a contract remained executory. The High Court, however, was given power under section 25(5) of the Companies Act 1963 to award compensation to the company or third parties for any loss or damage sustained by them because of the setting aside of the delinquent transaction. However, such compensation was not to cover loss in respect of anticipated profits to be derived from the performance of the contract in question.

The Companies Act 2019 returns to this topic and carries out a more radical reform by proposing a complete abrogation of the *ultra vires* doctrine, in certain circumstances. It provides that a company may be incorporated without an objects clause and in fact makes this the default situation. This implies that, for such a company, the doctrine of *ultra vires* becomes completely irrelevant. There is no objects clause in relation to which there can be a determination of excess of powers. The company then has the capacity of a natural person *simpliciter*.

On this topic, therefore, one sees a desirable evolution of company law doctrine to ease the doing of business and the protection of the reasonable expectations of business people who do business with companies. This radical proposal for reform enabled the formulation of other proposals for the simplification of the process of incorporation in Ghana. The Act has abolished the need to file a constitutive instrument as part of the incorporation process.

The single constitutive instrument of a company which, under the Companies Act 1963, is called "the Regulations" of the company is now to be called the "constitution", under the Companies Act 2019, and does not need to be registered with the Registrar of Companies in order to incorporate a company. Where the promoters of a company do not register a constitution for the company, the Second Schedule of the Act is deemed to be the company's default constitution, if it is a private company. The Third Schedule is the deemed constitution, if it is a public company. Finally, the Fourth Schedule is the deemed constitution, if it is a company limited by guarantee.

Evolution of Doctrine in relation to the Protection of the Rights of Individual Members of the Company and Minorities

Other reforms in the Companies Act 2019 adopt a remedy for minority shareholders which exists under Canadian and New Zealand legislation. It is the remedy of 'buy-out'. There are provisions in the Act which confer on shareholders who have opposed particular transactions of a company, but have been outvoted, the right to demand to have their shares bought out. This remedy provides an outlet for minimising dissension in a company and an additional relief against oppression of, or unfairness to, minority shareholders. The Business Law Reform Committee considered that Ghanaian law would be well-served by its adoption. The right is triggered in relation to certain transactions which need, under the Act, the approval of shareholders by special resolution, or, in the case of variation of rights, the written agreement of 75% of the shareholders. The transactions concerned are:

* Approving a "major transaction";
* Variation of class rights;
* Altering the company's constitution so as to vary or dispense with the objects or stated business activities of the company;and
* Approving an arrangement or merger or both under the provisions of the Act.

A shareholder who has voted against these transactions, but in respect of which the approval has gone through, is entitled to request that the company should purchase his or her shares at a fair value. The fair value is to be settled either by agreement between the company and the shareholder, or by arbitration in accordance with the provisions of the Act. The courts are given power to grant an exemption from the obligation of the company to purchase shares where a purchase of the shares of a dissenting shareholder would impose a disproportionately damaging obligation on the company. Also,the courts may grant an exemption where the company cannot reasonably be required to finance the purchase or it would not be just and equitable to compel the company to purchase the shares concerned. The Act makes provision for the re-instatement of shares if, within one year from the date of passing of the special resolution complained of by the dissenting shareholder, the company has been unable to carry out the proposed objects or any of the business activities contemplated under the special resolution.

In justifying a similar reform in New Zealand, the Law Commission there stated that their recommended provision was:

> "[b]ased on the view that some dealings have such far-reaching effects that they should be referred to shareholders. Shareholders should not find that massive transactions have transformed the company they invested in without warning. Clearly, unless the constitution of a company restricts its activities,all shareholders will have to accept a large measure of change. Normally that may be achieved over some time, permitting the shareholder who does not like the direction of the company to leave or to exercise his rights to call management to account. What we are concerned with is abrupt and substantial change which transforms the nature of the enterprise."[223]

Another reform embodied in the Companies Act 2019 and which is linked to the buy-out remedy is the provision requiring shareholder approval of major transactions of the company. This is a further

---

223   Para 499 of the 1989 Report of the New Zealand Law Commission, *Company Law: Reform and Restatement*, Report No. 9

provision which increases shareholder protection from abuse by the management of the company. To increase the influence of shareholders, certain transactions, characterised as "major", will require a special resolution before a company can validly enter into them. These are transactions involving:

- The acquisition or an agreement to acquire assets worth more than 75% of the value of the company before the acquisition or the agreement to acquire;

- The disposition or an agreement to dispose of assets worth more than 75% of the value of the company before the disposition or the agreement to dispose;

- A deal that has or is likely to have the effect of the company acquiring rights or interests, or incurring obligations or liabilities whose worth is more than 75% of the value of the company.

The definition of a "major" transaction does not, however, include an agreement by the company to give a charge, secured over assets of the company, the value of which is more than 75% of the assets of the company for the purpose of securing the repayment or the performance of an obligation[224]. The major transaction provision does not apply also to the appointment of a receiver under a charge instrument covering the whole or a substantial part of the property of the company[225].

The effect of the major transactions provision is to remove from the board of directors the authority to enter into such major transactions without the authorisation of the majority of shareholders. It therefore strengthens shareholder democracy.

These reforms in the Act build on the protection of minority and individual member rights already provided for by Professor Gower in the Companies Act, 1963. Section 218 of that Act provided for a remedy against oppression and prejudicial unfairness. He framed the provision to give a remedy to members or debenture holders of the company, not only on the ground that the affairs of the

---

224   See s.145(3) of the Companies Act, 2019
225   See s.145(5),

company were being conducted, or the powers of the directors were being exercised, oppressively, but also on the wider ground that such conduct of affairs or exercise of power was in disregard of the proper interests of members, shareholders, officers or debenture holders of the company. He also provided a remedy in respect of acts or threatened acts of the company which unfairly discriminated against, or were otherwise unfairly prejudicial to, one or more members or debenture holders of the company.

The buy-out and major transaction provisions in the Companies Act 2019 can thus be legitimately viewed as an evolution of doctrine intended to give protection to the rights of individual shareholders against oppression and unfairness by either management or the majority of shareholders. Such further protection is called for in the light of the abolition of the *ultra vires* doctrine in the circumstances already described. Shareholders are thus subject to substantial and rapid change which may radically change the nature of the company in which they invested.

These two examples of provisions in the Companies Act 2019, discussed above, are intended to illustrate the evolution of business law in relation to company law. The Act also contains new provisions on beneficial ownership of shares, including the establishment of a central register of beneficial ownership to be setup and maintained by the Registrar of Companies.

It is noteworthy that a parallel reform has taken place in the law of corporate insolvency and restructuring, as well. Based on recommendations made to Government by the Ghana Association of Restructuring and Insolvency Advisors ("GARIA"), a Corporate Insolvency and Restructuring Act, 2020[226] has also been enacted by Parliament which has a wider intended coverage area by providing a statutory framework for the restructuring of distressed companies to assist them to remain as going concerns, in addition to re-enacting the provisions of the Bodies Corporate (Official Liquidations) Act, 1963. The Corporate Insolvency and Restructuring Act, 2020 has indeed introduced a regime for the rescue of distressed companies, for the first time in Ghanaian

---

226 Act 1015

law. It thus plugs a glaring hole in the business law of Ghana. A distressed company can now go into administration through the appointment of an administrator who is given the responsibility of convening a committee of creditors to consider a restructuring plan that he/she puts together. If the committee of creditors agrees to the restructuring plan at a watershed meeting, the distressed company enters into a restructuring agreement with the administrator, who then becomes a restructuring officer, to implement the restructuring agreement. The Act also repeals and re-enacts the provisions on official liquidation of insolvent companies contained in the Bodies Corporate (Official Liquidations) Act, 1963 (Act 180),[227] although the new Act now allows private insolvency practitioners, in addition to the Registrar of Companies, to be an official liquidator, in the liquidation of insolvent companies.

The Incorporated Private Partnership

The final example of the evolution highlighted in this Chapter is that of the incorporated private partnership which was recommended for introduction into Ghanaian law by Professor Gower.

At common law, business people are at liberty to agree to pool their resources and investment for a common business purpose in a partnership. A partnership is a business unit by which two or more persons agree to carry on business together and share its profits. The English Partnership Act 1890 contains a classic definition of a partnership, affirming that: "Partnership is the relation which subsists between persons carrying on a business in common with a view of profit.[228]" A demerit of the partnership at common law, however, is that it is unincorporated. The unincorporated nature of partnerships was identified by Professor Gower as a problem in the context of the desire of government to promote indigenous small and medium scale enterprises. He explained his view as follows[229]:

---

227 I am leading a team of experienced lawyers to write a practitioner's book on the Companies Act, 2019 and the Corporate Insolvency and Restructuring Act, 2020, which we hope to publish in 2021.

228 See s 1(1) of the Act.

229 See *The Final Report*, para 25 at 6.

"...I believe that most small African businesses are not yet ready for limited liability trading. What they need is a fundamentally different type of organisation analogous to the partnership, with unlimited liability and without any separation of ownership and control. This, and this alone, can provide the needed simplicity without sacrifice of essential safeguards. But, and this is where the English conception of partnership does not meet the need, the business itself must be personified (i.e. incorporated) so as to afford a better possibility of survival from one generation to another, and a clearer separation between business and private assets. This is vital if African businesses are to expand. In every country incorporation is an important factor in commercial development and it is especially important in a country like Ghana with a system of family ownership. Unless the business can be clearly distinguished from the family there is little chance of profits being ploughed back sufficiently to allow for expansion or of the business escaping from dispersal on the death of its founder."

This view of Professor Gower arguably remains relevant in today's Ghana. His recommendation for the incorporation of partnerships was accepted by Government and the Incorporated Private Partnership Act 1962[230] was enacted to implement it. The mystery is why, following the enactment of the Act, there has not been a higher take-up rate of incorporated private partnerships by small and medium-scale enterprises in Ghana. This is a question worthy of investigation. The registration of business names under the Registration of Business Names Act, 1962 outstrips the registration of incorporated private partnerships. This probably is reflective of the alleged prevalent psychology within the local business community which is inclined towards individual effort, rather than the pooling of resources. If true, this alleged mindset needs to be overcome, in order to make progress in Ghanaian private enterprise.

---

230   Act 152

The enactment of the Incorporated Private Partnership Act 1962 is a further illustration of the evolution of business law in Ghana. It was meant to attune the law of partnership to the needs of Ghanaian society and business. Limited liability, in the hands of enterprises that are undercapitalised and whose accounting practices do not measure up to the high standards demanded by companies legislation, can be a snare to third parties. The limited liability company is thus not suitable for every enterprise. The combination of unlimited liability with incorporation in the incorporated private partnership provides an opportunity for enabling the growth of small and medium enterprises ("SMEs"), which currently remains underutilised,unfortunately.

Concluding remarks

It is clear that the reforms in contract law and company law,carried out by Government in the early years of Ghana's independence, have laid a solid foundation for the development of business law in this country. Business law, of course, has to continue to evolve in response to changing circumstances. Government has to monitor the business environment and provide the right regulatory environment. This implies both proactive and reactive action by Government. Consequently, administrative law, criminal law and regulatory interventions by Government have played and will increasingly play a role in business law.

Let us take, for example, the protection of personal data, which is of increasing importance in business, worldwide. It is indubitable that the collection, processing and exchange of information, particularly in a digital form, have fed a considerable expansion of the global economy in the contemporary world. However, the swirling of data around the world which has been enriching various stakeholders and contributing to economic growth should not be at the expense of the privacy of individuals. A fair balance has to be struck between the needs of government and business and the human right of individuals to protect their privacy.

The Government of Ghana has recognised this need for balance and enacted a regulatory framework for the protection of personal data. The relevant legislation is the Data Protection Act 2012[231]. The Act establishes a Data Protection Commission which is charged with responsibility to achieve this balance. All stakeholders win if the privacy of personal data is adequately protected. Businesses that rely on personal data can count on the goodwill of trusting customers, if the customers are confident that the privacy of their personal data has been protected in compliance with the standards laid down in the Data Protection Act. Equally Government will have the trust of its citizens if they are assured that their privacy will be protected and their personal data accessed only in carefully defined exceptional cases, in the public interest, within the limits set expressly or impliedly in the Constitution and the Data Protection Act 2012.

Government has enacted comparable regulatory legislation, such as for the banks, insurance companies, the electronic communication industry, the nuclear power industry and the securities industry. Business law is thus evolving, responding to the needs of these various sectors of the economy. It needs to be emphasised that Government has to endeavour to remain ahead of the game, in this evolutionary process. A further illustration of Government's endeavour to be ahead of the game in responding to the evolutionary challenges of business law is legislation enacted to modernise the regulation of banking in Ghana.

The regulation of banking has been in the Ghana news in recent times and probably deserves a brief mention here because of its topicality. The contract and company law rights and duties which underlie the business of banking are subject to the statutory rules currently contained in the Banks and Specialised Deposit-Taking Institutions Act, 2016.[232] This is the latest of a series of banking statutes which have been enacted in Ghana since Independence. It is a substantial piece of legislation consisting of some 160 sections which provide extensively for the Bank of Ghana's regulatory

---

231   Act 843
232   Act 930

authority over all matters relating to the deposit-taking business. This is not the place to assess the adequacy of this regulatory statute, except to mention its innovatory provision[233] that persons aggrieved by a decision of the Bank of Ghana, in respect of certain matters, are obliged to resort to arbitration, rather than to normal litigation. (This provision is reflective of the growth and evolution of alternative dispute resolution in this jurisdiction.) The significant fact is that only a few years ago, Parliament, recognising the need to stay ahead of the game, enacted legislation to enable the Bank of Ghana to exercise supervisory and regulatory powers over banks to ensure the stability of the banking and financial systems. It is pursuant to this statute that the Bank of Ghana has been able to exercise powers to avert its perception of impending turbulence in the banking sector.

This Chapter has been a broad brush endeavour to paint a landscape of the evolution of some aspects of business law in Ghana. I hope that I have succeeded in showing that business law cannot be static, but is rather a dynamic enabling framework within which enterprises can thrive and produce the goods and services needed by society. Periodic legislative interventions will be needed from Government to make the law fit for purpose. Judges can also make their contribution interstitially to enable the law to serve its purpose. If Government takes its eye off the ball, it can result in aspects of business law impeding investment, production and trading to the detriment of society. In sum, Government must, and be seen to, be proactive in fashioning policies, statutes and administrative measures which both facilitate and regulate the doing of business in the country.

---

233   See s. 141 of the Act.

THE COMPETITION LAW SCENARIO IN WEST AFRICA[234]

Introduction

None of the West African States operates a planned socialist economy; indeed, they all have market-based economies. Like all market economies, the economies in West Africa need competition law and policy to ensure their proper functioning in the interest of consumers and producers. It is thus of legitimate public policy interest to ascertain the health of competition law and policy in West Africa, at both the national and sub-regional levels (including the interactions between the national and regional policy process on this issue). Is there a culture of encouraging competition in the sub-region? If not, what policy measures need to be taken to foster and sustain competition in the markets of the sub-region?

Evolution of competition law in West Africa

One of my last projects, before retiring in 2003 from the Commonwealth Secretariat in London to serve on the Ghanaian Supreme Court Bench, was to put together a team to formulate a competition law for The Gambia. Several years down the line, the project eventually resulted in the Gambia's enactment of competition legislation. Ghana, however, still has no comprehensive competition legislation, in spite of having had a few draft statutes formulated in the past which never caught the fancy of policy makers as a priority matter. However, various pieces of legislation have been passed in the country which have an impact on competition and competitive behaviour in key markets. Examples are the Public Utilities Regulatory Commission Act, 1997[235] and the Protection against

---

234 This Chapter is based on a paper I delivered at the Third Biennial Conference on Competition and Regulation, organised by CUTS (Consumer Unity and Trust Society) of India in Delhi in November 2013.

235 Act 538

Unfair Competition Act, 2000[236]. Nevertheless, the country is yet to establish any entity or authority to monitor competition generally in the economy and to take action to arrest malpractices affecting the competitive process. One may speculate that the political directorate is not yet convinced that it is necessary to police uncompetitive behaviour actively. During the last two decades of the last century, the Ghanaian Government was 'force fed' with market liberalization ideas under the structural adjustment programmes administered under the Washington Consensus. It may be that the idea of the need for markets to operate efficiently to maximize consumer welfare has not been fully internalised within all the recesses of the political consciousness of the Ghanaian political directorate.

It appears ironic that the political directorate has taken this inactive stance, with regard to enacting an appropriate competition statute, since, in principle, skeptics of markets are rather those who should more actively monitor and regulate them. This holds true for some of the other West African States. Nigeria, after several false starts regarding the introduction of a national competition statute, finally succeeded in enacting the Federal Competition and Consumer Protection Act, 2019.[237]

Some of the other countries in the sub-region, especially members of the West African Economic and Monetary Union (WAEMU), have had competition statutes for a long time. Examples of such countries are Burkina Faso, Mali, Senegal and Togo. However, their implementation has been far from satisfactory. One of the main reasons for this is the way in which the national competition legislation of the WAEMU member states is linked to the WAEMU regional competition regime. Fortunately, this anomaly has been identified and the process of addressing it is being explored.

Overall, the performance of West African countries on competition enforcement needs a 'shake-up'. Given the resource constraints under which some of the governments are compelled to operate,

---

236 Act 589

237 For more information on Nigeria's Federal Competition and Consumer Protection Act, 2019, see A. Abiodun, "Competition Law in Nigeria" https://www.legalnaija.com/2019/12/competition-law-in-nigeria-ayotunde.html."

the role of civil society and international development partners becomes key in moving this agenda forward.

The foregoing implies that it is "A Time for Action" in West Africa, as the title of a CUTS International study of competition law regimes of select West African Countries, published in 2010, suggests. That study was an output of the 7Up4 Project on 'Strengthening Constituencies for Effective Competition Regimes in Select West African Countries'.

The 7Up4 project was a two-year research, advocacy and capacity building project which was launched by CUTs International in June 2008 and embraced 7 countries: Burkina Faso, The Gambia, Ghana, Mali, Nigeria, Senegal and Togo. According to the study, at the macro-economic level, all the seven countries had adopted policies intended to promote competition, such as enhancing private sector participation and the withdrawal of the State from key productive activities. This context of policy is, however, to be distinguished from specific competition laws. With respect to the latter, the project found that:

> "The project countries are at different stages as far as operationalising their competition laws is concerned, with two countries having no law and one law at an early stage of being made operational, while other countries have laws, but face different challenges on implementation. However, the countries without active competition laws have taken steps to develop them."[238]

Apart from legislation at the national level, there is need for a binding competition regime at the West African sub-regional level. At this level, there is the complication of having two distinct bodies as players. There is ECOWAS (the Economic Community of West African States), the larger and more comprehensive West African grouping of 15 States. In addition, there is WAEMU (West African Economic and Monetary Union) whose French acronym is UEMOA. This is a smaller grouping of Francophone/Lusophone countries

---

238 See *A Time for Action – Analysis of Competition Law Regimes of Select West African Countries* Vol I (CUTS, 2010) 11

which are all also members of ECOWAS. WAEMU's members are: Benin, Burkina Faso, Cote d'Ivoire, Guinea-Bissau, Mali, Niger, Senegal and Togo. WAEMU adopted a common external tariff before ECOWAS's current endeavour to achieve this objective. Additionally, as far as a competition regime is concerned, WAEMU adopted Regulation no. 02/2002/CM/UEMOA of May 23, 2002. The Regulation covers cartel agreements, abuses of dominant power, State aids and anti- competitive practices resulting from State policy.

The WAEMU Commission has dealt with a number of cases relating to airport services, motorcycles, flour-mills and State aids. WAEMU's Competition Commission's decisions take precedence over the national law of its member States.

As already indicated, ECOWAS, established by a **Treaty of the Economic Community of West African States** of 1975, which was revised in 1993, is the larger regional grouping covering West Africa. It has also formulated competition regulations, namely:

- Supplementary Act A/SA.1/06/08 adopting community competition rules and the modalities of their application within ECOWAS; and

- Supplementary Act A/SA.2/06/08 on the establishment, function of the regional competition authority for ECOWAS.

The first Supplementary Act vests authority in an ECOWAS organ to deal fairly comprehensively with the range of acts which should be of concern to a competition commission. Article 4(1) of the first Supplementary Act provides that the Act applies to agreements, practices, mergers and distortions caused by member States which are likely to have an effect on trade within ECOWAS. Article 4(2), however, provides for a number of exceptions to this scope of application, including: labour-related issues; collective bargaining agreements and other trade practices and agreements approved by a regional competition organ of ECOWAS, where these trade practices are authorised under the Supplementary Acts. Article 6 prohibits abuses of dominant power by one or more enterprises. Article 7 prohibits mergers and acquisitions where the resulting market share in the ECOWAS Common Market or any significant part of it results in abuse of dominant market position, resulting in a substantial reduction of competition. However, the prohibited merger or acquisition may be authorized, if the transaction concerned is in the public interest.

Article 8 prohibits State Aid which distorts or threatens to distort competition. However, it provides for exceptions where such aid is of a social character or if it serves to promote economic development of regions, favours culture and is in the Community interest. Article 13 establishes a Regional Competition Authority with a mandate to collaborate with existing competition authorities.

The existence of two different competition agencies at the West African sub-regional level poses challenges which need to be addressed. The challenges have not yet come to a head since it would appear that, in spite of the law in the books, the ECOWAS Regional Competition Authority is not yet functional. Nevertheless, thought needs to go into rationalizing the interrelationship between ECOWAS and WAEMU in their competition mandates and reviewing the existing competition regime of WAEMU. It has been observed, for example, that the existing WAEMU regime is over-centralised and would benefit from decentralization, as raised earlier in this paper.

The way forward

The construction of competition law regimes at both the national and regional or sub-regional levels in West Africa is very much work in progress. There is a need for much more interactive communication and conversation amongst the stakeholders both at the national and sub-regional levels on this matter. This conversation should feed into the design and implementation of sub-regional and national competition regimes that operate efficiently and with synergy among them. Jurisdictional conflicts should be minimized. National competition authorities should have a significant role to play in keeping with the principle of subsidiarity.

Ideally, and ultimately, only one sub-regional competition agency should deal with those competition issues that are best dealt with on the sub-regional level. A co-ordinated competition regime at the sub-regional and national levels, which is fair and thoroughly thought-through, would contribute to economic development and consumer welfare in the sub-region. Finally, it should be stressed that whatever competition institutions are established should be well-resourced to enable them implement their mandate efficiently.

CHAPTER 19

THE CASE FOR AFRICAN STATES' ACCESSION TO, OR RATIFICATION OF, THE UNITED NATIONS CONVENTION ON CONTRACTS FOR THE INTERNATIONAL SALE OF GOODS (VIENNA, 1980).[239]

This Chapter makes the case for more widespread African adherence to the United Nations Convention on the International Sale of Goods, 1980 ("CISG") on the ground that it represents an effort through the United Nations system to make available harmonised rules on the international sale of goods which are intended to have an international and universal reach. The Chapter begins with an introduction which briefly examines the origins of CISG and proceeds to discuss the relevance of CISG to Africa. It ends with a recommendation to African States to accede to, or ratify, the Convention.

Introduction: the origins of the Convention on Contracts for the International Sale of Goods

One of the recitals of the CISG is:

> "THE STATES PARTIES TO THIS CONVENTION ... BEING OF THE OPINION that the adoption of uniform rules which govern contracts for the international sale of goods and taking into account the different social, economic and legal systems would contribute to the removal of legal barriers in international trade and promote the development of the international trade..."

Of course, the international body, that assisted the States Parties to the Convention in their endeavour to attain these objectives of the removal of barriers in international trade and the promotion

---

239 This Chapter is based on a paper delivered at the First African Conference on International Commercial Law, Douala, Cameroon, in January 2011.

of the development of international trade, was the United Nations Commission on International Trade Law, "UNCITRAL". UNCITRAL was established by a General Assembly resolution of 17 December 1966, as a result of an initiative by the Hungarian Government. The Permanent Representative of Hungary to the United Nations submitted a *note verbale*[240] requesting an inclusion in the agenda of the nineteenth session of the United Nations in 1965 the following item: "Consideration of steps to be taken for progressive development in the field of private international law with a particular view for promoting international trade." In an explanatory memorandum that accompanied this request, the Hungarian Permanent Representative argued that though the provisions in the Charter of the United Nations required the General Assembly to initiate studies and make recommendations for the purpose of encouraging the progressive development of international law and its codification and the General Assembly had attained great achievements in this respect of public international law, UN organs had not till then handled the progressive development of private international law. He continued:[241]

> "For the present purposes what is meant by "the development of private international law" is not so much an international agreement on the rules of the conflict of laws as applied by national courts and arbitral tribunals as rather an unification of private international law mainly in the field of international trade (e.g. unification of the law on the international sale of goods or on the formation of contracts). Recently the United Nations has undertaken special efforts towards the development of international trade, having regard particularly to the general interest of the community of nations in the advancement of the developing countries. A thorough study of the legal forms of international trade, their possible simplification, harmonization and unification, would be well suited for this purpose. Governments, learned societies and international organizations have thus far done commendable work in this field. This work, however, is done mostly on a

---

240   236 See *United Nations Commission on International Trade Law Year book. Volume I:1968-70* (United Nations, New York, 1971) 5

241   *Ibid.*

regional basis and practically without the participation of representatives of the greatly interested States of Africa and Asia."

The Hungarian Government thus urged that the proposed item be included on the agenda for the nineteenth session of the United Nations. The Hungarian Government succeeded in initiating UN work on the unification of substantive private international law. A General Assembly resolution was passed in December 1965[242] which requested the Secretary-General to submit a comprehensive report, surveying work in the field of unification and harmonisation of the law of international trade and considering which United Nations organs and other agencies might be given responsibility for work in this area. The eventual establishment of UNCITRAL is traceable back to this initiative of Hungary. What needs to be stressed is that, right from the outset, this initiative dwelt on the need to bring the representatives of Africa and Asia into the shaping of the law that was to be the outcome of this harmonisation and unification process.

The UN General Assembly resolution which established UNCITRAL in 1966[243] prescribed its object as: "the promotion of the progressive harmonization and unification of the law of international trade" in accordance with the provisions of the resolution. One of the recitals of the resolution makes reference to the need to secure broader participation in the process of harmonization and unification of the law of international trade. It was thus to UNCITRAL that fell the task of organising a broader participation in the processes that eventually led to adoption of CISG. UNCITRAL did not start from scratch. Work had been done on the unification of the law of international sale of goods prior to its establishment. However, this work could not boast of the broad participation that the UN General Assembly was insisting on in 1966.

Right from the outset, Africa played an important role in the new organisation. For example, Ghana had the privilege not only of being elected one of the initial members of UNCITRAL, but also

242 General Assembly Resolution 2102 (XX) of 20 December 1965 in *UnitedNationsCommission on International Trade Law Yearbook. Volume I*:1968-70 at 18.

243 General Assembly Resolution 2205(XXI) of 17 December 1966. Ibid.

its representative then, Ambassador Emmanuel Kodjoe Dadzie, was elected its first Chairman.[244] I also had the privilege of being elected Chairman of UNCITRAL in 1978 and presiding over the session of UNCITRAL at which the rules on formation of contracts of international sales were adopted.

UNCITRAL, at its very first session in 1968, adopted as one of its priority items of work: the international sale of goods. It formulated this item of work as follows:[245]

> "International sale of goods:
>
> a. In general;
>
> b. Promotion of wider acceptance of existing formulations for unification and harmonization of international trade law in this field including the promotion of uniform trade terms, general conditions of sale and standard contracts;
>
> c. Different legal aspects of contracts of sale like:
>   i.   Limitations;
>   ii.   Representation and full powers;
>   iii. Consequences of frustration;
>   iv.   *Force majeure* clauses in contracts."

To pursue this work item, UNCITRAL decided at its second session in 1969 to establish a Working Group, composed of Brazil, France, Ghana, Hungary, India, Iran, Japan, Kenya, Mexico, Norway, Tunisia, USSR, the United Kingdom and the United States of America. It will be observed that three African countries were members of the Group. The remit of the Group was to consider, *inter alia*, the comments and suggestions by States in order to ascertain which modifications of the existing texts on uniform rules governing international sale of goods might render them capable of wider acceptance by countries of different legal, social and economic systems. Alternatively, the Group was to consider whether it would be necessary to elaborate a new text for the same purpose.

---

244   Ibid. 73
245   Ibid. 77

The existing texts on uniform rules governing international sale of goods were, of course: the Uniform Law on the International Sale of Goods (Corporeal Movables) ("ULIS"); and the Uniform Law on the Formation of Contracts for the International Sale of Goods (Corporeal Movables) ("ULF"). Both uniform laws had been adopted at the Diplomatic Conference on the Unification of the Law Governing the International Sale of Goods, convened by the Government of the Netherlands at the Hague in April 1964. The uniform laws were based on drafts prepared by the International Institute for the Unification of Private Law (which is usually referred to as "UNIDROIT"). UNIDROIT was established in 1926 by a multilateral treaty within the orbit of the League of Nations. It has been reported that UNIDROIT's work on international sale of goods contracts was initiated as a result of a suggestion by Ernst Rabel to Vittorio Scialoja, President of UNIDROIT in 1928.[246] UNIDROIT has, since then, achieved outstanding work in the area of the unification of private law; however, it has never succeeded in truly reflecting the whole world in the manner that the United Nations system has. Africa has always been either grossly underrepresented or not represented in its councils.

This fact was manifested in the extent of the representation that the Government of the Netherlands was able to achieve in the Diplomatic Conference that it convened in April 1964. Twenty-seven States signed the Final Act of that Conference. Of these, twenty-two were European; three Latin-American and two Asian. None was African. From these facts, one can understand why UNCITRAL resolved to ascertain what modifications of the texts adopted at the Hague might render them capable of wider acceptance by different countries with different heritages. At the deliberations at the Second Session of UNCITRAL in 1969 on the unification of the rules on international sale of goods, many representatives expressed the view that UNCITRAL's decision to consider ULIS and ULF did not imply that the Commission should limit itself to giving an opinion merely on whether their texts were satisfactory or not. They considered that though UNCITRAL should take full account

---

246 See P. Schlectriem, *Commentary on the UN Convention on the International Sale of Goods* (Oxford University Press, 1988) 1. (The latest edition is the Fourth Edition by Schlechtriem & Schwenzer)

of what ULIS and ULF had achieved, UNCITRAL should regard itself as being at liberty to chart a new course if the Hague texts were found to be unacceptable to a substantial number of States.[247] In sum, two schools of thought emerged at UNCITRAL with regard to the Hague texts: one view was that the texts were suitable and practicable instruments and a significant contribution towards the unification of law. Accordingly, there was no need to revise them before being put to the test in practice. The second view was that the Hague texts did not correspond to contemporary needs and realities and that it was therefore necessary to review them before they could be more widely applied. Protagonists of this view pointed out that the 1964 Hague Conference had been attended by only twenty-eight States and that none of them was a developing country.[248] It was in consequence of the interplay of these two schools of thought that UNCITRAL decided to establish its Working Group on the international sale of goods ("The Working Group on Sales").

CISG is largely the result of the meticulous work done by this UNCITRAL Working Group on Sales. One of the first issues tackled by the Working Group was on the sphere of application of the proposed uniform law. The issue was whether the UNCITRAL draft should follow the approach of article 2 of ULIS which directed the tribunals of contracting States to apply the Law to international sales without regard to the relationship between the sales transaction in question and a contracting State. This approach may be referred to as the universalist approach by which the uniform law is applied without the need to establish any relationship between the transaction and the *forum* state of the litigation, where it is a contracting state. The Working Group did not accept this approach, but modified it to combine the system of applying the law only when the places of business of both parties are in the territories of contracting States with the system under which the law is applied when the rules of private international law point to the application of the law of a contracting state. This combined system is what was eventually embodied in CISG. Thus CISGis applied to only

---

247 See *United Nations Commission on International Trade Law Yearbook. Volume I:1968-70* (op. cit) 97.

248 *Ibid.* 98.

sales transactions where there is a real connection between the transaction and a contracting State. CISG eventually came into force on 1st January 1988.

The relevance of CISG to Africa

The fact that a real connection between an international sale of goods transaction and a contracting State needs to be established before the CISG is applicable provides the first reason why African States need to ratify or accede to the CISG. If African traders and commercial lawyers are to get the benefit of the uniform rules of CISG, then African States will need to become contracting States. A further advantage of CISG, which should be of interest to African States, is that it minimises resort to the perplexing rules of private international law. Where the places of business of both parties are in the territories of contracting states, then private international rules are bypassed and the uniform rules of CISG are applied automatically.

Secondly, the concepts embodied in the CISG make for flexibility of the contractual system that is set out in it. This flexibility should commend it to African cross-border traders, African lawyers and African States. Moreover, CISG enables access by African cross-border traders to a system of modern harmonised rules. Through the practice of an increasing number of states and the scholarly as well as practical professional attention of an equally expanding pool of lawyers of many nationalities, this system of rules has now become, in effect, part of a *lex mercatoria*. Africa cannot afford to be isolated from this universal movement.

The flexibility of the contractual system embodied in CISG will be illustrated in this paper by presenting an overview of its system of remedies. Under the CISG, if a seller fails to perform any of his obligations under the contract of sale or under the convention, the buyer may:

1. Require performance by the seller of his obligations unless the buyer has resorted to a remedy which is inconsistent with this requirement (article 46(1));

2. Require, in appropriate circumstances, delivery of substitute goods, provided that the goods' lack of conformity with the contract constitutes a fundamental breach of contract and the buyer makes the request for substitute goods in conjunction with the notice that the convention requires to be given by a buyer who discovers a lack of conformity in the goods or the request is made within a reasonable time after such notice (article 46 (2));

3. Require the seller to repair any lack of conformity of the goods, unless this is unreasonable, having regard to all the circumstances (article 46 (3));

4. Give a *Nachfrist* notice, or, in other words, fix an additional period of time of reasonable length for the seller to perform his obligations (article 47);

5. Declare the contract avoided, if the seller's failure to perform his/her obligations under the contract or convention amounts to a fundamental breach or the seller fails to deliver the goods within an additional period of time fixed by the buyer in a *Nachfrist* notice;

6. Reduce the price "in the same proportion as the value that the goods actually delivered had at the time of delivery bears to the value that conforming goods would have had at that time";

7. Finally,claim damages in accordance with the provisions of the convention.

Conversely, if a buyer fails to perform his obligations under the contract or convention, the seller may:

1. As appropriate, require the buyer to pay the price, take delivery or perform his other obligations, unless the seller has resorted to a remedy which is inconsistent with such requirement (article 62);

2. Give a *Nachfrist* notice fixing an additional period of time of reasonable length for the performance by the buyer of his obligations (article 63);

3. Declare the contract avoided if the buyer's breach amounts to a fundamental breach or the buyer fails or refuses to perform during the *Nachfrist* period.

A prominent feature of this remedies regime is the primacy it accords to specific relief, in contrast with the common law approach of ordinarily only giving, to the party whose contract of sale has been breached, damages or damages combined with the right to repudiate. Under CISG, the innocent party can insist on performance by the party in breach. In other words, specific performance is more widely available under the convention than under the common law. This is a manifestation of the influence of civil law doctrines which take the maxim *pacta sunt servanda* more seriously than the common law. The common law is content to grant substitutional relief. In other words, the value of the promised performance is given to the innocent party in money (i.e. damages). In recognition of this common law approach and by way of a compromise, Article 28 of CISG was included in the convention. It provides as follows:

> "If, in accordance with the provisions of this Convention, one party is entitled to require performance of any obligation by the other party, a court is not bound to enter a judgment for specific performance unless the court would do so under its own law in respect of similar contracts of sale not governed by this Convention."

In other words, if the forum of the dispute is a common law court, it will not have to grant specific performance of a contract of sale, where under its national rules such specific relief would not be available. Article 28 is illustrative of the many compromises between civilian and common law approaches in the CISG. This is a feature of the convention which should commend it to African States composed, as they are, of both common law and civilian jurisdictions.

Another illustration of the features of CISG which should make it attractive to African States is the freshness of some of its approaches, at least from the standpoint of a common lawyer. Its Article 50 provides as follows:

> "If the goods do not conform with the contract and whether or not the price has already been paid, the buyer may reduce the price in the same proportion as the value that the goods actually delivered had at the time of delivery bears to the value

that conforming goods would have had at that time. However, if the seller remedies any failure to perform his obligations in accordance with article 37 or article 48 or if the buyer refuses to accept performance by the seller in accordance with those articles, the buyer may not reduce the price."

This article lays down a non-judicial remedy distinct from the remedy of damages, which is separately provided for. The buyer may resort to it unilaterally, without a prior judicial adjudication, but if the seller considers that it has been invoked wrongfully, he may go to court to challenge the price reduction or the quantum of it. The non-judicial character of the remedy of reduction of price is the main difference between it and the remedy of damages. A buyer may only claim damages and, unless and until a court or arbitral tribunal has accepted this claim, the damages remain unliquidated. However, a claim to reduce the price is liquidated by the buyer's unilateral quantification of it, subject always to any challenge in the courts. This is a quick and handy remedy in the hands of a buyer in an international sales transaction and provides further evidence of the flexibility of the contractual regime embodied in the CISG.

The final illustration that this paper will offer on the flexibility of the remedies regime contained in CISG is the idea of the *Nachfrist* notice. From a common law standpoint, the introduction of articles 47 and 63, derived from the German law notion of *Nachfrist,* is a refreshing innovation that places a flexible remedy in the hands of a party to an international sale of goods transaction. *Nachfrist* is a German law idea according to which if a party is in breach, the innocent party may set him an additional period of time within which he should perform his obligations. If at the end of this additional period of time, the party in breach has still not performed, then the innocent party can terminate the contract by avoidance. In CISG, the *Nachfrist* idea is adopted in relation to delivery by the seller and also the buyer's obligation to pay the price and take delivery.

If the seller fails to deliver on time, this will not necessarily constitute a fundamental breach, within the meaning of CISG. He will thus not be entitled to avoid the contract without more. He can only avoid the contract if the non-delivery has caused him detriment substantially depriving him of his expectation under the contract and if this substantial detriment was foreseeable. Where a buyer is uncertain whether the non-delivery has caused him such substantial foreseeable detriment, he can resort to article 47 to "fix an additional period of time of reasonable length for performance by the seller of his obligations." The consequence of fixing such additional period for performance is that the buyer acquires the right, pursuant to article 49 (1)(b) to declare the contract avoided, "if the seller does not deliver the goods within the additional period of time fixed by the buyer in accordance with paragraph (1) of article 47 or declares that he will not deliver within the period so fixed."

Similarly, the seller may, pursuant to Article 63, "fix an additional period of time of reasonable length for performance by the buyer of his obligations." The seller may then declare the contract avoided, pursuant to Article 64(1)(b) "if the buyer does not, within the additional period of time fixed by the seller in accordance with paragraph (1) of article 63, perform his obligation to pay the price or take delivery of the goods or if he declares that he will not do so within the period so fixed."

Recommendation to African States regarding the CISG.

Africa needs to increase its intra-African as well as extra-African trade as part of its development strategy. Discerning African politicians have been stressing that what Africa needs is trade and not aid. As some particular African trade economists have observed:

> "Most African countries and their citizens now fully appreciate and recognise the need for integrating into the global economy and the multilateral trading system especially through effective involvement in WTO Agreements and negotiations."[249]

---

249 See Onguglo, Murigande and Mburu, *Preparing African Countries to Benefit from Continuous International Trade Negotiations and Complex Agreements*. 3. www.uneca.org/aec/documents

They go on to assert that:

> "The demand for trade negotiations support by African countries also arises from the growing importance of international trade as an engine of growth and development, accounting for an important and, in some countries, increasing share of their domestic wealth creation. In 2004 for example, the share of exports of goods and services in gross domestic product (GDP) was about 28% for the world as a whole, 23% for developed countries, and 43% for developing countries. This ratio was 36% in the case of African countries in 2004 as compared to 26% in 1995."[250]

An important factor in any successful African trade expansion would be the establishment and maintenance of an appropriate legal framework. CISG is an available element in this appropriate legal framework. It is in this context, that I would like to make a strong recommendation to the African Governments which have not yet ratified or acceded to the CISG, to do so. The CISG is a legal framework that was made universally acceptable through the instrumentality of UNCITRAL. African States have from the outset played an active role in UNCITRAL and therefore its products deserve legitimacy in the councils of Africa. There is indubitably a nexus between development and meaningful reform of the legal framework for international trade[251]. African States would thus be well advised to consider the products of UNCITRAL.

Conclusion

This Chapter has traced the origins of CISG in ULIS and ULF, whose texts were deliberately transformed in the councils of UNCITRAL, from their original Eurocentric focus to make the resulting product more universally acceptable. This universal ambition and aspiration of the framers of CISG and the participation of representatives of African and other developing countries in the transformation

---

250 *Ibid.* At 6.

251 Cf.L. Castellani, "International Trade Law Reform in Africa" in (2008)10 *Yearbook of Private International Law*. 547 at 548.

process are a strong argument in favour of its adoption by African States. Another reason for African States to join the harmonisation movement represented by CISG is the sheer kinetic energy that has been generated in the past couple of decades towards universality in cross-border sale of goods law, manifested in the ratification and accession process of the CISG.

The current parties to CISG include the following States whose significance in world and African trade is indubitable[252]: Argentina, Australia, Austria, Belarus, Belgium, Canada, Chile, Cuba, Czech Republic, Denmark, Finland, France, Germany, Greece, Hungary, Israel, Italy, Japan, Lebanon, Mexico, Netherlands, New Zealand, Norway, Poland, Republic of Korea, Russian Federation, Serbia, Singapore, Spain, Sweden, Switzerland, Turkey, Ukraine and the United States of America. The African States which have so far ratified or acceded to the Convention are (as of October 2020): Benin,Burundi,Cameroon,Congo,Egypt,Gabon,Guinea,Lesotho, Liberia, Madagascar, Uganda and Zambia. Ghana has signed the Convention, but has not yet ratified it. In all there are, as of October 2020, 94 parties to the Convention.[253]

---

252 See Status. *United Nations Convention on Contracts for the International Sale of Goods (Vienna, 1980)* at www.uncitral.org/uncitral/en/uncitral_texts/sale_goods/1980CISG_status. html.

253 The number of parties as of the date of delivery of this paper in January 2011 was 76..

CHAPTER 20

OBSERVATIONS ON ARBITRATION[254]

Introduction

Arbitration is of increasing importance to lawyers practising in Ghana. This Chapter has accordingly been included in this compendium in the expectation that practising lawyers will pay heed to the messages contained in it. The Chapter is in two parts: Part A deals with arbitral clauses, whilst Part B deals with the current Ghanaian law on the enforcement and recognition of arbitral awards under the Convention on the Recognition and Enforcement of Foreign Arbitral Awards, commonly known as the New York Convention.

A. Drawing up of arbitration clauses

Why opt for an arbitration clause?

Arbitration clauses are useful devices in relation to certain categories of transactions. For instance, transnational transactions often raise issues of trust in relation to the courts of the host state. The foreign investor or foreign party to a transnational transaction may be diffident about confiding its disputes to the courts of the host state for their resolution, fearing bias against foreigners. On the other hand, the host state, local or Ghanaian parties to transnational transactions may equally be diffident about agreeing to settle their disputes in foreign courts.

In an earlier career as an adviser, at the Commonwealth Secretariat, to many developing member states of the Commonwealth in their investment transactions with transnational corporations, our

---

254 This Chapter is based on two papers delivered by the author at a workshop on International Commercial Arbitration,organised by the Ghana Arbitration Centre in Accra, October 2015; and at a Webinar presentation to the Ghana Judiciary in June 2020, respectively.

team always incorporated an arbitration clause in the agreements embodying these transactions, to resolve this issue of trust. Inserting an arbitration clause gives greater assurance to parties to such transactions that their disputes will be resolved fairly and by adjudicators who are sufficiently knowledgeable about the issues in contention.

The historic compromise our team struck in all the agreements we advised on was to insert a clause for international arbitration, while insisting on a choice of law clause which applied the law of the host state to the transaction. This compromise met with the agreement of the parties in all the transactions we advised on. More recently, however, a phenomenon has emerged which may require a re-consideration of this historic compromise. Arbitrators under international arbitration clauses, in adjudicating disputes between parties, have sometimes purported to apply interpretations of the law of the host state different from what the courts of the host state have put on it. This is problematic and is an issue that will be discussed later.

Arbitration clauses can also be useful even in relation to purely domestic or national transactions. The attractive feature of an arbitral award is that usually there is no appeal from it. In other words, the parties reach finality quicker than in litigation before the courts. Secondly, most arbitration clauses give the parties a say in who the adjudicators are and provide for more confidentiality, where sensitive information of commercial import is involved in a dispute. The parties' participation in the selection of the arbitrators gives them confidence that the outcome will be fair. It also enables them to choose adjudicators with the appropriate experience in commercial or investment matters to resolve their disputes efficiently.

Proactivity in the drawing up of the arbitration clause

Arbitration clauses should be drawn up before any dispute between the parties have arisen. Ideally, they should be embodied in the parties' substantive agreement. The clause should be customised to fit the circumstances of the particular parties. In drawing up the clause, the parties 'lawyers should endeavour to design an efficient, expeditious and cost-effective mode of resolving all possible disputes that might arise in relation to the parties' transaction. Above all, the lawyers must ensure that the clause is enforceable. Drawing up an unenforceable arbitration clause is unpardonable. This is where knowledge of the New York Convention comes in handy.

The New York Convention

For an arbitral award to be enforceable under the New York Convention, it must be in writing. Secondly, it must cover disputes that are arbitrable. The public policy of particular States determines what disputes are non-arbitrable. The parties to an arbitration clause must also have the capacity to agree to arbitration. If under the governing or proper law of a contract, a party lacks capacity, a clause agreed by it will not be enforceable.

Article 2(1) of the Convention provides that:

> "Each Contracting State shall recognize an agreement in writing under which the parties undertake to submit to arbitration all or any differences which have arisen or which may arise between them in respect of a defined legal relationship, whether contractual or not, concerning a subject matter capable of settlement by arbitration."

Article 2 further provides that:

> "2. The term "agreement in writing" shall include an arbitral clause in a contract or an arbitration agreement,signed by the parties or contained in an exchange of letters or telegrams.
>
> 3. The court of a Contracting State, when seized of an action in a matter in respect of which the parties have made an agreement within the meaning of this article, shall, at the request of one of the parties, refer the parties to arbitration, unless it finds that the said agreement is null and void, inoperative or incapable of being performed."

Institutional or ad hoc arbitration

Parties are at liberty to choose between institutional and *ad hoc* arbitration. Institutional or administered arbitration refers to arbitration which is conducted under the auspices of an arbitration body such as the International Chamber of Commerce or the Ghana Arbitration Centre. Arbitration institutions provide certain support services for arbitrators, such as appointing arbitrators, if a party defaults in making an appointment, setting up the hearings and making payments to the arbitrators.

However, the actual arbitration remains in the charge of the arbitrators. They still determine the merits of the case. Where the parties do not have experience of international commercial arbitration, it is preferable for them to choose institutional arbitration to enable the institution to backstop the arbitration process. If a good arbitration institution is chosen, it can bring its experience and knowledge to bear on the procedural aspects of the arbitration process and manage the process well.

In *ad hoc* or non-administered arbitration, the onus of running the arbitral proceedings is borne by the parties themselves, without the intervention of any arbitral institution. After the arbitrators have been chosen by the parties, the burden of running the proceedings devolves on to them, of course, at the cost of the parties.

Place of arbitration

Parties should choose a place of arbitration in their arbitration clause. It is prudent to choose a New York Convention State to ensure enforceability of the arbitration commitment as a matter of treaty law.

The place of arbitration should also be a State whose courts are not known to obstruct international arbitration. It should be remembered that the law of the place of arbitration will govern the procedural law of the arbitration.

Arbitration rules

Whether the parties choose institutional or *ad hoc* arbitration, it is prudent to choose a set of arbitration rules and adopt the model clause recommended for those rules. If parties do not choose existing arbitration rules, they will need to draw up their own detailed rules to provide the procedural framework for the arbitration proceedings. This may not be a wise move, unless the parties have access to specialised advice. The statutory law of the forum state of the arbitration may provide some default provisions, if the parties fail to set out their own rules.

Scope of the clause

The clause should be drafted to cover as wide a spectrum of disputes as possible to avoid arguments later as to whether a given dispute falls within the scope of the clause or not. Thus the clause should cover not only disputes "arising out of the contract", but also disputes "relating to" or "in connection with" the contract.

Finally, choice of law clause

Apart from the arbitration clause itself, the parties are well advised to insert a choice of law clause in their contract, if it is an international one. A choice of law clause selects the substantive law to be applied to the contract. If the contract is to be performed in Ghana, it is best to choose the law of Ghana.

I spoke earlier of the historic compromise whereby an international arbitration clause is combined with a choice of the host state's law. This compromise threatens to be undermined by the conduct of international arbitrators in refusing sometimes to accept the interpretation of the host state's law by its national courts. This is an issue of sovereignty. The law of the host state is what its courts declare it to be and not what arbitrators think it is. To remedy this emerging trend, there may be need to strengthen the choice of law and arbitration clauses by language which requires the arbitrators to accept the interpretation of the law by the courts of the legal system chosen as the proper law of the contract in question.

B. Current Ghanaian law on enforcement and recognition of arbitral awards, especially in relation to the New York Convention[255]

The current law

The legal framework for the enforcement of arbitral awards in Ghana is set out in the Alternative Dispute Resolution Act 2010 (Act 798), which is based on the 1985 UNCITRAL Model Law on International Arbitration, as amended in 2006. The Memorandum to the Act's Bill stated that its object was to: "bring the law governing arbitration into harmony with international conventions, rules and practices in arbitration, provide the legal and institutional framework that will facilitate and encourage the settlement of disputes through alternative dispute resolution procedures;..."

However, the Act did not adopt all the provisions of the Model Law. It modified some of them and introduced some homegrown ones as well, particularly on customary arbitration. The Act covers both domestic and international arbitration as well as other methods of ADR. It expressly excludes, from its ambit, matters relating to the national or public interest, the environment, and the enforcement and interpretation of the Ghanaian Constitution.

It gives the High Court extensive powers in relation to arbitrations. By s40, unless otherwise agreed by the parties, the High Court may, on application on notice to the other party by a party to arbitration proceedings, determine any question of law that arises in the course of the proceedings, if the Court is satisfied that the question substantially affects the rights of the other party.

Foreign arbitral awards are enforced under the Alternative Dispute Resolution Act 2010 (Act 798) by leave of the High Court or by a common law action (i.e. by writ, see e.g. *Grinaker –LTA Ltd. V Stype Investment Ltd.*).[256] Under s57 of Act 798, no distinction is made

---

255 This is a reduction into writing of a Webinar presentation made by the author to the Judiciary of Ghana in June 2020, under the auspices of the International Council for Commercial Arbitration, the Judicial Training Institute of Ghana and the International Chamber of Commerce, Africa Commission.

256 Unreported decision of the High Court, Accra, dated 30th November 2006, Suit No.34/2006)

between domestic and foreign awards. They are both enforced, by leave of the High Court, "in the same manner as a judgment or order of the Court to the same effect." Leave will be refused "where, or to the extent, that a person against whom the award is sought to be enforced shows that the arbitrator lacked substantive jurisdiction to make the award."

Thus, both under statute and at common law, foreign and international arbitral awards are enforceable in Ghana. There has, however, been no legislation implementing the International Convention on the Settlement of Investment Disputes, unlike the New York Convention. Accordingly, ICSID awards have to depend on the general provisions of the Alternative Dispute Resolution Act 2010.

The main practical issue arising is the procedure for securing such enforcement and the attitude of the Ghanaian judiciary to such enforcement. The principal relevant provision of the Alternative Dispute Resolution Act is s59 (1) which provides as follows:

"59. Enforcement of foreign awards (1) The High Court shall enforce a foreign arbitral award if it is satisfied that

a. the award was made by a competent authority under the laws of the country in which the award was made;

b. a reciprocal arrangement exists between the Republic of Ghana and the country in which the award was made; or

c. the award was made under the international Convention specified in the First Schedule to this Act or under any other international convention on arbitration ratified by Parliament; and

d. the party that seeks to enforce the award has produced

    i.   the original award or has produced a copy of the award authenticated in the manner prescribed by the law of the country in which it was made;

    ii. the agreement pursuant to which the award was made or a copy of it duly authenticated in the manner prescribed..."

S 59(1) of Act 798 (set out above) thus deals with the enforcement of foreign awards. Subsection (3) sets out defences. It provides as follows:

> "Despite subsection (1) the court shall not enforce a foreign award if
>
> a. The award has been annulled in the country in which it was made;
>
> b. The party against whom the award is invoked was not given sufficient notice to enable the party present the party's case;
>
> c. A party, lacking legal capacity, was not properly represented;
>
> d. The award does not deal with the issues submitted to arbitration; or
>
> e. The award contains a decision beyond the scope of the matters submitted for arbitration."

There are significant differences between these defences and those available under Article V of the New York Convention. Responding to these differences, Prof. Richard Oppong has suggested that in cases coming within the New York Convention, Article V rather than s 59(3) should apply.

He argues:

> "The ADR Act does not contain a provision dealing with conflicts between the provisions of the Act and international instruments such as the NYC. However, it is submitted that applying the maxim *lex specialis derogat legi generali,* which is recognised as a principle of interpretation in Ghanaian law,in cases falling within the scope of the NYC, Article V shall be the governing law of the defences that are available…"[257]

---

257 See Richard Oppong: *The Government of Ghana and International Arbitration* (Wildy, Simmonds & Hill Publishing, 2017).114

Article V is set out below:

"1. Recognition and enforcement of the award may be refused, at the request of the party against whom it is invoked, only if that party furnishes to the competent authority where the recognition and enforcement is sought, proof that:

a. The parties to the agreement referred to in Article II were, under the law applicable to them, under some incapacity,or the said agreement is not valid under the law to which the parties have subjected it or, failing any indication thereon, under the law of the country where the award was made; or

b. The party against whom the award is invoked was not given proper notice of the appointment of the arbitrator or of the arbitration proceedings or was otherwise unable to present his case; or

c. The award deals with a difference not contemplated by or not falling within the terms of the submission to arbitration, or it contains decisions on matters beyond the scope of the submission to arbitration, provided that, if the decisions on matters submitted to arbitration can be separated from those not so submitted, that part of the award which contains decisions on matters submitted to arbitration may be recognised and enforced; or

d. The composition of the arbitral authority or the arbitral procedure was not in accordance with the agreement of the parties, or, failing such agreement, was not in accordance with the law of the country where the arbitration took place; or (e) The award has not yet become binding on the parties, or has been set aside or suspended by a competent authority of the country in which, or under the law of which, that award was made.

2. Recognition and enforcement of an arbitral award may also be refused if the competent authority in the country where recognition and enforcement is sought finds that:

    (a) The subject matter of the difference is not capable of settlement by arbitration under the law of that country; or

    (b) The recognition or enforcement of the award would be contrary to the public policy of that country."

Get Technologies Ltd v Bankswitch Ghana Ltd,[258] illustrates a successful application for leave to enforce an award. It was granted quickly under the Alternative Dispute Resolution Act. (The Application was not opposed). The application was filed on 12th July 2017 and leave to enforce granted on 28 July 2017.

In contrast, in *Get Group Fze v Bankswitch Ghana Ltd,*[259] the application for leave, which was opposed, took well over a year to dispose of. (Proceedings to annul the award in the country of the seat of the arbitration did not help). In the course of her ruling, the High Court judge said: "In principle when a court is called upon to enforce an arbitral award, the court is not required to undertake a re-assessment of the facts in order to make a determination. That function is typically outside the scope of the court's enforcement duties."

General message to judges: expedition should be the name of the game

The action of judges on enforcement applications can contribute to the strengthening of judicial comity with arbitral tribunals and foreign courts if they deal with them expeditiously. A desirable approach is facilitation within the limits of the law. It should be emphasised that an award covered by the New York Convention is presumed to be binding and the burden is on the respondent in an

---

258 Unreported ruling of the High Court, dated 28th July 2017(Suit No .GJ/1041/17)

259 Unreported ruling of the High Court dated 6th July 2017 (Suit No.GJ242/2016)

application for leave to enforce to persuade the Court not to grant leave.[260]

Hardly any caselaw on the New York Convention itself in Ghana.

The main relevant case on the New York Convention is: *The Republic v High Court (Commercial Division) Accra; Ex parte Attorney-General (Zenith Bank, Interested Party).*[261] An issue arose in this case as to whether the High Court could validly grant a Garnishee Order Nisi in respect of an international arbitral award which had not been recognized and confirmed by a court in Ghana.

The facts of the case were as follows: in an earlier case of *Attorney-General v Balkan Energy Ghana Ltd & Ors*[262], the Supreme Court had held that a power purchase agreement ("PPA") entered into between the Government of Ghana and Balkan Energy (Ghana) Ltd was unconstitutional and unenforceable because it had not been laid before Parliament and approved by Parliament, as required by Article 181(5) of the 1992 Constitution. Balkan Energy Ghana Ltd. had, on 23rd December 2010, initiated arbitration proceedings against the Government of Ghana under the auspices of the Permanent Court of Arbitration at the Hague. At these proceedings, the Ghana Government raised the point that the PPA needed Parliamentary approval under article 181(5) of the 1992 Constitution. However, this approval had not been sought and therefore the PPA was invalid,as having been executed in breach of a constitutional provision.

The Government of Ghana argued before the arbitration tribunal that non-compliance with the constitutional provision made the PPA invalid, including its arbitration clause, and consequently the arbitral tribunal had no jurisdiction over the dispute before it.

The Arbitral Tribunal, however, held that it had jurisdiction. However, the Tribunal expressed a willingness to take account of

---

260   See Redfern and Hunter, *International Arbitration*, (Oxford University Press, Oxford, 6th Ed. 2015) 622-3.

261   Unreported Supreme Court ruling dated 10th April, 2019

262   [2012] 2 SCGLR 998

the Supreme Court's interpretation of the constitutional provision in question, when it was delivered.

The Attorney-General had, in June 2010, issued a Writ of Summons in the Commercial Division of the High Court, Accra, claiming a declaration that the PPA is an international business transaction that needed Parliamentary approval and was unenforceable because it did not have such approval. The Plaintiff also claimed that the arbitration agreement contained in the PPA was an international business transaction and was also in breach of article 181(5) and therefore unenforceable.

After the institution of the suit, the Plaintiff (the Attorney-General) applied to the High Court to refer to the Supreme Court for interpretation the following two questions:

> "Whether or not the Power Purchase Agreement dated 27th July 2007 between the Government of Ghana and Balkan Energy (Ghana) Limited constitutes an international business transaction within the meaning of Article 181(5) of the Constitution.
>
> Whether or not the arbitration provisions contained in clause 22.2 of the Power Purchase Agreement dated 27th July 2007 between the Government of Ghana and Balkan Energy(Ghana) Limited constitutes an international business transaction within the meaning of Article 181(5) of the Constitution."

The High Court refused to refer the questions. Accordingly, the Attorney-General applied to the Supreme Court to exercise its supervisory jurisdiction over the High Court to quash its decision not to refer. In its Ruling of 2nd November, 2011, the Supreme Court did indeed quash the decision of the learned High Court judge and referred the two questions set out above to itself. The Supreme Court then proceeded to hold the PPA to be unconstitutional and unenforceable. This view of the law was however not accepted by the arbitral tribunal. These facts from these earlier proceedings are vital to an appreciation of the dispute in *The Republic v High Court*

(Commercial Division) Accra; Ex parte Attorney-General (Zenith Bank, Interested Party).[263]

In the event, the majority of the Supreme Court held that the action brought by the Attorney-General failed on a procedural issue. The Supreme Court held that *certiorari* did not lie because the High Court acted within jurisdiction in granting the Order Nisi. It was open to the Attorney-General to show to the High Court that the alleged debt of the Government of Ghana had not yet accrued. However, two Supreme Court Justices dissented, contending that as of the date of the institution of the garnishee proceedings, there was no debt recognisable within the jurisdiction of Ghana, since it emanated from an arbitral award which had not been registered or enforced in Ghana.

They relied on s59 of the Alternative Dispute Resolution Act, 2010[264] which in their view:

> "enjoins specific steps to be taken to register an arbitral award in the High Court of Ghana, before an arbitral award may be recognised or enforced in Ghana. This is in accordance with the provisions of the New York Convention, specifically incorporated into Ghana's domestic law by Act 798. To the extent that there had not been any enforcement proceedings regarding the arbitral award on the strength of which Zenith Bank instituted the garnishee proceedings, there was no debt enforceable in Ghana."

Although this statement of the law is not contained in the majority opinions and therefore not necessarily a binding statement of the law, it raises an issue of importance in relation to the New York Convention, worthy of discussion. As only the dissenting Justices based their opinion on this provision, there is not yet a binding Supreme Court interpretation of it. Moreover, the dissenting Justices found that, at the time of the initiation of the Garnishee proceedings, the Government of Ghana had already, in any case, paid the arbitration award to the awardee.

---

263   Unreported Supreme Court ruling dated 10th April, 2019
264   Act 798

In fact, the Interested Party in the *certiorari* action contended as follows: by Article III of the New York Convention, an arbitral award can be enforced in any of the contracting states. Accordingly, the recipient of the award did not need to come to Ghana to either confirm the award or enforce it. Since the recipient had filed applications in South Africa and the US to confirm and enforce the award and had attached the assets of the Government of Ghana in South Africa and France, this was sufficient evidence of a debt due to the recipient of the award from the Government of Ghana to justify the interested party applying for a Garnishee Order against the Government of Ghana.

An issue that arises from the narration above is thus: can an arbitral award confirmed in a foreign jurisdiction be regarded as a source of obligation under Ghanaian law, without compliance with section 59 of the Alternative Dispute Resolution Act 2010? This is an issue that is yet to be determined by the Supreme Court. However, it is submitted that the right position should be that foreign arbitral awards which have not yet complied with section 59 of the Alternative Dispute Resolution Act 2010 should not be recognised as a source of obligation in the Ghanaian jurisdiction. Failure to adhere to this position would encourage circumvention of Ghanaian mandatory provisions. Moreover, Article III of the New York Convention explicitly provides that each contracting state shall recognise arbitral awards as binding and enforce them in accordance with the rules of procedure of the territory in which the award is relied on.

Moreover, the facts of the case under discussion raise strongly the issue whether under Article V (II) of the New York Convention enforcement of the award in Ghana would not be against public policy. In the English case of *Soleimany v Soleimany*,[265] a dispute arose between a father and son, both Iranian Jews, who had entered into a transaction involving the smuggling of carpets out of Iran in breach of Iranian laws. Their dispute was submitted to the Court of the Chief Rabbi in London for arbitration. That Court made an award under Jewish law, ignoring the illegal purpose of the transaction.

265　[1999] QB785

The English Court of Appeal refused to enforce the award, noting that the award on its face referred to an illegal object of the parties' transaction, and therefore it would be against public policy for it to be enforced. The Court said:[266]

> "The Court is in our view concerned to preserve the integrity of its process, and to see that it is not abused. The parties cannot override that concern by private agreement. They cannot by procuring an arbitration conceal that they, or rather one of them, is seeking to enforce an illegal contract. Public policy will not allow it."

Soleimany v Soleimany draws attention to the public policy exception to the enforcement of foreign arbitral awards. Article 5(2)(b) of the New York Convention allows a court to refuse recognition of or enforcement to an award where such recognition or enforcement would be contrary to the public policy of the forum country. The facts of *The Republic v High Court (Commercial Division) Accra; Ex parte Attorney-General (Zenith Bank, Interested Party)* illustrate a situation where the enforcement of the arbitral award in question would be against public policy. This is obviously because there is a binding Supreme Court judgment in the Ghanaian jurisdiction which states that the agreement sought to be enforced in the award is unconstitutional and unenforceable. It would surely be against public policy to enforce an arbitral award in direct conflict with a judgment of the highest court of the land, which has pronounced on the illegality of the transaction sought to be enforced!

Conclusion

It is hoped that this Chapter has demonstrated the importance for practising lawyers and national judges to digest the New York Convention and to be fully abreast with the transnational case law on it. More generally, as the world becomes ever more interdependent, international arbitration is increasingly important. Therefore, lawyers practising within particular jurisdictions, such as Ghana, will need to pay attention to the mechanics, tactics and received knowledge on international arbitration.

266　At 800

Index